THE SESAME EFFECT

The Sesame Effect details the wide-ranging work of Sesame Workshop and its productions across the world. With an emphasis on impact and evidence from research on projects in low- and middle-income countries, the book tells the stories behind the development of an international family of Muppet characters created for the locally produced adaptations of Sesame Street.

Each chapter highlights the educational messages of international co-productions and presents the cultural context of each project. Readers will learn about the specific needs of children living in a given locale, and will gain insights into the educational drivers of each project. These projects often deal with difficult issues, from race relations in the United States, to HIV/AIDS education in South Africa, to building respect across cultural divides in the Middle East. Readers will learn how local productions have helped build a new mindset that values the importance of early childhood education, and how Sesame Street promotes a brighter future by building children's academic skills, encouraging healthy habits, and by fostering attitudes that counter negative stereotypes and create appreciation of and respect for others.

The Sesame Effect shows how, when magnified across the millions of children touched by the various international programs, the Sesame Workshop and its projects are making a difference around the world.

Charlotte F. Cole is Executive Director of Blue Butterfly Collaborative, a nonprofit organization that helps producers in low- and middle-income countries use the transformative power of children's media to promote international development aims in education, health and peace building. Formerly Senior Vice President of Global Education at Sesame Workshop, she oversaw the education and research conducted on international co-productions of Sesame Street from 1994–2013.

June H. Lee is Vice President of International Research at Sesame Workshop, where she oversees the research associated with Sesame Street's international projects.

THE SESAME EFFECT

The Global Impact of the Longest Street in the World

Charlotte F. Cole, editor with
June H. Lee, associate editor

Routledge
Taylor & Francis Group

NEW YORK AND LONDON

First published 2016
by Routledge
711 Third Avenue, New York, NY 10017

and by Routledge
2 Park Square, Milton Park, Abingdon, Oxon, OX14 4RN

Routledge is an imprint of the Taylor & Francis Group, an informa business

Library of Congress Cataloging-in-Publication Data
Names: Cole, Charlotte F., editor. | Lee, June H., editor.
Title: The Sesame effect : the global impact of the longest street in the world / Charlotte F. Cole, editor ; June H. Lee, associate editor.
Description: New York, NY : Routledge, 2015. | Includes bibliographical references and index.
Identifiers: LCCN 2015027144 | ISBN 9781138806900 (hardback) | ISBN 9781138806917 (pbk.) | ISBN 9781315751399 (ebook)
Subjects: LCSH: Sesame Street (Television program) | Sesame Workshop. | Television in preschool education.
Classification: LCC PN1992.77.S43 S37 2015 | DDC 791.45/72—dc23
LC record available at http://lccn.loc.gov/2015027144

ISBN: 978-1-138-80690-0 (hbk)
ISBN: 978-1-138-80691-7 (pbk)
ISBN: 978-1-315-75139-9 (ebk)

Typeset in Bembo
by Apex CoVantage, LLC

To Joan Ganz Cooney, whose magnificent idea has changed the world by bringing the happiness of learning to millions of children everywhere

CONTENTS

TABLES

FIGURES

PLATES

ABOUT THE AUTHORS

Cairo Arafat is the Managing Director of Bidaya Media in Abu Dhabi, which is working with Sesame Workshop in producing the new version of Iftah Ya Simsim. She was previously Education and Research Director for the Palestinian Sesame Street program, Shara'a Simsim. Cairo has worked in the area of children's development, education, and rights with Save the Children, UNICEF, and a host of other organizations.

Sashwati Banerjee leads Sesame Workshop's educational mission in India. As Founding Managing Director of Sesame Workshop India, she spearheads Galli Galli Sim Sim (the Sesame Street program in India). Under her leadership, the organization has developed and implemented innovative programs that have demonstrated impact on children's educational and developmental outcomes. Sashwati Banerjee is deeply committed to human rights and serves on the Board of Point of View, an organization that promotes the points of views of women using media, arts, and culture, and CREA a feminist human rights organization based in New Delhi, India.

Ameena Batada is Assistant Professor in the Department of Health and Wellness at the University of North Carolina Asheville, where her teaching and research focus on health equity, community health promotion, and health communication. She was Director of Education, Research, and Outreach for Sesame Workshop India from fall 2009 to summer 2011.

Jean Baxen is Professor and Head of School at the University of the Witwatersrand School of Education, South Africa. She is author of numerous research reports, peer-reviewed papers, and book chapters on aspects of education in South Africa. She is author of *Performative Praxis: Teacher Identity and Teaching* in the

Context of HIV/AIDS (2010) and co-editor of the volume HIV/AIDS in *Sub-Saharan Africa: Understanding the Implications of Culture and Context* (2009). Jean Baxen is an active member of the education community in South Africa and sits on a number of editorial boards, national advisory committees, and review panels.

Jorge Baxter is Regional Director for Sesame Latin America. Baxter first came to Sesame as Director of Education in 2009. Baxter previously worked as an education specialist at the Organization of American States and in 2012 co-founded MobilizArte, a Latin American organization focused on film and education for social change. He is currently pursuing a Ph.D. in international education policy at the University of Maryland.

Lewis Bernstein's association with Sesame Workshop began in 1972 when he came on board as Director of Research working alongside Jim Henson and Jon Stone to integrate entertainment and education. Through the forty years that followed, Lewis Bernstein served as Vice President of Global Sesame Street Productions, Executive Producer of both the United States and the Israeli/Palestinian versions of Sesame Street, and the Executive Vice President of Education, Research, and Outreach. He holds a Ph.D. from Columbia University in communications research, an M.A. from Hebrew University in communications, and a B.A. from Queens College, CUNY, in psychology.

Jeanette Betancourt is Senior Vice President of U.S. Social Impact at Sesame Workshop. She directs all community outreach initiatives designed to increase family engagement and impact at-risk children's school readiness, health, and social/emotional wellbeing. She has degrees in speech and language pathology, bilingual reading, and an Ed.D. in special education.

Abigail Bucuvalas is Director of Global Social Impact at Sesame Workshop. She leads content development and outreach activities for Sesame health programming around the world, including the company's multi-country water, sanitation, and hygiene initiative. She manages Sesame Workshop's project in Nigeria and oversees curriculum and content development in West Africa and Latin America. She received an Ed.D. in health education and Ed.M. in international educational development from Columbia University Teachers College.

Shantimoy Chakma joined Sesame Street's Bangladeshi co-production Sisimpur in May 2004 and currently oversees program design and implementation as its program director. He brings a wide range of experience to the project, including teaching, research, curriculum and material development, and film and television production. Shantimoy holds a master's degree in early childhood development from the Institute of Educational Development of BRAC University in Bangladesh. For the last three years, he has also been teaching various early childhood development modules at BRAC University and other educational institutions as visiting faculty.

Charlotte F. Cole is Co-Founder and Executive Director of Blue Butterfly Collaborative, a non-profit organization that uses children's media to advance international development aims. Prior to co-founding the collaborative, Cole was Senior Vice President of Global Education at Sesame Workshop in New York where she oversaw the education and research activities associated with international co-productions of Sesame Street. She received her doctorate in human development and psychology from the Harvard Graduate School of Education. She served as the first review and commentary editor of the *Journal of Children and Media* and her research appears in publications such as the International Journal of Behavioral Development and Communication Research Trends.

Lilith Dollard is Senior Educational Content Specialist at Sesame Workshop. She currently manages educational content development for international co-productions of Sesame Street in South Asia. Lilith holds a master's in international education development from Teachers College, Columbia University.

Nada W. Elattar, Director of Global Social Impact at Sesame Workshop, has worked for a number of prestigious international organizations throughout the Middle East and North Africa, namely the United Nations World Health Organization, the United Nations World Food Programme, and the Johns Hopkins University's Center for Communication Program's Communication for Healthy Living project. Nada holds a bachelor's degree in health education from San Francisco State University and a master's of public health from the Johns Hopkins Bloomberg School of Public Health.

Sayed Farhad Hashimi is Director of Education and Research for Baghch-e-Simsim, Sesame Workshop's program in Afghanistan. He holds a bachelor's degree from American University of Afghanistan (AUAF) and has over 15 years of experience in development programs, including some ten years' experience in children programing in Sesame Project and in Save the Children.

Janice Fuld is Associate Director of Education at WNET, New York Public Media, where she oversees evaluation efforts for the education department and assesses the impact of the department's initiatives. Before joining WNET in 2007, Janice developed curricula, designed educational content, and conducted research and training sessions for educational websites, television programs, and museums. She worked on international adaptations of Sesame Street, including Takalani Sesame in South Africa. She has a B.A in psychology from Bryn Mawr College and a master's in educational technology from the Harvard Graduate School of Education.

Joan Ganz Cooney, Co-Founder of Children's Television Workshop (renamed Sesame Workshop, June 2000) and Originator of the preschool educational series, Sesame Street, served as President and Chief Executive Officer until 1990. She is currently Chairman of the Executive Committee of Sesame Workshop's Board of Trustees and in November 2007 introduced the Joan Ganz Cooney Center at Sesame Workshop, dedicated to investigating the potential of digital media to help children learn and collaborating with educators, media producers, policymakers, and investors to put this research into action.

Yeh Hsueh is Associate Professor in the Program of Educational Psychology and Research at the University of Memphis. His research areas are children's development and teachers' professional development in the changing culture and society. He has worked as a content consultant and program evaluator for Sesame Workshop's co-productions in China since 1998.

Zainab Kabba is an educator from New York City. She has a combination of both technical and pedagogical training and has leveraged this knowledge in the area of media and education in both K-12 classrooms and higher education institutions. She has experience in the field of education research and development, designing and managing education initiatives in parts of Africa and the Middle East. Her research interests lie at the intersections of education, media, and religion. She holds a B.S. in information systems and an M.A. in computing in education. She is currently a Ph.D. candidate in the Department of Education, University of Oxford.

Jennifer A. Kotler is Vice President of Research and Evaluation at Sesame Workshop. She oversees research design, methodology, assessment, and data analysis for formative and summative evaluations across a variety of media platforms. Jennifer graduated from Cornell University with a B.S. in human development and family studies. She went on to receive her master's in human development from the University of Kansas and a Ph.D. in child development and family studies from the University of Texas at Austin.

June H. Lee is Vice President of International Research at Sesame Workshop. She directs all formative research and impact evaluations for Sesame Workshop's international projects and works with partners around the world to elevate the rigor of the company's research. She has also overseen content development and community- and school-based projects in Asia. June received her Ph.D. in human development and family sciences from the University of Texas at Austin, where her work focused on the contexts and effects of children's media use.

Alyaa Montasser is a clinical psychologist at Flo Chi Integrative Medicine in Cairo, Egypt. As the first Director of Education for Alam Simsim, the Egyptian adaptation of Sesame Street, she has led the program's educational and research activities over the project's history. She received her doctorate from Mannheim University in Germany. She is the owner of Malak's Honey, a non-profit organization that produces Egyptian honey for health, whose proceeds from sales go directly to helping people in need of medical care who would otherwise go untreated.

Ayobisi Osuntusa is Project Manager of Sesame Square in Nigeria. In this role, she oversees all programmatic operations and activities for the TV show and outreach projects. She develops scripts, games, and instructional materials for audio and visual media resources with input from local tribes and zones and through maintaining relationships with government establishments, media agencies, and the private sector. In addition, Ayobisi Osuntusa has more than 21 years of experience as a teacher and teacher trainer in public, private, and Islamiyya school systems. Her observations of the gaps between educational opportunities she had as a child in America and what is currently available in Nigeria continue to drive her to institutionalize change in education.

Mathangi Subramanian is a writer and educator who currently works for UNESCO's Mahatma Gandhi Institute for Education for Peace and Sustainable Development in New Delhi, India. She is the author of three books for children and teens and the co-editor of an academic volume about immigration and education in the United States. A former US public school teacher, senior policy analyst at the New York City Council, and Fulbright-Nehru scholar, she worked at Sesame Workshop for five years. She earned a B.Sc. from Brown University and received her doctorate in communications and education from Columbia University Teachers College.

Rosemarie T. Truglio is Senior Vice President of Curriculum and Content at Sesame Workshop. She is responsible for the development of the interdisciplinary curriculum on which Sesame Street is based. Previously, she oversaw all educational research pertaining to program development, the results of which informed both the production and creative decisions for how to enhance the entertaining and educational components of linear and interactive content. She received a Ph.D. in developmental and child psychology from the University of Kansas, and a B.A. in psychology from Douglass College, Rutgers University.

Muhammad Zuhdi, Ph.D. is Senior Lecturer at the Faculty of Education, State Islamic University Syarif Hidayatullah Jakarta, Indonesia. From 2006 to 2012, he served as Director of Education, Research, and Outreach for Jalan Sesama (the Indonesian co-production of Sesame Street), overseeing the content development for the educational TV series as well as printed learning materials for preschool-aged children in Indonesia. He received his Ph.D. in curriculum and instruction from McGill University in Montreal.

ACKNOWLEDGMENTS

We begin our acknowledgments with thanks to the over 150 million children Sesame Street reaches annually. Sesame Street has been created for them and this book would not have a purpose were it not for the hope and inspiration they offer.

Many people were part of the completion of this book and we are grateful to them all. First we would like to thank our family, friends, and co-workers whose patience and support are at the heart of what has made the completion of this book happen. We are also deeply indebted to the many people at Sesame Workshop who paved the way for the success of Sesame Street internationally. Much of what we have written has been motivated by the many talented individuals behind the company's international efforts. Some, like Gerry Lesser and Ed Palmer, who are no longer living, have been instrumental; their contribution to the first international co-productions still impacts the ways teams engage and move through the production process. This early work was furthered by the former president of Sesame Workshop, Gary Knell, and his keen interest in the global arena; his leadership inspired many of the projects discussed in these pages. We are also deeply grateful to the foresight and passion of Baxter Urist, who headed Sesame Workshop's international division years ago and who believed in the power and potential of Sesame Street to promote international development aims. The team that supported him, including Bunny Lester, Steve Miller, David Jacobs, John Higgins, Lisa Annunziata, Natasha Lance Rogoff, Renee Mascara, and Yolanda Platon, was also a big component of these efforts. Also part of that group are Gregg Gettas, a friend and extensive international traveler, whose knowledge goes well beyond Vygotsky's zone of proximal development, Cooper Wright, who we are particularly grateful to for her reminder of the importance of listening to the universe, and Brett Pierce, with his cheerful support and inspiration.

Thanks go to Lewis Bernstein, the former Executive Vice President for Education, Research, and Outreach who was instrumental in making this book a practical reality. We are grateful, too, to Allison Gutknecht, whose efficiency helped in uncountable ways.

Sherrie Westin, Sesame Workshop's Executive Vice President of Global Impact and Philanthropy, saw the potential of this book in its early stages and has continued to support it along with others in her department including Ellen Lewis, Beatrice Chow, Solange Van Loo, and Phil Toscano. David Chan, Estee Bardanashvili, Naila Farouky, Veronica Wulff, Miranda Barry, Rocio Galarza, Jocelyn Leong, and Dina Guadalupe also played important roles in inspiring the content of this book at various times in the history of its making and, through their moral support and insights, helped to deliver on its practical realities.

Thanks too to Gail David, whose editorial input has been a delight and thought provoking. Sue McCann Brown's detailed review of many of the chapters greatly improved their final versions. Ellen Buchwalter provided important verification regarding funders and other specifics. And Anna Genina, Sandra LeBlanc, Taska Carrigan, Daryl Mintz, Quintin Oliver, and Shari Rosenfeld reviewed some content and offered helpful commentary.

Thanks also to our editor at Routledge, Linda Bathgate, who went well above and beyond any call of duty, generously providing her time, insights, and general moral support, which has moved this project from an idea we had imagined many years ago to its current reality.

Additionally, we would like to mention all of our many colleagues, both in the US as well as the many, many people who have worked on co-production teams throughout the world. We have learned much from them and are indebted for their insights, thoughts, and opinions and for reminding us of the importance of context, experience, and the unique contributions of all.

Special thanks also extend to Evan Cheng who has been a wonderful cheerleader and husband to the associate editor.

And finally, the editor would like to give a special call-out to her eight siblings (and their wonderful spouses) and the foundation growing up with such extraordinary, generous, noisy, and kind individuals that has meant in providing energy for this endeavor; to her son Luis to whom she has learned much; and to her husband, Scott Budde, whose encouragement and optimism have remained unending in his true understanding of the value of playfulness and in being in touch with one's "inner Muppet." And lastly, appreciation goes to the Sesame Street character, Hoots the Owl, whose wise words ignited this project. Sometimes "you have to put down the ducky if you want to play the saxophone."

FOREWORD

Writing this foreword is, in many ways, an opportunity to look back.

I've had the privilege of helping Sesame Street take root and grow for the last almost half century. What began as a television show to help American preschoolers learn now spans multiple media and makes a difference for over 156 million children annually worldwide. In fact, Sesame Street is "the longest street in the world," benefiting more children in more countries across more cultures through more channels than any program in history.

And all this amidst a backdrop of dizzying change. The last half century has been witness to turmoil and innovation at an unprecedented pace. The technological transformations alone that continue to reshape media (and every other aspect of our lives) have been no less than stunning. But despite all the changes, or perhaps because of them, Sesame Street's vision, our vision and values, have remained constant.

What are these core convictions? Three rise above the rest: no matter our country or cause, we all want better for our children; education is the way to that better future; and media—the right kind of media—can be used effectively to help children learn.

This is what galvanized us in the late 1960s when Sesame Street began, a time in this country of great social change—and what has galvanized so many others around the world in similar times of hope and promise. This is why the South African Sesame Street, Takalani Sesame, was only possible in a post-apartheid nation; why it could withstand withering condemnation when it was the first to take on the stigma of HIV/AIDS. This is what was behind Northern Ireland's Sesame Tree, created in the wake of the Good Friday Agreement, to encourage a new generation of children to be open to and curious about others as a bridge to peace and stability. And while it saddens me as I write this today with yet more bloodshed in the region, this is what propelled Rechov Sumsum/Shara'a Simsim, the ground-breaking co-production to foster tolerance and mutual respect among Israeli and Palestinian children, inspired by the long-ago handshake between Yitzhak Rabin and Yasser Arafat on the White House lawn.

But as this remarkable volume makes clear, the adaptability of the Sesame Street model, the way it lends itself to the unique circumstances of local contexts, and its capacity to provide common ground for polarized camps, only partially explains our success through the years. The rest of the story, without which, frankly, the first would lose meaning, is because Sesame Street works.

Sesame Workshop has always been a laboratory for learning. And everything we've learned tells us that what began as a hunch is spot on: Sesame Street, in all its iterations, makes a meaningful, measureable difference in children's lives.

I'm delighted to have the most recent evidence together in this volume, adding to the collection begun with the 2001 publication of *"G" is for Growing: Thirty Years of Research on Children and Sesame Street*.[1] With *The Sesame Effect*'s emphasis on efficacy and impact, it tells the story of our international work, animating the development of a family of Muppets created for more than 30 indigenously produced adaptations. We learn in depth about the ways these Muppets—created to capture in-country qualities and respond to in-country needs—are moving the needle on some of the most intractable issues of our times: educating girls in Egypt and Afghanistan; promoting mutual respect and understanding in areas long defined by conflict; reducing the stigma of HIV/AIDS in South Africa; joining the fight against malaria in Tanzania; increasing access to and elevating the status of early childhood education in India, Bangladesh, and Indonesia; and so much more.

What a valuable contribution this volume makes. Conventional wisdom might have conceded that children learn from media, but they nonetheless persist in assigning that learning to the negative only—children learn violence from media, they learn crassness and unchecked consumerism. Perhaps this book will finally debunk the myth. The right kind of media is indeed an important intervention, an effective tool for development and a proven ally of education. In short, the right kind of media matters.

For this, we have countless individuals to thank. And because the list itself would fill volumes, I'll limit myself to only a few involved directly with this book—namely, Charlotte Cole, the book's editor, whose leadership has been essential to an approach that emphasizes the importance of cultural specificity and the use of listening as a diplomatic tool. Charlotte Cole has helped us all view Sesame Street as a two-way street, where we learn as much or more from our co-producing partners as they from us. Perhaps her greatest contribution comes from her steadfast belief that any content area, however bold, as HIV/AIDS in South Africa certainly first was, can be tackled in the service of children. And to the many critics who say our work is only "a drop in the bucket," she reminds us that a single droplet of tint, with a bright enough hue, can change the color of a bucket's contents entirely.

I also want to thank Lewis Bernstein, who was behind this project from the beginning and helped to spearhead it as the Workshop's former Executive Vice President of Education, Research, and Outreach. I've known Lewis since he joined the Workshop as a young man in 1972, and while he has been instrumental in so many of our efforts, his contributions as one of the architects of the Workshop's research model, as well as the use of Sesame Street to teach tolerance and mutual respect to children in Israel and Palestine, have been trailblazing of the highest order.

And finally, one last acknowledgement. We often speak of the impact our co-productions have on children. But there is a special category of "adults" for whom the process of developing programming has ripple effects that go far beyond any single effort. I want to recognize the visionary writers, directors, producers, researchers, performers, and others who continue to bring Sesame Street to children under the most difficult of circumstances. The very fact of a co-production in Kosovo, for example, while Albanian and Serbian tensions were high, or in Afghanistan while war persists, or Israel and Palestine, speaks to the desire among even the most deeply estranged colleagues to build a better future for their children. The very fact of a co-production—the demands of making decisions and reaching compromises—gives colleagues opportunities to work closely together, often for the first time, and sometimes quite literally shoulder to shoulder to manipulate Muppets. Clearly, Sesame Street doesn't exist in a vacuum; we don't pretend it can solve the many problems of the world. But we know unequivocally, through almost 50 years of research and experience, that it can contribute to the solutions.

In 1966, when I conducted a study for the Carnegie Corporation, out of which came a proposal for the creation of Sesame Street, there was no such thing as a "Theory of Change." But just because we didn't call it that didn't mean we were any less intentional about our approach. Today, it's perhaps best captured in these lines:

> If children experience the joy of learning, it's more likely they'll be lifelong learners. If they learn healthy habits, it's more likely they'll grow up healthy and strong. If they gain a sense of themselves and an appreciation of others, it's more likely they'll engage others with respect and understanding. It's that simple and that complicated. Sesame Workshop is using the power of media—and the power of Muppets—to help all children reach their highest potential, and in so doing, make a better world for us all.[2]

That simple and that complicated. In 1989, in a television special celebrating the 20th anniversary of Sesame Street, Jim Henson and I sat down to talk about our work. We spoke briefly about the evolution of our international efforts, and my sense of surprise when the Germans first approached us to do a full-out co-production, not a dubbed version, because I always thought of Sesame Street as uniquely American. (What a delight to have been wrong—Sesamstrasse in Germany and Plaza Sésamo in Mexico, two of the earliest co-productions, are still on the air after more than 40 years.) But as I explained at the time, I was never more thrilled than when Sesame Street co-productions aired in the Arab world and then in Israel. As a result, we knew that Arab and Israeli children would have the same pedagogical experience in their early years, and my dream was that "one day, the Arabs and the Israelis would be at the negotiating table together and one of them would say to another some line of Bert and Ernie's, and they'd pick up the routine and peace would break out in the Middle East!"[3]

While said in jest, in our heart of hearts, this is what moved us at the beginning and continues to motivate us today—to use our characters to help establish the building blocks of peace, of which letters and numbers, and more overtly, messages of respect and understanding, are essential. There's certainly no shortage of need in this world. I'm forever grateful to those who've joined with us to use Sesame Street to respond to these needs, and to the authors of this book for telling the story, now—and looking ahead in this foreword—for generations to come.

Joan Ganz Cooney

Notes

1. Fisch, S.M. and Truglio, R.T. Eds (2001) *"G" is for Growing: Thirty Years of Research on Children and Sesame Street*. Hillsdale, NJ: Lawrence Erlbaum Associates.
2. David, G. (2008) *Increase the Odds*. Sesame Workshop Annual Report, New York.
3. Hosted by Bill Cosby, "Sesame Street: 20 Years and Still Counting!" aired on NBC, April 7, 1989.

INTRODUCTION

Charlotte F. Cole and June H. Lee

SCRIPT RADIO EPISODE #20: Baghch-e-Simsim (Sesame Garden) Afghanistan

KAJKOAL: (A MUPPET CHARACTER) Salaam friends, once again it is me the cute and sweet Kajkoal. Do you know where I am right now? I will tell you myself; right now I am in a clinic. I have an appointment to visit the doctor and ask a question about how a person can become a doctor. I am waiting for my turn. [EFFECT OF KNOCKING THE DOOR WITH FINGER]

DR. NASRIN: Come in! [EFFECT OF DOOR OPENING AND CLOSING]

KAJKOAL: Salaam, Dr. Auntie, I am the cute and sweet Kajkoal from Baghch-e-Simsim.

DR. NASRIN: Welcome, Kajkoal Jan, tell me, what is your problem?

KAJKOAL: [LAUGHS] Doctor! I don't have any problem. I have a question I wanted to ask you.

DR. NASRIN: What is the question, Kajkoal Jan?

KAJKOAL: Doctor! How could you become a doctor?

DR. NASRIN: Well, I always wanted to be a doctor. When I was younger, I went to school and I studied a lot day and night.

KAJKOAL: And now you are a doctor! Wow! That was pretty simple! It doesn't sound hard to be a doctor at all!

DR. NASRIN: No, Kajkoal Jan, I wasn't a doctor yet! After that I went to university, I studied medical lessons for several years there.

KAJKOAL: And now you are a doctor! University is quite challenging!

DR. NASRIN: [LAUGHS] It was, Kajkoal, but I wasn't a doctor yet! After that I worked with many experienced doctors, so finally I became a doctor.

KAJKOAL: [Surprisingly] Wow, Doctor Auntie, you have worked very hard. You have studied a lot to become a doctor.

DR. NASRIN: Kajkoal Jan, to learn something, you have to work very hard, and try a lot. I tried a lot to become a good doctor.

KAJKOAL: Dr. Auntie! Thanks for answering my question. You really are a very good doctor. When I need to visit a doctor, I will definitely come to you.

DR. NASRIN: Good bye, Kajkoal! Come back for a check-up soon!

Kajkoal is a Muppet character who appears on Baghch-e-Simsim, a version of Sesame Street produced in Afghanistan. (Baghch-e-Simsim means "Sesame Garden" in the Dari language.) Like his American counterpart, Grover, Kajkoal is a happy, curious character, whose zany antics entertain as they inspire. The segment above comes from the radio version of the series and is an example of the way in which Sesame Street's magic reaches children in Kabul and beyond.

The curricular messages extended in that simple exchange are multiple: it is a segment about jobs and occupations, working hard to obtain a goal, and the importance of visiting a doctor. It's also about curiosity and posing questions. In short, it is about a range of educational objectives related to skills children need to help prepare them for life-long learning.

Such segments, while simple, are far from simplistic in their design and execution. For children living in a country where only 32% of the adult population (and only 18% of females) are literate (UNESCO, 2014) and where many children, particularly girls, lack access to high-quality education opportunities (UNICEF, 2013), they are part of a much bigger effort to provide a meaningful learning experience to young children who might not otherwise have such opportunity.

The locally produced Sesame Street television and radio programs, which have aired in Afghanistan on TOLO TV (Dari language) and LEMAR TV (Pashto language) and various radio stations since December 2011, have a particularly potent power to transform the lives of the children they reach because they present content that reflects the daily-life context in which they live. They give children tools that build their cognitive and socio-emotional wellbeing. And by modeling, through a combination of Muppet pieces, animations, and locally produced live action documentaries, accomplishments, positive communication, and productive ways of coping with life's challenges, they offer hope for the future.

Kajkoal's adventures, and how and why they are presented in the context of Sesame Workshop's international co-productions, are, along with the stories of his many Muppet friends, the subject of the pages that follow. Collectively, the ensuing chapters describe the process for creating over 30 indigenous adaptations of Sesame Street. The book details what has come to be known as *The Sesame Effect*, that is, what research has told us about the worldwide impact of these co-productions.

The book describes Sesame Workshop's international work focusing on the successes in low- and middle-income countries. The chapters highlight the educational messages that international co-productions of Sesame Street forward and describes what research says about the measurable impact these projects have made. The various chapters present the cultural context of each project and provide a sense of the specific needs of children living in a given locale and the ways these are tended to by the programs' educational visions and production achievements.

With an emphasis on impact and evidence from research on projects in low- and middle-income countries, the book tells the stories behind the development of an international family of Muppets characters created for the indigenously produced adaptations of Sesame Street. It describes how the production of these characters and their related projects galvanize individuals living in challenging parts of the world to work toward something that serves to build a brighter future for children.

Many of these projects deal with difficult issues, something which Sesame Street has never shied away from. From race relations in the United States, to HIV/AIDS education in South Africa, to building respect across cultural divides in the Middle East, the programs have responded to the challenging environments that have precipitated their need. Building productive programming has taken the dedication of individuals from varying groups who are willing to engage in such projects and who commit to finding a common ground. Often that shared philosophic base is children themselves and the motivating force behind wanting to build a better future for them. The result has been that Sesame Street has served as a catalyst for broader societal change. As the chapters that follow detail, the projects have contributed to building a new mindset that values the importance of early childhood education and its long-term benefit to society.

And it is working! Research has shown that in a small but significant way, Sesame Street promotes a brighter future by building children's academic skills, encouraging healthy habits, and by fostering attitudes that counter negative stereotypes and foster appreciation of and respect for others. When magnified across the millions of children throughout the world the program reaches annually, it is clear that Sesame Street is making a meaningful difference.

Overview of Contents

Part I, The Global Sesame Effect, provides an introduction to Sesame Workshop's international co-production process and the way its impact has been measured. The first chapter, authored by the editor, Charlotte Cole, provides an overview of Sesame Workshop's international approach. It highlights the way producers in countries throughout the world have adapted a model developed in the United States to create culturally relevant, entertaining educational content.

Sesame Workshop's Theory of Change and its measured impact is the focus of the second chapter which has been jointly authored by Charlotte Cole and June Lee. The chapter details the complexities of bringing together expertise in education, child development, media research, international relations, and cultural context to study Sesame Street's large-scale media efforts in an international context.

The chapters in Part II, Meeting Children's Educational Needs, which comprise the core of the book, provide insights into the theoretical underpinning of the various Sesame Street projects. With an emphasis on low- and middle-income countries, they speak to the practical mechanics of executing projects in challenging parts of the world. Each chapter has a specific geographical focus overlaid with a different content theme. Chapter 3, by Jennifer Kotler, Rosemarie Truglio, and Jeanette Betancourt, who respectively head the Workshop's Content Research, Content and Curriculum, and US Social Impact groups in the United States, focuses on the company's domestic work and describes the ways in which Sesame Street continues to meet children's changing educational needs through a range of distribution platforms.

Chapters 4–7 each focus on a different aspect of core curricular areas. Authored by a mix of US-based personnel and various educators, researchers, and others who have worked on these projects in-country, the chapters provide an in-depth window into the specifics of the conception, execution, and evaluation of Sesame Workshop's projects in low- and middle-income countries. Chapter 4, by June Lee, Yeh Hsueh, Muhammad Zuhdi, Shantimoy Chakma, Sayed Farhad Hashimi, and Lilith Dollard, provides a prospective on Sesame Workshop's work around basic academic/cognitive skills through the lens of our projects in Asia. Health is a focus of Chapter 5, which highlights our work in Africa and has been written by Abigail Bucuvalas, Zainab Kabba, Jean Baxen, Janice Fuld, and Ayobisi Osuntusa. It details such accomplishments as the creation of Kami, a Muppet who is HIV positive, who was created as a vehicle for presenting a specially designed HIV/AIDS education curriculum.

The prosocial realm is the topic of both Chapters 6 and 7, which respectively speak to gender equity and empowerment as promoted in our Arabic-language programming and mutual respect and understanding as elucidated through our work in the Middle East and elsewhere. Both of these topics are central to the core values of Sesame Street and its aim of heightening children's appreciation for diversity while understanding our common humanity. Chapter 6 is authored by

Charlotte Cole, Alyaa Montasser, June Lee, Cairo Arafat, and Nada Elattar; Chapter 7 is co-written by Charlotte Cole and Lewis Bernstein.

The final section, Part 3, A Sustainable Future: Community and Partnerships, takes a more focused look beyond television. Whereas the chapters in Part II describe the application of the co-production process in different regions from the perspective of specific curricular themes, the two chapters in the final section present insights into the extension of Sesame Street programming into the community and the ways in which that helps to promote long-term sustainability of the projects. Chapter 8, by Ameena Batada, Sashwati Banerjee, and Mathangi Subramanian describes the Galli Galli Sim Sim project in India and its rich extension into the community through specific community-engagement projects. Chapter 9, written by Jorge Baxter, speaks to the evolution and sustainability of Sesame Workshop's international work, providing insights from Latin America as a case study.

References

UNESCO (2014). International literacy data, 2014. Retrieved from http://www.uis.unesco.org/literacy/Pages/literacy-data-release-2014.aspx.

UNICEF (2013). Afghanistan: Basic education and gender equality. Retrieved from http://www.unicef.org/afghanistan/education_2206.htm.

PART I
The Global Sesame Effect

1

.29: THE GLOBAL SESAME EFFECT

Charlotte F. Cole

Education is the most powerful weapon which [we] can use to change the world.

Nelson Mandela, 2003

Muppets, the playful furry creatures that populate the preschool television series, Sesame Street, have proven an ideal vehicle for helping children learn everything from counting and literacy to complex social values. This is because, in the Sesame Street context, they are specially designed to forward specific educational goals. The friendly vampire Count von Count, in his enthusiasm for counting, models a love of numbers and mathematics; the oppositional Oscar the Grouch, in his contrary way of liking things that others dislike, helps children value different perspectives; and as a group, Muppets, who come in all shapes, sizes, and colors, potently illustrate that it doesn't matter what you look like or where you come from, all people are worthy of respect.

This is a book about how these Muppets are being used to advance goals of the international development community in low- and middle-income countries (LMICs). It describes the Global Sesame Street Effect and the ways in which localized adaptations of a children's media program are being used to reach underserved children with important education, health, and peace-building messages. It is the story of a production process that galvanizes energies, builds common ground, and drives toward education solutions. By enlisting an arsenal of locally created Sesame Street Muppets—which includes a vibrant Indian schoolgirl, an endearing South African meerkat, an engaging Indonesian orangutan, and many other local characters who are introduced in the pages that follow—this international development vehicle has made, and continues to make, a measurable difference in the lives of millions of children throughout the world.

The power of Sesame Street as an agent of change is derived from the essence of what makes Sesame Street Sesame Street. It's fun, furry, informative, and flexible.

Fun in that it entertains as it teaches; furry in that it artfully utilizes the antics, adventures, and personalities of signature Muppet characters to communicate; informative in that it presents foundational elements of learning in developmentally appropriate and accessible ways; and flexible in that its production process allows for, and indeed values, context as a factor for achieving educational results. With initiatives in over 30 countries, Sesame Workshop works with local partners to offer children across the globe high-quality content that educates as it entertains. The programs present messages local educators identify as important for children in a given locale: girls' education in Afghanistan, India, and Bangladesh; boys' empowerment in Palestine; HIV/AIDS messaging in South Africa; malaria education in Tanzania; and many other educational domains in many other places. These areas of focus directly align with objectives defined by the international development community, including efforts to provide universal primary education for all, increase gender equity, combat HIV/AIDS, malaria, and other diseases, and promote peace building (United Nations, 2013).

While progress has been made since the turn of the century in improving the lives of the world's children, more than 58 million are out of school and millions more attend under-resourced school programs with limited materials and insufficiently trained teachers (GMR and UNESCO, 2014). But with improvements such as reductions in the mortality rate for children under age five and a decline in the disparities in primary school enrollment between boys and girls (United Nations, 2013; UNICEF, 2014), there is a positive story to be told that underscores the importance of continuing to focus efforts on achieving these development aims. Children everywhere need to be literate, they need to be healthy, and they need to learn positive ways of engagement and kindness toward others. The international versions of Sesame Street offer these basics by building on young children's natural joy in learning and by providing messaging that is relevant to and reflective of individuals' own life experiences. And they do this through local applications of a production model that elicits this type of change. This is, in essence, the "Global Sesame Street Effect."

The size of the effect has been quantified by two researchers at the University of Wisconsin at Madison who, in their examination of the impact of Sesame Street's international co-productions, found an overall effect size,[1] that in statistical speak, is .29 (Mares and Pan, 2013). That's a number quantifying the size of the impact of Sesame Street. It is generated through a formalized statistical process (called "meta-analysis") that is essentially a systematic "study of studies" that, in this case, synthesized data from 24 research reports from 15 countries representing over 10,000 child participants. Taken together, the results of these studies show that across countries and programs, Sesame Street is having an impact on children's learning that is about equivalent to the size of the effect of other early childhood interventions outside the US (Nores and Barnett, 2010). As Mares and Pan conclude, there is, however, one important difference: Sesame Street reaches millions of children daily and in this respect has a very large worldwide impact.

To translate the .29 concept into more user-friendly terms, it's useful to delve into the specific findings of the 24 individual studies incorporated in the Mares and Pan report and to look, as well, at research that wasn't a part of the analysis. Focusing on low- and middle-income countries and regions of conflict and post conflict, this book provides the story behind and context for what we know about the global Sesame Street effect within specific educational content areas; it unpacks the findings and provides commentary on what data tell us about impact and the continued potential of these programs to educate children in need.

A Shared International Experience

The use of children's media to promote social change arguably has its underpinnings in the visionary stance of Joan Ganz Cooney, the creator of Sesame Street, over four decades ago. Her insightful report (Cooney, 1966) to the Carnegie Foundation (the philanthropy that ultimately provided some of Sesame Street's first funding) describes an experimental project to determine if the relatively new medium, television, could be used as a vehicle for educating children.

Her ideas were very much an outgrowth of their historical context. The proposal, which was written in the late 1960s, was in line with the tenets of President Lyndon B. Johnson's Great Society program and the declared "War on Poverty" (Johnson, 1964). A basic supposition was that education is an equalizer and a way to elevate children out of poverty.

Behind Cooney's experiment was the belief that children were learning from television. Observing children watching television made it clear that they were quick to pick up advertisement jingles and the like; she, therefore, reasoned that children might learn information of value through the same means. Children were drawn to television and, like it or not, were watching it. Her idea was to capitalize on the attraction to the medium (applying some of the same genius Madison Avenue had utilized to sell products) to build a program that presented a series of short, well-focused segments that would "advertise" content (such as learning how to count and recite the alphabet). The ultimate aim was to use television to help prepare preschoolers for school.

The thinking was radical in many ways. At the time, television had been deemed a "vast wasteland" by Newton N. Minow, the commissioner of broadcasting, in a famous speech at the convention of the National Association of Broadcasters (1961). The potential of television as an educational tool was highly questionable. Yet Cooney persisted, operating under the belief that it is not television itself that is inherently bad; it's whether the content transmitted is of educational worth.

The use of television to simultaneously teach and entertain was just one of Sesame Street's innovative elements. Its production approach was also groundbreaking. To achieve her goals, Cooney brought together experts from a range of fields. Not only did she enlist some of the most creative minds (such as the famous puppeteer Jim Henson and versatile musicians such as Joe Raposo), but she also built a team that included the world's leading experts in education such as Harvard University's Gerald Lesser and researcher Edward Palmer. Her idea was that professionals from these three domains (production, education, and research) would not just consult with each other, but would work together over the course of the entire project. What emerged from this thinking is something that later became known as the Children's Television Workshop Model (now referred to, after the company changed its name in 2000, as the Sesame Workshop Model; Mielke, 1990). Educators and researchers were integral members of the production team who worked side by side with the series' writers, puppeteers, actors, and others.

The program was bold in other respects. Its diverse cast of characters from different racial backgrounds living and working together in an urban neighborhood setting was very much designed to speak to the contemporary racial divide in the US and present an aspiration for how life could be. Yet, this vision was regarded as so radical at the time that the broadcast of Sesame Street was initially banned in one state, Mississippi, because some members of the State Commission on Educational Television were opposed to airing the series due to its integrated cast. In the words of one member of the commission quoted in a New York Times article, "Mississippi was not yet ready for it" (1970).

The willingness to engage in courageous and sometimes controversial efforts has become a signature element of Sesame Street's approach domestically. It has also driven much of the company's work internationally. With programs supporting difficult issues such as gender equity, HIV/AIDS education, and mutual respect and understanding in regions of conflict and post conflict, Sesame Workshop has occupied challenging educational arenas in different parts of the world. The pathway that enabled this level of action begins with the production model that Sesame Workshop employs to create content. The approach and its application have been detailed by others (Lesser, 1974; Palmer et al., 1976; Gettas, 1990; Cole et al., 2001; Fisch and Truglio, 2001) but are worth summarizing in these pages, particularly with respect to the way they have been applied over the years globally.

Figure 1.1 provides a pictorial representation of the components of the model. The diagram shows overlapping circles depicting three distinct groups of professionals: producers, educators, and researchers.[2] The groundbreaking element of the model lies in the fact that the groups of professionals—each with distinct roles— are brought together over the course of an entire production process. Prior to Sesame Street there was certainly both educational television and television for entertainment, but educational television tended to be developed without the distinct aim of entertainment and vice versa. Early in its history, educational television typically did not fully exploit the use of the visual medium. One notion was simply to bring the camera into the classroom—filming a teacher at a chalkboard, for instance—rather than visually representing concepts on the screen. At the time, TV for children in the United States was dominated by animated cartoons, situation comedies (some of which, like *Bewitched*, *The Andy Griffith Show*, and *The Beverly Hillbillies*, are still viewed in syndicated re-runs today) and a mix of other programming. There were studio classics such as *Captain Kangaroo* and *Romper Room*, both

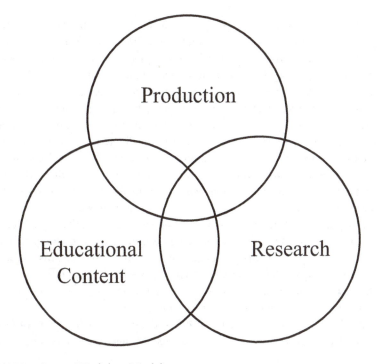

FIGURE 1.1 Sesame Workshop Model
Source: Truglio and Fisch, 2001, xv

long-running shows which had some educational strengths, but none of these efforts were developed with the depth and scientific rigor of Sesame Street.

The careful planning and attention that had been given to developing Sesame Street paid off. Almost from the beginning, it was deemed a success. Recognition surfaced in the journalistic media in a big way, as evidenced by the appearance of Sesame Street on the cover of *TIME* magazine (Plate 1.1).[3] Its educational value, though debated by some, was mostly heralded in a positive light, including within the formal education sector where the studies of the Educational Testing Service (Ball and Bogatz, 1970; Bogatz and Ball, 1971) and others highlighted its value in meeting explicit curricular aims (Lesser, 1974).

The heightened profile generated an interest from broadcasters in other countries—most notably those in Germany, Brazil, Mexico, and Canada—who liked the idea of Sesame Street, but wanted versions of the program that reflected their own educational priorities, pedagogic orientation, and cultural sensibilities. What resulted over time was the development of an international co-production model that enabled the creation of localized versions of Sesame Street that retained the identifiable essence of the original version while taking on distinct qualities from the different locales in which they were produced. Sesame Street was not the first to engage in this type of approach. *Romper Room*, for example, while a very different show from Sesame Street, is particularly interesting in the context of the Sesame Workshop's international model in that it was one of very few (and early) children's programs with a "franchise" format that enabled localization—using hosts and children from a given locale—at both a regional (domestic) and country-by-country level (Langdon, 1978; Terrace, 2008; Moran, 2010). But Sesame Street took this approach to new heights with the development of now over 30 adaptations of the series. Like Sesame Street in the United States, a mix of puppet scenes, live-action documentaries, and animation segments comprise the productions'"magazine" formats; the difference lies in the characters and settings, as well as projects' educational frameworks which are determined by specialists from a given country or region. Consequently, a multinational family of Muppets has emerged who populate environments that are reflective of the culture in which they were developed. While the characters live on a street in an urban neighborhood in the United States, elsewhere they inhabit such diverse places as a plaza in Mexico, a marketplace in South Africa, and a train station in Norway. Thus, as a group, the productions share a united Sesame Street structure, but take on unique qualities of their own. As a result, when children across the world view Sesame Street, they share a common experience that is also relevant to their own cultural context (Cole et al., 2001).

Table 1.1 provides a list of current co-productions, their language of broadcast, the date of first broadcast, and associated Muppet characters. The cultural

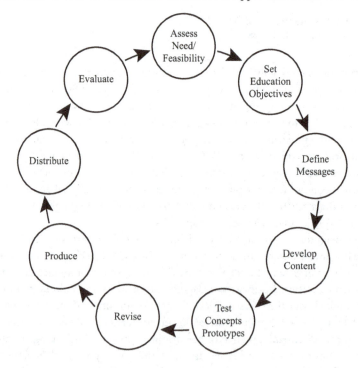

FIGURE 1.2 Production process

TABLE 1.1 Past and current co-productions and character names

Country of origin / Language(s)	Series title / Year of first broadcast	Muppet character names
Afghanistan *Dari and Pashto*	Baghch-e-Simsim/2011	Elmo; Bart (Bert); Hadi (Ernie); Shaw Parr (Big Bird); Khajoor (Cookie Monster); Kajkoal (Grover); Gom Gom (Oscar); Pari (Prairie); Zeba (Zoe), Rukhsaar (Rosita); Shaarmac (Telly); Khwaaga (Businka from Ulitsa Sezam); Gulguly (Tuktuki from Sisimpur); Khushaal (Khokha from Alam Simsim); Laala (Lola from Plaza Sésamo); Zari
Australia *English*	Open Sesame/2004	Ollie
Bangladesh *Bangla*	Sisimpur/2005	Halum; Tuktuki; Ikri Mikri; Shiku; Elmo; Raya
Brazil *Portuguese*	Vila Sésamo/1972 & 2007	Garibaldo; Bel; Retired: Gugu
Canada *English (with some French)*	Sesame Park/Sesame Street Canada/1973	Basil; Louis; Chaos; Dodi; Katie
China *Mandarin*	Zhima Jie/1998 & Big Bird Looks at the World/2010	1998: Da Niao; Xiao Mei Zi; Hu Hu Zhu 2010: Da Niao; Lily; Elmo
Denmark *Danish*	Sesamgade/2009	Elmo
Egypt *Arabic*	Alam Simsim/2000	Nimnim; Filfil; Khokha
Finland *Finnish*	Seesamtie/1997	Alfa; Romeo
France *French*	1, Rue Sésame/1978	Mordicus; Toccata; Trepido

(Continued)

TABLE 1.1 Continued

Country of origin/Language(s)	Series title/Year of first broadcast	Muppet character names
France *French*	5, Rue Sésame/2005	Nac; Griotte;Yoyo; Georges; Olive; Elmo
Germany *German*	Sesamstrasse/1973	Samson; Finchen; Pferd;Wolle; Bert; Ernie The following are retired: Tiffy; Rumpel; Buh; Lena; Moni; Felicitas Filu; Gustav Zobi, Kami
Ghana *English*	Teacher training modules/2011	
Gulf *Arabic*	Iftah Ya Simsim/2015	No'man; Shams; Melsoon; Gargur; Melsoon
India *Hindi, Gujarthi, English, Marathi, Tamil, Telugu*	Galli Galli Sim Sim/2006	Aanchoo; Boombah; Chamki; Googly; Toto; Elmo; Grover; Khadoosa; Raya; Zoonie; Dhenchoo; Bollywood Hero
Indonesia *Bahasa Indonesia*	Jalan Sesama/2008	Jabrik; Momon; Putri;Tantan; Elmo
Israel *Hebrew*	Rechov Sumsum/1983	Kippi; Moshe Oofnik
Israel *Hebrew*	Rechov Sumsum/2006	Noah; Brosh; Avigail; Sivan; Gruvi; Moshe Oofnik; Elmo
Israel/ Palestinian Territories *Hebrew/Arabic*	Rechov Sumsum/Shara'a Simsim/1998	Kippi; Moshe Oofnik; Dafi; Haneen; Kareem
Israel/Palestine/Jordan *Arabic, Hebrew*	Sippuray Sumsum(Israel)/ Hikayat Simsim(Palestine, Jordan)/2003	Israel: Noah; Brosh Palestine: Haneen; Kareem Jordan:Tonton;Juljul

(Continued)

Country of origin/Language(s)	Series title/Year of first broadcast	Muppet character names
Japan *Japanese*	Sesame Street/2004	Elmo; Pierre; Cookie; Mojabo; Big Bird; Grorie; Teena; Meg; Arthur
Jordan *Arabic*	Hikayat Simsim/2007	Juljul; Tonton
Kosovo *Albanian, Serbian*	Rruga Sesam/Ulica Sezam/2004	No local Muppets[1]
Kuwait *Arabic*	Iftah Ya Simsim/1979	No'man; Melsoon; Yaqut; Abla
Mexico (Latin America) *Spanish*	Plaza Sésamo/1972	Abelardo; Pancho; Lola; Elefancio; Gaby; Elmo; Señor Lechuga; Modesto Microfono; Vicent; Baron Purpura
The Netherlands *Dutch*	Sesamstraat/1976	Pino; Tommie; Ienie Mienie; Purk; Angsthaas; Stuntkip
Nigeria *English, Hausa*	Sesame Square/2011	Kami; Zobi
Northern Ireland *English*	Sesame Tree/2008	Archie; Samson and Goliath; Claribelle; Hilda; Potto; Weatherberries
Norway *Norwegian*	Sesam Stasjon/1991	Max Mekkar; Alfa; Bjarne Betjent; Py
Pakistan *Urdu*	Sim Sim Hamara/2011	Rafi Peer[2] puppets: Rani; Munna; Haseen; Baaji; Aienna; SW/Henson puppets: Elmo, Baily
Philippines *Tagalog and English*	Sesame!/1983	Pong; Kiko Matsing
Poland *Polish*	Ulica Sezamkowa/1996	Bazyli; Beata; Pędzipotwór
Portugal *Portuguese*	Rua Sésamo/1989	Poupas; Ferrao; Tatatita
South Africa *See language note below[3]*	Takalani Sesame/2000	Moshe; Zikwe; Zuzu; Neno (Elmo); Kupukeji; Kami

(Continued)

TABLE 1.1 Continued

Country of origin/Language(s)	Series title/Year of first broadcast	Muppet character names
Russia *Russian*	Ulitsa Sezam/1996	Zeliboba; Kubik; Businka
Spain *Spanish* *Catalan*	Barrio Sésamo (Barri Sèsam) Barrio Sésamo: Monstruos Supersanos/1979	1979: Caponata; Perezgil 1983: Espinete; Don Pimpón 1996: Vera; Gaspar; Bluki; Bubo 2012: Elmo; Blas (Bert); Epi (Ernie); Triqui (Cookie Monster); Coco (Grover); Rosita, Dr. Rooster
Sweden *Swedish*	Svenska Sesam/1981	Animated Puppets: Fia Jannson; Hansson
Tanzania *Kiswahili*	Kilimani Sesame/2007	Kami; Moshe; Neno; Zikwe; Zuzu
Turkey *Turkeish*	Susam Sokagi/1989	Minik Kus; Gulec; Kirpik
United Kingdom *English*	Play with Me Sesame/2004	Domby; Kit

1 The Kosovo project used an adaptation of Sesame Workshop's Open Sesame program which features "classic" Sesame Street Muppets such as Bert and Ernie. The program included locally produced live action segments.

2 Sim Sim Hamara was produced in partnership with Rafi Peer, a Lahore-based production company which specializes in puppetry. The program included a mix of Henson and Rafi Peer puppets.

3 South Africa: TV Seasons 1–3: Zulu, Sotho, English, Afrikaans, Nguni, and Xhosa (code switching); Season 4: Tshivenda, Sepedi, Setswana, Zulu, and English (each episode in each); Season 5: Afrikaans, Xhosa, Sotho, Tsonga, and English (each episode in each language); Seasons 6–10: English, Afrikaans, Zulu, Tshivenda, Sepedi; with radio broadcast in 11 official languages.

specificity of these programs is at the heart of their success educationally. Each is developed through the application of a flexible production process (summarized in Figure 1.2) that begins with a needs assessment, includes the creation of an educational framework, which is then, in turn, used as a structure for developing content that is tested and refined before it is distributed. Ideally, the process also includes research to assess impact and provide lessons learned for future production; when possible, this summative research is commissioned to an outside agency to promote greater objectivity of the assessment.

The idea that children learn within a cultural context has been well established by psychologists such as Rogoff (2003), who have carefully documented environmentally based differences in children's development. Such researchers have illustrated that while children throughout the world pass through some similar developmental milestones—for example, at about age one children across the world learn to walk—important differences in performance can be directly traced to the child's learning context. It is honoring this mix of nature and nurture that has been a key to Sesame Workshop's international success.

At the core of Sesame Street's international work is a production process that has proven to be an excellent blueprint for creating culturally specific content throughout the world. Internationally, the key aspects of the success of this approach lie in its flexibility, experimental essence, and dependence on collaboration of experts from a range of fields at nearly every stage of production. To gain a better sense of how this process is applied, it is worth unpacking each of its various elements.

Need and Feasibility

Sesame Workshop has prided itself in only going places where the organization is welcomed by local champions who see the value and potential of Sesame Street programming to help meet critical needs of young children. Initially, there was some surprise that Sesame Street would be of interest outside of the United States. The program had been intentionally designed to meet the needs of American children and seemed—from the setting, to the characters, to the educational content—something quintessentially American. As Joan Cooney framed it in an interview (mentioned in the foreword to this book) with Jim Henson that aired on NBC, "if you recall, it was very American and sort of 'hip' American . . . so it sort of caught me by surprise when the Germans came to us and said, 'Can we do a coproduction?;' not just dub it; a real coproduction" (20 and Still Counting, 1989).

In fact, the early development of Sesame Street in Germany is a good example of the way in which Sesame Workshop's international model emerged. As with Sesame Street in the United States, the program began with input from educators who worked to set its educational plan. The discussions reflected the sensibilities of the time. One key difference in the educational thrust of the German series has been, since the beginning, its orientation toward pro-social relationships with cognitive elements more implicitly represented. Early learning practices focused on a "kindergarten" ideal (see Fröbel, 1826/1902) that emphasized a different kind of approach than was common in the States. The explicit alphabet and counting segments, which had grown to become a signature element of the American program, were of less interest to the German educators who emphasized learning through discovery and play (Lesser, 1978). The discussions were inspired by the country's cultural climate that had emerged in the post-WWII era, and were in keeping with a drive to encourage questioning of authority. Educators wanted to instill a healthy skepticism of dogma and passive acceptance by teaching children to challenge the status quo. (And in fact, the opening song for the show prompts children to question.)

The producers of the program that resulted, Sesamstrasse, created characters such as an engaging brown bear the size of America's Big Bird (known as Samson), Tiffy the Bird, and others who appear along with live action films and animations within the framework of a show format that is distinctively Sesame Street. This format, however, evolved over time. From 1973 to 1978 the show consisted of mostly American segments (initially, live-action sequences produced in Germany were inserted into a dubbed version of the US show). Starting in 1978 the German team created their own studio segments sparked by a growing sensibility that the audience needed more characters from their own cultural background. In the late 1970s American segments accounted for about 50% of the program and slowly decreased to about a third by the late 1990s (Sandra LeBlanc, 2015, personal communication).

The series has been kept up to date and sustained over the years with newly produced episodes in much the same way Sesame Street in the US is refreshed yearly. Changes such as the creation of new characters and the "retiring" of others also keeps the program current. The German producers have initiated innovations such as an animated series—known as *Ernie und Bert im Land der Träume* (whose English title is *Bert and Ernie's Great Adventures*)—which has been exported to other countries including the United States. More recently, the show's broadcaster, Norddeutscher Rundfunk (NDR; North German Broadcasting) created a "spin off" known as *Eine Möhre für Zwei* (*A Carrot for Two*) which debuted in 2010 on the KIKA network and includes some of Sesamstrasse's characters.

The programs in Brazil, Canada, and Mexico[4] were developed with a similar orientation, although the specifics of their historical courses differed.[5] Over the years and across countries, the initial stages of development of international co-productions have included different components depending on the needs and complexities of the country or region where the program was created. Sometimes the process has taken years, as was the case in South Africa where senior executives started traveling to South Africa as early as 1992 on a fact-finding trip. The project began to take hold in 1993 after the Workshop received grants from the Ford Foundation and W.K. Kellogg. The initial stage included a fellowship program for six South Africans who came to the United States in 1994 for a six-month training session where they were resident at the Workshop's New York offices. Full production of the television program, which has been supported through the generous contributions of several organizations including the United States Agency for International Development, Sanlam (a South African insurance company), the Mai Family Foundation, and South African Airways, as well as through partnerships with the South African Department of Basic Education and SABC, did not commence until 1999 or begin broadcasting until 2000.

Setting the Educational Objectives

The use of educational advisory boards to assist in educational programming was not new at the time Joan Cooney established a group of experts in the formative stages of developing Sesame Street. But as Lesser (1974) explains, the first board of advisors for Sesame Street differed from the traditional in that they were substantially more involved in the development process. The idea was not just to rubber-stamp a product created by others, but instead to provide a significant educational framework to guide the creation of content produced (p. 42).

Domestically in the United States, the process used in the early days of Sesame Street has continued today. Each year, Sesame Workshop's education team brings together advisors to discuss the educational focus for that season. While the program has always maintained a "whole child approach," in that it provides learning across the full spectrum of child development domains, in a given year the series has maintained a special focus on specific curricular areas. These have included everything from health and nutrition in response to the obesity crisis in the United States, to targeted messages to promote resilience and coping with trauma. (Chapter 3, which presents some of Sesame Street's recent domestic achievements, details the progression of these different educational foci on the more recent programs, and Lesser and Schneider (2001) present the earlier curricular history beginning with Sesame Street's first season.)

Internationally, the process has unfolded in a similar fashion, with the first season of a given project generally covering a broad range of curricular goals and subsequent seasons presenting core curricular objectives enhanced by special educational initiatives. While there are differences in the developmental course of each project, they all have generally adhered to a basic process that is similar to that used in the United States. Most have begun with an advisory meeting that has shaped the project's educational architecture on the basis of what educational experts deem are the critical needs of children that Sesame Street can help meet.

Interestingly, many Sesame Street co-productions have begun at (or near) junctures of revolutionary shift in a given country or region. Ulitsa Sezam in Russia started broadcast in 1996 after Mikhail Gorbachev's Perestroika movement (which began in the late 1980s) had begun to take hold and drive toward a new more open society; Takalani Sesame in South Africa started to air in 2000 in the advent of the country's post-apartheid era. The Rechov Sumsum/Shara'a Simsim project in the Middle East started after the 1993 Oslo accords, a time of hope and optimism with respect to the Israeli/Palestinian situation. The project in Kosovo followed Resolution 1244 of the UN Security Council which authorized an international civil and military presence. These events, which are markers of paradigmatic shifts in thinking, resulted in the need for new educational resources to reflect changes in the community and the civic lives children were to confront as they grew older. Sesame Street was one way to help address these new needs.

The ability of the Sesame Workshop Model to provide a structure to enable educators to plan for a very different future is one of the key strengths of this process. The development of the curriculum for Ulitsa Sezam, Russia's Sesame Street, provides an example of the flexibility of the process, its value as a tool for developing culturally specific, meaningful educational content, and its capacity as a vehicle for delving into uncharted educational territory. As has been typical of most Sesame Street projects, at the beginning a small group of (in this case, Russian) educational specialists met with the production team to determine an educational plan. The format of this meeting, which took place in Moscow in June 1995, was similar to those executed for Sesame Street programs in other parts of the world. Using a broad definition of "education," in addition to teachers, it included artists such as a composer, a writer, and a journalist, as well as participants representing a diversity of academic fields, such as psychology, physics, ecology, gender education, special education, musicology, pediatrics, and technology.

The approach was flexible enough to accommodate the creation of a relevant and effective educational plan to help children prepare for their future in a new more democratic society. The curriculum contained messages about making choices, learning about democratic institutions, and becoming aware of Russia's diverse society. The process worked because of its commitment to bringing together a spectrum of people with varied backgrounds and expertise to determine the educational plan alongside artists, producers, and others involved in the creative process. To paraphrase an observation of one of the Russian advisors who attended: no single person could articulate an effective plan for the future, particularly because none of the Russians present had grown up in an open society, yet collectively, diverse minds were more likely to come close (Genina personal communications, 1995, 2015).

The Curricular Framework

After the curriculum meeting, the next step in the Sesame Workshop process is the creation of the curriculum document—or as it is known on some projects— the educational framework. It summarizes the results of the education advisory meeting and outlines the specific educational aims for the project (Cole et al., 2001). In short, it is a list of what educators hope children will learn from exposure to Sesame Street.

For many of the projects, the document articulates the range of skills that would awaken children's abilities across cognitive, affective, and social learning domains. Elements such as critical thinking, creative thought, and problem solving are, in many of the documents, seen as the foundation upon which learning in specific topic areas (such as literacy, mathematics, health, and ecology) can best take place.

Many of the projects continue in the tradition of the American counterpart, providing educational opportunities that value a range of learning styles and types of intelligence. For most of the projects, the educational underpinning is very similar, but the distinction lies in what is prioritized in the program content as well as the context in which the learning is presented. This makes sense when you consider the interplay between the natural developmental milestones children across the world pass through (such as learning to walk at about one year) and the way these are intertwined with the influence of the context in which they live (which dictates elements such as language(s) learned and other skills).

A comparison of the curricular plans for various projects reveals that, while there are differences in the ways they are structured and in the specifics of the educational goals represented, most of the documents are more similar than they are different. The distinction across projects, therefore, takes hold in three different ways:

1. the context in which a given skill is presented;
2. the pedagogy underlying a given skill; and
3. the priority and emphasis given to different educational domains.

With respect to context, there are many dimensions that underscore this variation. The most obvious, of course, is the language (or languages) of production. The same skill presented in English will differ when presented in any of Sesame Street's different program languages. Delving a little further, though, it is easy to see how the learning context differs for even something as basic as counting skills, which are a part of most Sesame Street curricula. They take on a distinct twist when segments are developed by creative teams in different parts of the world. A numeracy objective, such as counting to 20, may be worded similarly in the different curricular documents, but when presented on the screen have a very different execution. Counting fruits, for example, may mean apples in the United States but mangos in South Asia. Because writers and the creative team use the curriculum as a launching point for developing culturally appropriate content, the same educational objective is concretized in a unique fashion by the various teams who bring to the process their own creative ideas and their own cultural contexts, experiences, and sensibilities that, in turn, shape the content developed.

The result is a fascinating array of Sesame Street segments from different co-productions that present the same curricular objective in unique ways. Such segments can look very similar at their conceptual and script stage, yet once produced take on a very different form. There are, for example, segments from several co-productions designed to encourage hand washing (before meals, after going to the bathroom, etc.). Each demonstrates hand washing with people at sinks and other places cleaning their hands. The various segments, though, are distinct as the children featured, the plumbing shown, and other indigenous elements give each a signature form. A piece produced for Plaza Sésamo in Mexico, for example, includes a beautifully decorated ceramic sink which is quite different from a line of white porcelain sinks filmed in a Russian elementary school for Ulitsa Sezam. Egypt's Alam Simsim extends the learning further with a live action documentary showing a young boy's careful ablutions prior to prayer. Additionally, a Sesame Street live action film made for Planet Water's Water for Life community outreach project (a partnership with J.P. Morgan) in rural Indonesia depicts children washing their hands at a Planet Water Aqua Tower (Sesame Workshop, 2012).

A look inside the curricular content of the various programs demonstrates the second distinction: the pedagogic approach. Over the years it has accommodated a spectrum that has included sometimes oppositional methodologies such as learning the A, B, Cs (a famous aspect of the America program) to a more constructionist (see Vygotsky, 1980) approach (which scaffolds literacy learning through contextualization opportunities, rather than through the presentation of isolated skills) advocated by some educators (and used on several of the programs). As educational methods change or go in and out of fashion, both in the United States and elsewhere, Sesame Street series are able to accommodate differences.

For example, in the United States during the 1990s, the concept of inventive spelling was introduced on the program. At that time, literacy experts advocated introducing content that would respond to a relatively new pedagogical approach that focused on the developmental stages of learning to spell. This included a step of having children learn to spell phonetically by sounding out words and putting the sounds they heard on paper even if the resulting "word" on the page was spelled wrong (Lutz, 1986). The idea was that this "inventive spelling" stage is an interim step to learning correct spelling in English and encouraging children to engage in inventive spelling was a way to engage them in learning how to spell.

One attempt to introduce this approach to teaching spelling on Sesame Street was an animated segment featuring a cat. With a voiceover sounding out the first letter of the word "cat" ("kah"), the word is first presented on that screen spelled with a "k." The "k" is eventually erased by the cat's tail and replaced with the correct letter "c." While the inventive spelling pedagogy (an attempt to match the sound to the symbol, even if the wrong symbol is used) was well represented and the segment is artfully produced, a concern grew about incorrectly spelling words on the screen. Subsequently, educators working on the team determined that it might be confusing to viewers and agreed that the inventive spelling approach was better suited to classroom learning, where it could be mediated, than on television, where it might mislead some viewers. The approach was no longer recommended for televised Sesame Street content.

Internationally, co-production projects have made similar adjustments over the years. Alterations to Sisimpur's (Bangladesh) approach to literacy provides one example. The producers began with a phonetic orientation that highlighted the connection between individual sounds and symbols; in later seasons of the program, at the advice of Bangladeshi literacy experts, the team moved to a more holistic approach that emphasized the context of words.

The third distinction, regarding priority areas of focus, underscores another advantage of the flexibility of Sesame Workshop's production approach. It allows teams to tailor their curricular emphasis to the specific, contemporary needs of the children in their target audiences. Consequently, across the different co-productions and, indeed, over the long-term history of a given project, different issues have been presented on different programs. Thus, the process allows for the production of curricular content that may be appropriate in one context, but not others. One outcome of this process was an HIV/AIDS education curriculum for the South African version which excited controversy in the United States (US Politicians Attack, 2002). This same process also prompted a live human birth on the Norwegian program (something that would not have been considered on many programs). The impact of many of these varied efforts is presented in greater depth in later chapters of this book.

The Production Process

The seamless tie between education and engagement, which is a signature element of Sesame Workshop's productions, takes wing from the very beginning of the production process. The careful attention paid to elements such as defining the Muppet characters, determining the setting for the program, developing content, and conducting formative research, are all key aspects for forging the indistinguishable linkage between learning and fun.

Defining Muppet Characters

Most of the international co-productions of Sesame Street have their own indigenously devised Muppet characters. The creation of local characters started with some of the earliest international programs where the teams were particularly sensitive to any kind of cultural imperialism and the fact that characters like Big Bird had become American cultural icons (Cole et al., 2001). The creation of Tiffy the Bird, for example, who emerged on Sesamstrasse in 1978 (replacing Big Bird) was a way to ensure that the program was truly German in nature. Interestingly, dubbed versions of the Bert and Ernie segments that appeared on the American program were still included in the German and other programs. These segments were distinct from those that had included Big Bird and other characters in that they took place in a "limbo" set, which is outside the urban American Sesame Street setting, and have, therefore, a more neutral look and feel. The result was that

German children watching Sesamstrasse knew Bert and Ernie as their own, and even today people who grew up watching the series outside the US borders are sometimes surprised to learn that these beloved characters were originally from the United States.

On the various programs that have been developed, a great deal of thought has been given to the creation of the core characters. The various Muppets (listed in Table 1.1) fall into different categories. There are some that are more humanoid than animal-like (in the way Bert and Ernie are). These include characters such as Putri from Indonesia, Chamki from India, and Tuktuki from Bangladesh. Others are inspired by animals (typically indigenous animals), such as South Africa's Moshe, who is a meerkat (the size of Big Bird), Bangladesh's Halum (a Bengal tiger), Mexico's Abelardo (a colorful parrot), Palestine's Kareem (a rooster), and Indonesia's Tantan (an orangutan).

Still others are "monster" characters in the way the rod puppets, Grover, Elmo, and Zoe, and the sack puppet, Cookie Monster, are. These include characters such as Lola (who appears on Plaza Sésamo in Latin America), Neno (an Elmo look-alike who is a central character on Takalani Sesame), and the Palestinian, Haneen, who are all rod puppets, as well as South Africa's Zikwe who is a sack puppet (like Cookie Monster). Notably, several of the programs have "grouch" characters who have been inspired by America's Oscar. These include Mexico's Poncho and Israeli's Oofnik. Still other puppets have more abstract origins, such as Russia's Zeliboba, a full-body puppet who is characterized as a Russian tree spirit.

All the characters have been developed with educational sensibilities in mind. As will be elucidated in later chapters, many take on targeted interests and abilities that are specifically designed to model competencies and sensibilities derived from a given educational plan. Just as in the United States (as noted in the opening pages of this chapter), characters such as Count von Count, who was designed to promote mathematics learning, and Oscar the Grouch, whose contrary ways prompt appreciation of different perspectives, the various international characters afford specific learning opportunities that punctuate key aspects of a project's educational framework. For example, India's Chamki is a vibrant, curious girl who models a love of learning and participation in education, key elements of the Indian program's curriculum. Hilda, an Irish hare who appears on Northern Ireland's Sesame Tree, likes to explore and discover. She is used as a vehicle to transport children to different geographical places to promote learning about the region's diversity. Kami, a Muppet who is HIV positive, has been used to provide children living in South Africa (and elsewhere) a vocabulary for talking about HIV and AIDS.

Defining the Setting

Like the creation of the puppet characters, the production team pays careful attention to developing the program setting. The sets need to service a given project's educational goals and provide fodder for rich story design. For this reason, the teams design the sets so that they scaffold specific educational opportunities while permitting a diversity of potential experiences and activities. Devising this aspect of the production becomes a kind of puzzle that is solved in different ways on different programs.

The Alam Simsim project in Egypt, for example, maintained a special focus on literacy. Its set (like some of the other co-productions) includes a small library (see Plate 1.2). The inherent strength of incorporating this element into the set design is that any segment that takes place in the library naturally carries with it an implicit literacy message, as the characters are surrounded by books and other markers of literacy that become a part of the plot. Other curricular aspects are intrinsic in the settings in other ways, for example, several of the programs (including Alam Simsim) underscore healthy eating with the inclusion of a store (or on some programs a merchant cart) where fruits and vegetables are sold. Messages about the importance of play, exercise, and fresh air are reinforced by sets that include parks, playgrounds, or other recreational elements (see Plate 1.2). Similarly, a sense of community, which is central to many of the programs, has been extended in different places in different ways: a marketplace on Takalani Sesame, South Africa; a train station on Sesam Stasjon in Norway, and a plaza on Plaza Sésamo in Mexico, for example.

Creating and Reviewing Content: Contending with Cultural Differences

Translating an educational objective into content for Sesame Street (whether it is in video, audio, print, or other form) is a complex task that not only requires mastery of the creative craft, but also necessitates a keen understanding of the educational message to be conveyed. For video, audio, and most other platforms this typically begins at the script-writing (or concept) stage. Writers write material to present a given concept outlined in the program's curriculum. This is then reviewed by an education team, which provides comments on the strength of the educational messaging on its developmental appropriateness and potential entertainment value.

At its best, the script review process involves a dynamic exchange between the educators working on the project—who help define the educational messages— and creative personnel, who ensure that material is engaging and fun. When the process is most successful, this is a seamless integration of the education and entertainment sides rather than separate aspects of a whole. When done well, it looks very simple, but it is, like any artfully executed endeavor, far from easy.

On Sesame Street's international co-productions in low- and middle-income countries, much attention is paid to building the capacity of local teams to successfully engage in this dynamic. Critical to training in this regard is helping teams learn the skill of transforming the educational goals outlined in the project's curricular framework into content that is both developmentally appropriate, educationally sound, and entertaining. Over the years, Sesame Workshop's international education team has also developed a series of practical guidelines for creating content within a range of curricular areas (see Table 1.2 for a list). These guidelines provide basic information about a given content area and offer tips on how to present material. But while these types of resources can inform the team and inspire ideas, there is no magic formula for creating good content.

Even with training and other materials, the best way teams learn the process is by engaging in it. When the projects are in their earliest stages, scripts, concept ideas, and prototypes are reviewed by a team of individuals on the New York staff. This review sometimes uncovers interesting cultural differences that emerge across the local and US-based staff and the process results in thought-provoking exchanges between members of the teams collaborating on a given project. Some of the more animated discussions have to do with the balance between whether a point is or isn't consistent with "Sesame Street" values or the Sesame Street brand versus aspects that concern cultural sensitivities or interpretation.

Safety, for example, is one place that often generates rich dialogue. There is a common understanding that the Sesame Street approach strives to model safe practices. In the United States, for example, when children are in vehicles, they are shown wearing safety belts and wearing bicycle helmets when riding a bike. Yet in different contexts what constitutes "safe" practice differs with some elements lacking relevance in some places. Over the years, questions have emerged, for example, around modeling safety belt usage in places where most cars are not equipped with them or using bike helmets in a locale where they are difficult to buy and beyond the financial reach of many viewing families.

Negative modeling is often another issue that arises (and this frequently relates to safety issues). The Sesame Street approach emphasizes showing children what to do, rather than what not to do. Instead of, for example, a message such as "don't touch a sharp knife" if there is an instance where cutting something is part of the script, the action itself would be completed by an adult with children appropriately distanced from the activity. While these points have been debated with

TABLE 1.2 Guideline topic areas

Character building	Family and home	Multilingualism
Computers	Feelings and emotions	Music
Conflict resolution	Gender	Numbers
Cooperation	General health	Optimism
Death	Healthy foods	Reading and writing
Disabilities	HIV/AIDS	Road safety
Divorce	Identify	Safety
Entering social groups	Immunization	Sanitation
Environment	Letters and words	Science
Ethnicity and culture	Moral development	

some teams who argue that children effectively use such instruments in appropriate contexts (and indeed, in certain cultures young children safely manage sharp objects—see for example, Rogoff's (2003, 168) picture of a child using a large machete), because the visual images are so powerful, the thinking is that it is best to avoid depictions that could prompt children to engage in unsafe practices, particularly when unsupervised.

In a similar vein, modeling healthy eating can be a challenge as what is considered good nutrition in one place may differ in others, and the importance of modeling good eating habits has, itself, evolved over the history of the program. Sesame Street generally avoids the depiction of candy and other treats, favoring fruits and vegetables. Yet there are many contexts (for example, birthdays and other celebrations) where sweets and other foods are appropriate. Consequently, the depiction of sweets in segments is sometimes a topic of debate. The preferred orientation, which evolved over time, is to teach children that such foods are "sometimes" foods that can be enjoyed in moderation. But this mantra, now forcefully adopted by the cookie-obsessed Cookie Monster character, is a relatively recent practice that emerged as a response to the obesity epidemic in the United States (and other countries) and the creation of Sesame Workshop's healthy habits curriculum (Cole et al., 2010).

Debate also occurs when teams select material from Sesame Street's international library of segments for inclusion in their programs. (In addition to newly produced content, most of the international co-productions include material originally produced for the US or other co-productions; this shared material is then dubbed into the local language and incorporated into the magazine format of a given episode.) As part of a selection process, the production team in Afghanistan, for example, solicited input from parents. After parents screened one piece—a segment from the United States where the Muppet character Ernie "barks" and encourages his sidekick, Bert, to join him in acting like a dog—the team opted out of using the segment, citing that in Afghanistan many people consider dogs unclean (Sesame Workshop, 2011). Similarly, in Pakistan, the production group edited a piece where the character Elmo was at a petting zoo and some of the animals in the scene were pigs. Members of the team noted that pigs are considered in their culture unclean (Sesame Workshop, 2011) and they opted for content that didn't include reference to anything porcine.

Avoiding political overture has also been a tricky element of the content review process. An example from Palestine provides some insight. In a joint Palestinian–Israeli production of Sesame Street created in the 1990s, the Palestinian team developed an alphabet animation that included a depiction of the Palestinian flag. The Israeli team objected to the picture. Separate versions were then made of the animated piece for broadcast in different regions, with one version using a generic race car-like checkered flag.

The beauty of the Sesame Street process is that it allows for such discourse and for compromises to be made. While not everyone is happy with the final decision in every case, there is an effort to engage in a process that enables different ideas and sensibilities to be weighed. The success of Sesame Workshop's international programs is attributable to the commitment all parties make to this process. All share the aim of producing content that effectively reaches, teaches, and engages young children.

Formative Research

The use of research to inform the production process has, since its origin, been a signature element of the Sesame Workshop Model (Fisch and Bernstein, 2001). This has also been true internationally, although the depth of usage of formative research has varied across projects. Integrating formative research requires careful planning, a ready infrastructure, and an ability to execute research in an efficient manner. The process is quite different from conducting academic research.

Formative research is used for a variety of purposes:

1. to provide background information on a specific topic;
2. to gauge the audience's knowledge about a given topic (in order to develop material at the right level); and
3. to determine the setting, characters, and other basics for a program; test comprehension of educational messages; and measure engagement and the entertainment value of content and formats.

At the heart of this process is a commitment to the experimental approach that Cooney defined in her initial concept of Sesame Street (Lesser, 1974). Over the course of four decades, each new season has been conceived of as "experimental" in nature. Such an approach has many advantages, particularly with respect to a creative process. It allows teams to try new ideas, however unconventional, and test their worth. Indeed, much of the longevity of the program can be attributed to this mentality as it promotes risk taking and innovation. It also inherently respects the audience for which the program is intended as the research process brings the voice of the child into the production as it moves forward.

Internationally, the formative research process has been used to sharpen approaches to difficult issues and better understand reactions to and comprehension of content as it has been developed. Teams have also tested entire episodes of international co-productions to gain generalized lessons to apply to future production. While in some international contexts the use of formative research has been more challenging due to funding and scheduling constraints, when it has been well integrated into the production plan, it has proven an invaluable asset.

The development of the HIV/AIDS educational curriculum in South Africa (which is presented in greater detail in Chapter 5 of this book), provides a good example of the way formative research has been effectively applied on a co-production. The process began with an extensive literature review (Fox et al., 2000a, 2000b) that brought together basic statistics about HIV/AIDS (such as gender discrepancies in incidence rates) and best practices regarding education approaches (particularly given the target age of the Sesame Street viewers). Next, the team tested children's and caretakers' knowledge of the disease. This was particularly helpful in that it provided baseline information and assisted the team in orienting the messaging to the correct developmental level. For example, from interviews with children they learned that, while many understood that AIDS was something negative and some alluded to the stigma attached to being HIV positive, many children lacked even the most basic understanding that AIDS is a disease and how it is transmitted (Segal et al., 2002). Launching from this information, the production team devised segments that provided age-appropriate information to help children learn that AIDS is a "disease in the blood," that "you can't catch HIV by touching someone," and that you can be friends with people who are HIV positive. The research also uncovered a need for providing strategies for coping with the disease. In response, the team developed content that modeled practical approaches such as creating a "memory box" to remember a loved one.

As explained in greater detail in Chapter 5, the baseline research also helped in the creation of a Muppet character. Kami, as she came to be known, was purposefully designed to be female (due to the historically disproportionate number of women in South Africa who are HIV positive), a Muppet "monster" puppet with humanoid (rather than animal-like) features to emphasize that AIDS is a human disease, and vibrant (to counter the belief that all people with the disease are sickly). Messaging for adults—which was designed to provide strategies for talking to children about HIV and AIDS—was derived from formative research that showed that there was a "culture of silence" around the disease and a need to de-stigmatize having the disease or knowing someone infected (Segal et al., 2002).

Another example of the effective use of formative research comes from a global road safety campaign that was completed in partnership with Global Road Safety Partnership (GRSP). The project aimed to develop a series of public service announcements to be televised internationally. Because the idea was to create content that would be relevant across a broad array of regional, cultural, and other contexts, the production team conducted a multi-country formative research study that solicited feedback on two levels. Educational content specialists from different countries reviewed the content for its relevance and researchers also interviewed children in two countries (Jordan and India) to solicit their reactions to preliminary versions of the visual content. Of particular concern was a thumbs-up gesture used at the end of the animation (Plate 1.3). The research concluded that, although there were a few places in the world that the gesture is considered rude, the advisors felt that, in the context of the animation, the gesture would be interpreted in a positive light as the (Grover) character's affect is clearly positive and he is using the signal in a fashion similar to the way it is used internationally by pilots and others to communicate that everything is OK (see Morris et al., 1979). The formative review process also helped to shape these animations in other ways. At the request of content reviewers in the Middle East, the team revised the clothing a maternal character is wearing: her shirt was elongated to create a longer tunic that covered her body more modestly (Plates 1.4a and b).

Distribution

While television has typically been the driver of various co-production projects in most countries, it is not the only platform used to carry Sesame Street content and in some places has not been the lead platform. A teacher education project that launched in 2012 in Ghana, funded by the Innovation Development Progress (IDP) Foundation, is one good example of a non-television project. The program, comprised of ten ten-minute videos and an accompanying printed manual, was designed for use as a training tool for IDP's Rising Schools Program; the project had no television broadcast component (although the videos can be viewed on YouTube).

Table 1.3 presents the range of platforms used for various current co-productions. Notably, a few (such as Afghanistan, India, and South Africa) have strong radio components that have proven to be particularly valuable in locales where access to television (due to factors such as limited electricity and other infrastructure concerns) is an issue. The programming is specially designed for the medium, and is not merely an audio version of the television program.

Print materials have also shown to be an effective way to reach some populations. As noted and more fully detailed, for example, in Chapter 8's discussion of the Indian co-production, teams have developed low-tech innovations, such as printed mats, games, and other low-cost materials that more easily reach children and caregivers in under-resourced environments than higher-tech media. The use of the various platforms is further detailed in the chapters that follow.

Summative Evaluation

Whereas formative research helps the production team as content is being developed, summative evaluation assesses educational effects after content has been distributed. Over the years, Sesame Workshop has commissioned numerous studies to evaluate the impact of its international projects. The ensuing chapters present the context for and commentary on the results of these and other studies of the company's various international projects.

In low- and middle-income countries, the process for commissioning these studies is complex. As further elucidated in this book, across the history of these studies, Sesame Workshop has improved techniques for the design and implementation of summative research. The organization has, for example, developed a body

TABLE 1.3 Current co-productions and their media platforms

Project	Broadcast TV	Radio	Digital media (mobile phone, tablet, website, and social media)	Community/School Engagement				
				Print	DVD/Community viewings/listening	Teacher training	Parent workshops	Awareness workshops
Afghanistan	✓	✓					✓	✓
Bangladesh	✓						✓	✓
Brazil	✓		✓	✓	✓			
China	✓		✓	✓	✓	✓	✓	
Germany	✓		✓					
The Gulf	✓		✓	✓		✓		
India	✓	✓	✓	✓	✓	✓	✓	
Indonesia	✓		✓	✓	✓	✓	✓	
Israel	✓		✓	✓	✓	✓		
Latin America	✓		✓	✓	✓		✓	
The Netherlands	✓		✓					
Nigeria	✓		✓	✓	✓	✓		
South Africa	✓	✓	✓	✓		✓		

of sample questionnaires for use with young children, created training programs to hone data collectors' interviewing and recording techniques, built skills in data analysis, provided formats for report writing, and developed templates for budgeting various types of research. This material, as well as the associated training programs, has been an integral part of Sesame Workshop's engagement and has been a needed step that has sometimes been overlooked by other organizations commissioning large-scale studies of impact.

One reason other organizations cite for a more hands-off approach to evaluative research has been a legitimate concern over the objectivity of data collection and analysis. Yet, the counter argument (in favor of some involvement in the summative process) is also of value. Researchers need to understand the structure and content of the media intervention in order to develop a sound research design. Additionally, in many of the countries where Sesame Workshop has programming, it can be difficult to find researchers who are experienced in studying the impact of children's educational media resulting in the added need for training to build capacity in study design, data collection, analysis, and communication of findings. As Sesame Street co-productions sit at the intersection of four major fields—early childhood development, education, media, and international development—it is difficult to find research expertise in all these areas simultaneously. As a kind of compromise, Sesame Workshop therefore steps in to fill the gaps with researchers as necessary by scaffolding a procedure that supports research efforts on the ground, while still enabling researchers who have not been attached to the production process to drive the process. In different contexts we have been more and less successful at facilitating this process with varying degrees of independence depending on an array of factors.

For a project in the Middle East (Cole et al., 2003), for example, Sesame Workshop's role was more hands on than has been the case elsewhere. Our level of involvement stemmed from a need to serve as a bridge between the various groups involved (in this case Israelis and Palestinians; see Chapter 7 for a more complete discussion). On other projects, for example, one in Indonesia (Borzekowski and Henry, 2010) we provided feedback on questionnaires that mapped on to program content, but researchers worked independently to design the study, collect data, and analyze effects.

The point, however, about objectivity is critically important, and one we do not take lightly. As the field of children's media research has broadened in low- and middle-income countries, there are increasing opportunities for studies of Sesame Street (and other programs) to be conducted more independently. Further, as the interest in research impact has increased, funding agencies (such as USAID) are more apt to commission their own studies on a project-by-project basis. This is a welcomed development as it not only underscores the recognized value of impact research, but also provides another avenue for gaining information on effects.

All studies, whether or not they are commissioned by Sesame Street, can benefit from the lessons we've learned over the years. As further discussed in the ensuing chapters, across the various studies we have gleaned some best practices for engaging in the process of evaluating educational impact. It is essential, for example, to begin with a well-conceived educational framework. Having a clear sense of a project's educational focus is the only way to conduct a study that truly examines impact and answers the question of whether or not a program successfully attained its educational goals. Additionally, as any given season of a Sesame Street production presents only a subset of the educational objectives outlined in the project's framework, it is important to conduct an extensive analysis of content prior to commencing a study. This ensures that the objectives researched match those presented in the program and those targeted in a given production season. The benefit of employing a combination of qualitative and quantitative methodologies when designing studies of impact is also something that has become apparent in our work. While each methodology is fallible in some way, taken together they enhance overall understanding. It is worth mentioning that more recently there has been growing emphasis in the field of international development on evidence-based practice and interventions, which has, in turn, favored quantitative research rather than qualitative studies and has pushed for randomized design as a gold standard (see Parker, 2010). While such efforts are laudable in that they have done much to advance the field and encourage more data-driven practices, Sesame Workshop maintains the importance of an inclusive research approach that embraces a compendium of methodologies to benefit from the learning that results from the strengths of different processes.

As the Mares and Pan (2013) meta-analysis highlights, studies of Sesame Street's educational impact show that children are learning from Sesame Street. The chapters that follow delve into the specifics of the findings from both the studies presented in the Mares and Pan analysis and others, highlighting what we have learned about working in various low- and middle-income countries and the strengths and weakness of different co-production projects in promoting specific educational aims. In particular, these pages speak to Sesame Street's successes and limitations in supporting key aspects of the international development agenda, including the need for high-quality basic education materials, improved health communication, and peace-building efforts.

Conclusion

Children learn from a range of influences that include family, friends, school, and community. The various media platforms—from print, to television, to hand-held devices and other new technologies—are only one band in that spectrum. Yet, given the time children spend interfacing with media of all kinds, children's engagement with various media platforms has an important hold on what and how children learn. Whether by design or unintentionally, children are swayed by the media they are exposed to. As educators, we have an obligation to exploit the positive value of media and build content that purposefully delivers on an educational promise.

In low- and middle-income countries, delivering on this education promise is all the more critical due to the accessibility of television, radio, and other media and because of the millions of children who lack access to high-quality formal educational experiences who can potentially benefit from well-conceived and intentionally designed educational media. Given the scarcity of high-quality educational resources, media are an efficient and effective way to reach and teach young children. Sesame Street's projects in LMICs have worked to help support international education, health, and democracy and governance development goals by delivering culturally relevant, high impact, developmentally appropriate content.

While Mares and Pan (2013) have quantified the size of the Global Sesame Effect (.29), which is a helpful step in understanding impact, the pages that follow dig deeper to define its specifics and offer insights from research about the strengths and weaknesses of Sesame Workshop's international work. The various initiatives highlighted can be assessed both in terms of their effectiveness in educating children and with respect to the contributions they make to the societies in which these children live. As the opening quote from Nelson Mandela reminds us, "education is the most powerful weapon which [we] can use to change the world," and luckily we have a family of carefully developed, locally specific Muppets to assist in that effort.

Notes

1. As measured by Cohen's d, a statistic used to provide a standardized comparison of effect size: see Cohen (1988).
2. The diagram itself is illustrative of the time period in which Sesame Street was developed. The use of a Venn diagram, borrowed from the field of mathematics and invented in the late 1800s, was popularized, with the introduction of set theory, in the 1960s and was a commonly used conceptual device to represent similarity and differences across categories (Henderson, 1963).
3. Interestingly, about the same time Newsweek completed a photoshoot for a cover featuring Cooney that was never circulated because a bigger story hit; while the edition included a story about Sesame Street (TV's switched-on school, June 1, 1970), Newsweek elected to use an alternate cover (Sesame Workshop, January 2015, internal communication).
4. Chapter 9 includes a detailed description of the development of Plaza Sésamo in Mexico.
5. It was ultimately the Brazilian program Vila Sésamo that was the first to broadcast in October, 1972, followed by Mexico's Plaza Sésamo in November of the same year. The Canadian (Sesame Street Canada, which later became Sesame Park) and German, Sesamstrasse, both first aired a month later in January 1973 (Cole et al., 2001, 154).

References

20 and Still Counting (1989). Sesame Street: 20 and still counting. NBC television special, April 7. Produced by Jim Henson Company, Jim Henson Productions, and Children's Television Workshop.

Ball, S. and Bogatz, G.A. (1970). *The first year of Sesame Street: An evaluation.* Princeton, NJ: Educational Testing Service.

Bogatz, G.A. and Ball, S. (1971). *The second year of Sesame Street: A continuing evaluation.* Princeton, NJ: Educational Testing Service.

Borzekowski, D.L.G. and Henry, H.K.M. (2011). The impact of Jalan Sesama on the educational and healthy development of Indonesian preschool children: An experimental study. *International Journal of Behavioral Development,* 35, 169–79.

Cohen, J. (1988). *Statistical power analysis for the behavioral sciences* (2nd ed.). Hillsdale, NJ: Lawrence Erlbaum Associates.

Cole, C.F., Richman, B., and McCann Brown, S. (2001). The World of *Sesame Street* Research. In S. Fisch and R.T. Truglio (eds), *'G' is for growing* (pp. 147–79). Mahway, NJ: Erlbaum.

Cole, C.F., Arafat, C., Tidhar, C., Zidan Tafesh, W., Fox, N., Killen, M., Ardila-Rey, A., Leavitt, L., Lesser, G., Richman, B., and Yung, F. (2003). The educational impact of Rechov Sumsum/Shara'a Simsim: A *Sesame Street* television series to promote respect and understanding among children living in Israel, the West Bank and Gaza. *International Journal of Behavioral Development,* 27, 409–22, DOI:10.1080/01650250344000019.

Cole, C.F., Kotler, J., and Pai, S. (2010). Happy healthy Muppets: A look at Sesame Workshop's health initiatives around the world. In P. Gaist (ed.), *The role of non-governmental and community-based organizations in improving global public health* (pp. 277–95). New York: Springer Scientific Publications.

Cooney, J.G. (1966). *The potential uses of television in preschool education: A report to Carnegie Corporation of New York.* Unpublished report.

Fisch, S. and Bernstein, L. (2001). Formative research revealed: Methodological and process issues in formative research. In S. Fisch and R.T. Truglio (eds), *"G" is for growing* (pp. 39–60). Mahway, NJ: Erlbaum.

Fisch, S. and Truglio, R.T. (eds) (2001). *"G" is for growing.* Mahway, NJ: Erlbaum.

Fox, S., Oyosi, S., and Parker, W. (2000a). *Children, HIV/AIDS and communication in South Africa: A literature review.* Johannesburg: Cadre.

Fox, S., Oyosi, S., and Parker, W. (2000b). *Children, HIV/AIDS and communication in South Africa: A bibliographic review.* Johannesburg: Cadre.

Fröbel, F. (1826/1902). *Education of Man* (trans. W.N. Hailmann). New York: Appleton.

Gettas, G.J. (1990). The globalization of Sesame Street: A producer's perspective. *Educational Technology Research and Development,* 38(4), 55–63.

GMR and UNESCO (2014). *Progress in getting all children to school stalls but some countries show the way forward: Education for All global monitoring report (GMR): Policy paper 14/fact sheet 28,* http://unesdoc.unesco.org/images/0022/002281/228184E.pdf.

Henderson, D.W. 1963). Venn diagrams for more than four classes. *American Mathematical Monthly,* 70(4), 424–6, doi:10.2307/2311865.

Johnson, L.B. (1964). *Annual message to the congress on the state of the union,* January 8, http://www.americanrhetoric.com/speeches/lbj1964stateoftheunion.htm.

Langdon, D. (1978). Romper Room takes its own advice: 'Do Bee' the longest-running kids' program on U.S. television. *People,* 9(5), February 6, http://www.people.com/people/archive/article/0,,20070134,00.html.

Lesser, G.S. (1974). *Children and Television: Lessons from Sesame Street.* New York: Random House.

Lesser, G.S. (1978). *International trip reports*, volume I. Unpublished report.

Lesser, G.S. and Schneider, J. (2001). Creation and evolution of the Sesame Street curriculum. In S. Fisch and R.T. Truglio (eds), *"G" is for growing* (pp. 25–38). Mahway, NJ: Erlbaum.

Lutz, E. (1986). *Invented Spelling and Spelling Development.* ERIC Digest. ERIC Clearinghouse on Reading and Communication Skills.

Mandela, N. (2003). *Lighting your way to a better future.* Speech given at University of Witwatersrand, Johannesburg, South Africa, July 16, http://www.mandela.gov.za/mandela_speeches/2003/030716_mindset.htm.

Mares, M.L. and Pan, Z. (2013). Effects of *Sesame Street*: A meta-analysis of children's learning in 15 countries. *Journal of Applied Developmental Psychology*, 34, 140–51, DOI: 10.1016/j.appdev.2013.01.001.

Mielke, K.W. (1990). Research and development at the Children's Television Workshop. *Education Technology Research and Development*, 38(4), 7–16.

Minow, N. (1961). *Television and the public interest.* Speech delivered at the National Association of Broadcasters, Washington, DC, May 9, http://www.americanrhetoric.com/speeches/newtonminow.htm.

Moran, A. (2010). Global franchising, local customizing: The cultural economy of TV program formats. In A. Moran and M. Keane (eds), *Cultural adaptation* (p. 12). London: Routledge.

Morris, D., Collett, P., Marsh, P., and O'Shaughness, M. (1979). *Gestures: Their origin and meanings.* London: Cape.

New York Times (1970). Mississippi agency votes for a TV ban on *Sesame Street*, May 8, http://query.nytimes.com/mem/archive/pdf?res=F10F1EF8385C107B93C1A9178ED8544875F9.

Newsweek (1970). TV's switched-on school, June 1, 71.

Nores, M. and Barnett, W.S. (2010). Benefits of early childhood interventions across the world: (Under) investing in the very young. *Economics of Education Review*, 29, 271–82, http://dx.doi.org/10.1016/j.econedurev.2009.09.001.

Palmer, E.L., Chen, M., and Lesser, G.S. (1976). Sesame Street: Patterns of international adaptation. *Journal of Communication*, 26(2), 108–23.

Parker, I. (2010). The poverty lab: Transforming development economies, one experiment at a time. *New Yorker*, May 17, http://www.newyorker.com/magazine/2010/05/17/the-poverty-lab.

Rogoff, B. (2003). *The cultural nature of human development.* New York: Oxford University Press.

Segal, L., Cole, C.F., and Fuld, J. (2002). Developing an HIV/AIDS education curriculum for Takalani Sesame, South Africa's Sesame Street. *Early Education and Development*, 13(4), 363–78.

Sesame Workshop (2011). *Notes on some content review challenges on international co-productions.* New York. Sesame Workshop.

Sesame Workshop (2012). Planet Water, http://www.planet-water.org/wwd-sesame.

Terrace, V. (2008). Encyclopedia of television shows, 1925 through 2010 (2nd ed.). Jefferson, NC: McFarland.

Truglio, R.T. and Fisch, S. (2001). Introduction. In S. Fisch and R.T. Truglio (eds), *"G" is for growing.* Mahway, NJ: Erlbaum.

UNICEF (2014). *Millennium development goals (MDG) monitoring*, http://www.unicef.org/statistics/index_24304.html.

United Nations (2013). *Millennium development goals report*, http://www.un.org/millenniumgoals/pdf/report-2013/mdg-report-2013-english.pdf.

Vygotsky, L.S. (1980). *Mind in society: The development of higher psychological processes*. Cambridge, MA: Harvard University Press.

2

MEASURING THE DIFFERENCE

Charlotte F. Cole and June H. Lee

Don't forget to count!
  Count von Count's advice to Big Bird, 1985, Sesame Street Presents: Follow that Bird

In many ways, the longevity of Sesame Street can be traced to its long-standing dedication to heeding the Count's advice to remember to "count." It is through our commitment to counting and measuring that we are able to assess the difference that Sesame Street is making in the lives of children around the world. As discussed in Chapter 1, when conceiving of the program in the late 1960s, Joan Ganz Cooney, the founder of Sesame Workshop and innovator behind Sesame Street, proposed an experiment to determine whether or not the relatively new medium—television—could be used to help prepare young children for school (Cooney, 1968). This investigative orientation, which culminated in Sesame Street's first season with a comprehensive study completed by the Educational Testing Service (Ball and Bogatz, 1970), has continued to the present and is arguably the single most important factor in Sesame Street's lasting impact. It is this experimental approach and the seamless integration of research into the production process that has enabled Sesame Street's creators to take risks and test the ideas that work and revise or dismiss those that don't. It has also brought credibility to the program both domestically and abroad as the methodology behind the creation of Sesame Street has been recognized as scientifically rigorous. With over 1,000 published studies (Truglio and Fisch, 2001, xvii) of Sesame Street domestically and a significant body of research on Sesame Street's international co-productions, the program sits as the world's most researched children's media endeavor.

Yet, studying the impact of a large-scale sociological force such as Sesame Street is complex. While other media endeavors are measured against yardsticks, such as ratings and reach, Sesame Street is additionally assessed with respect to its ability to catalyze change in knowledge, attitudes, and behaviors. Internationally, understanding the program's educational impact—particularly in low- and middle-income countries (LMICs), the area of focus for this book—takes on an even greater order of magnitude. The study of program impact requires the management of a compendium of factors that necessitate advanced levels of expertise. To be executed well, evaluations need to employ best practices in child development, pedagogy, media research, cultural specificity, and statistical analyses. In addition to a keen and refined grasp of the educational goals of a particular Sesame Street intervention, the study of impact also demands knowledge of a given target audience and the intricacies of that audience's access or exposure. Given that much of Sesame Street's programming serves children living in low-resource contexts, regions of conflict or post conflict, and places with significant infrastructure challenges, this is a tall order. Furthermore, as many of the co-productions have specific areas of curricular focus—some of which are contentious (such as mutual respect and understanding across group divides, HIV/AIDS, and gender equity)—there is also often a need for specific expertise in a given content domain. Thus, given these complexities, at just about every juncture there are issues to be resolved. Yet, despite methodological concerns and other limitations, a body of research has emerged that highlights the educational value of Sesame Street programming. It also underscores how research efforts in some of the more challenging curricular arenas are in need of refinement and continued rigor, as we advance both our understanding of the impact of Sesame Street's work and how to study its effects in LMICs.

This chapter examines the intricacies of studying the educational impact of Sesame Street's international co-productions in LMICs. Critical to the discussion is a Theory of Change that has been applied across the various international endeavors. The chapter also presents issues surrounding the research instruments measuring impact. Using examples from a selection of curricular areas—literacy and math, health, and mutual respect and understanding—the chapter describes various approaches to research design and analysis that relate to the study of impact as a whole, as well as concerns within specific educational domains. It also presents insights gained from research on the cultural impact of Sesame Street as well as thoughts regarding the challenges of measuring exposure. It closes with a discussion of implications and recommendations for the future.

Theory of Change

Effective examinations of impact begin with clear conceptions of the kind of change that is anticipated (Weiss, 1995). Sesame Workshop's Theory of Change for international co-productions (Figure 2.1) describes the impact that its projects aim to have and the strategies employed to do so. At its heart, our theory is based on the

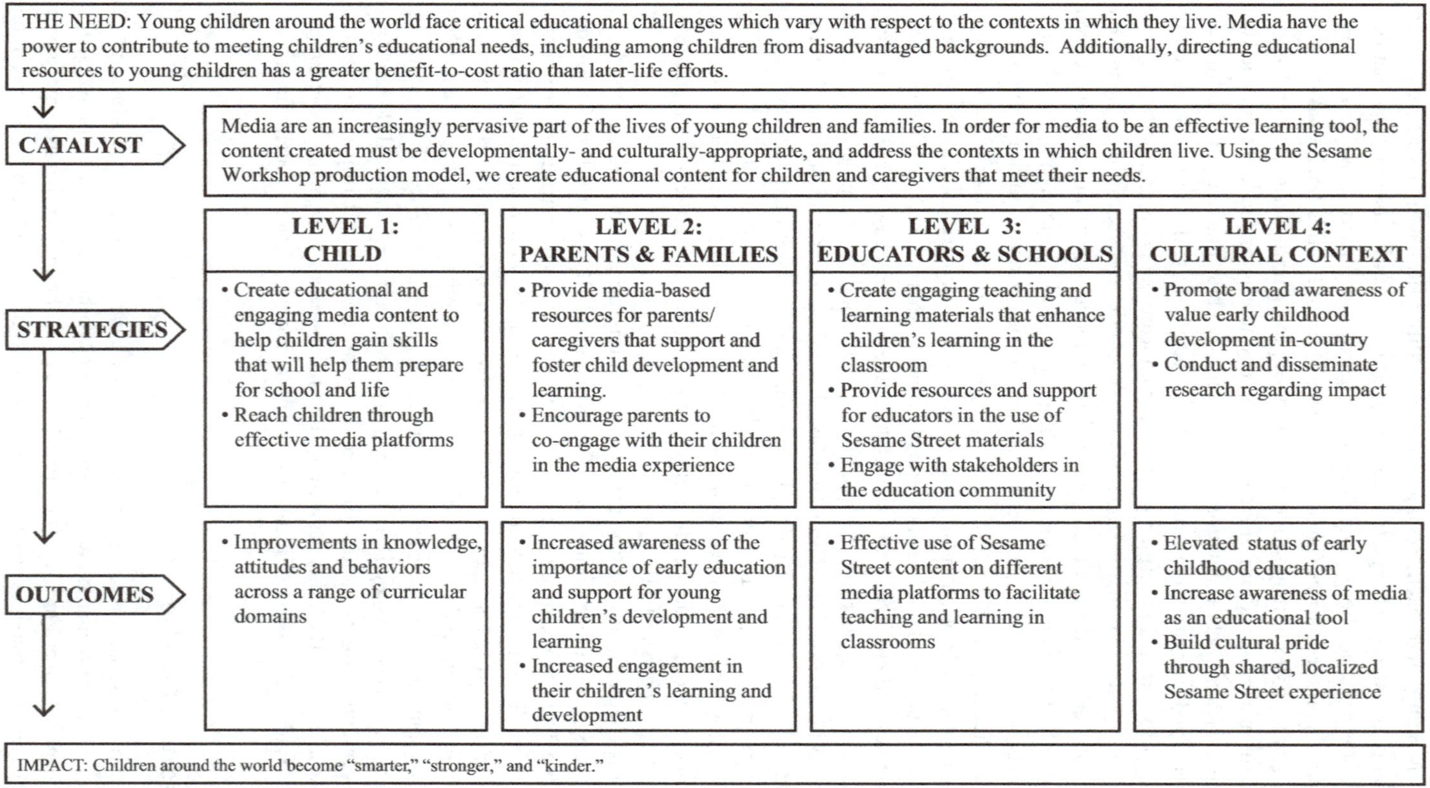

THE NEED: Young children around the world face critical educational challenges which vary with respect to the contexts in which they live. Media have the power to contribute to meeting children's educational needs, including among children from disadvantaged backgrounds. Additionally, directing educational resources to young children has a greater benefit-to-cost ratio than later-life efforts.

CATALYST

Media are an increasingly pervasive part of the lives of young children and families. In order for media to be an effective learning tool, the content created must be developmentally- and culturally-appropriate, and address the contexts in which children live. Using the Sesame Workshop production model, we create educational content for children and caregivers that meet their needs.

	LEVEL 1: CHILD	LEVEL 2: PARENTS & FAMILIES	LEVEL 3: EDUCATORS & SCHOOLS	LEVEL 4: CULTURAL CONTEXT
STRATEGIES	• Create educational and engaging media content to help children gain skills that will help them prepare for school and life • Reach children through effective media platforms	• Provide media-based resources for parents/caregivers that support and foster child development and learning. • Encourage parents to co-engage with their children in the media experience	• Create engaging teaching and learning materials that enhance children's learning in the classroom • Provide resources and support for educators in the use of Sesame Street materials • Engage with stakeholders in the education community	• Promote broad awareness of value early childhood development in-country • Conduct and disseminate research regarding impact
OUTCOMES	• Improvements in knowledge, attitudes and behaviors across a range of curricular domains	• Increased awareness of the importance of early education and support for young children's development and learning • Increased engagement in their children's learning and development	• Effective use of Sesame Street content on different media platforms to facilitate teaching and learning in classrooms	• Elevated status of early childhood education • Increase awareness of media as an educational tool • Build cultural pride through shared, localized Sesame Street experience

IMPACT: Children around the world become "smarter," "stronger," and "kinder."

FIGURE 2.1 Theory of Change

company's mission statement and the belief that exposure to Sesame Street content helps children grow "smarter, stronger, and kinder" (Sesame Workshop, n.d.).

The theory acknowledges that media are an increasingly pervasive part of the lives of young children and families; when developmentally and culturally appropriate, media can be an effective catalyst for addressing children's educational needs. For Sesame Street, the child is the primary focus of most projects, but the Theory of Change recognizes the importance of the contexts—family, school, and the broader culture—in which children live. Derived from the ecological model of human development and the belief that development is greatly influenced by one's environment (Bronfenbrenner, 1992; Bronfenbrenner and Morris, 1998), our strategy accommodates learning in these four levels. Children gain and sustain knowledge, attitudes, and behaviors from the context in which they live; parents, educators, and community are all part of an ever broadening, enabling environment that influences a child's growth. Therefore, Sesame Workshop not only creates media content to reach children where they are, it also provides resources for caregivers (parents and educators) for use in homes, schools, and other environments so that the child's learning is supported and connected across contexts. Additionally, as our content is delivered on a massive scale, international co-productions of Sesame Street not only effect change at the level of children and the adults who care for them, but also at a broader societal level where they elevate the status of early childhood education, augment focus on important health issues, increase awareness of media as an educational tool, and help to build cultural pride.

At each level, we employ a range of strategies to achieve desired outcomes. At the level of the child (Level 1 in Figure 2.1), we create content for multiple platforms that results in improvements in knowledge, attitudes, and behaviors across a range of curricular domains. For parents and caregivers (Level 2), we aim to elevate engagement with children's learning by providing resources that foster interactions and that build awareness and knowledge. At the level of the educator (Level 3), we provide engaging materials that help teachers enhance children's learning in the classroom, support professional development, and engage educational stakeholders. Lastly, at the broader community level (Level 4), we promote the value of early childhood education not only through our content, but also through the execution and dissemination of research that illustrates impact.

Measuring Outcomes

Evaluating the impact of this approach is multi-faceted. It starts with defining what is to be measured, applying instruments to assess those factors, collecting information (data) about those factors, and then analyzing differences between those who have been exposed and those who have not to a given Sesame Street project. To facilitate this process, many of Sesame Workshop's projects in low- and middle-income countries begin with the creation of monitoring and evaluation plans that

TABLE 2.1 Excerpt from Jalan Sesama's monitoring and evaluation plan

Result (1) Use television to help Indonesian children ages 3–6 learn basic skills that help prepare them for entry into primary school

Indicators[1]	Method	2009 (10/1/2008–9/30/2009)	
		Target	Actual
(a) Completion of educational framework for the project	1) Completion of content seminar to determine educational goals	Date for completion: 1) Jan 2009	Date completed: 1) Jan 2009
	2) Document summarizing educational objectives	2) Mar 2009	2) Apr 2009
(b) Reach of *Jalan Sesama* among the target audience			
Measured by assessing the reach of Jalan Sesama, as indicated by the % of mothers/caregivers of children ages 3 to 6 who:	Reach survey: A nationally representative survey of caregivers of children ages 3 to 6 to assess awareness and perceptions of Jalan Sesama. Respondents are interviewed individually, in person.		
1. have heard of Jalan Sesama (by urban/rural area)		Overall: 23% Rural: 17% Urban: 30%	Overall: 64% Rural: 62% Urban: 72%
2. say their children have watched Jalan Sesama (by urban/rural area)		Overall: 23% Rural: 17% Urban: 30%	Overall: 47% Rural: 45% Urban: 55%
3. report that their children watch Jalan Sesama regularly (at least once a week) (by urban/rural area)		Overall: 17% Rural: 6% Urban: 17%	Overall: 43% Rural: 41% Urban: 50%

Result (1) Use television to help Indonesian children ages 3–6 learn basic skills that help prepare them for entry into primary school

| Indicators[1] | Method | 2009 (10/1/2008–9/30/2009) | |
		Target	Actual
4. report that they watch Jalan Sesama regularly (at least once a week) with their child (by urban/rural area)		Overall: 10% Rural: 6% Urban: 13%	Overall: 36% Rural: 34% Urban: 43%
5(i) USAID Indicator: number of learners benefiting from USG-supported pre-primary education (TV)		2,587,875 children (1,293,938 boys 1,293,937 girls)	5,362,210 children★ (2,679,357 boys 2,682,853 girls)
(c) Perception of Jalan Sesama as being educational, entertaining, and Indonesian Measured by the % of parents (who are aware of Jalan Sesama) who agree that Jalan Sesama is:	Reach survey: A nationally representative survey of caregivers of children ages 3 to 6 to assess awareness and perceptions of Jalan Sesama. Respondents are interviewed individually, in person.		
1. entertaining		Entertaining: Overall: 25% Rural: 25% Urban: 25%	Entertaining: Overall: 90% Rural: 91% Urban: 90%
2. educational		Educational: Overall: 25% Rural: 25% Urban: 25%	Educational: Overall: 95% Rural: 96% Urban: 94%
3. reflects Indonesian culture and values		Indonesian: Overall: 25% Rural: 25% Urban: 25%	Indonesian: Overall: 75% Rural: 80% Urban: 72%

(Continued)

TABLE 2.1 Continued

Result (1) Use television to help Indonesian children ages 3–6 learn basic skills that help prepare them for entry into primary school

Indicators[1]	Method	2009 (10/1/2008–9/30/2009)	
		Target	Actual
(d) Demonstrate measurable positive educational impact among the target audience Children's exposure to Jalan Sesama will be linked to outcomes in the following domains: 1) Literacy, including: • Increased ability to identify letters • Increased ability to recognize letter sounds 2) Mathematics, including: • Increased ability to count • Increased ability to identify numbers 3) Cognitive skills, including: • Increased ability to identify colors • Increased ability to identify shapes 4) Environmental awareness, including: • Increased understanding of concepts related to the environment	Controlled experimental study: a study where children are randomly assigned to exposure groups (none, low, and high); measures of educational outcomes are taken before and after exposure, and scores among the exposure groups are compared.	Children exposed to Jalan Sesama will perform at higher levels on tests of at least one curricular area (literacy, math, cognitive skills, environmental awareness, health and safety, and social development). These gains will be evidenced at $p < .05$ level of significance.	RESULTS FROM THE EXPERIMENTAL STUDY[2] **Target met: children with high exposure performed better than those with no exposure in math, cognitive skills, environmental awareness, safety, and cultural awareness.** 1) Literacy: • Letter recognition (not significant) • Early reading/writing (not significant) 2) Mathematics • Number recognition ($p < .01$) [No exposure = 5.7, Low exposure = 6.6, High exposure = 7.5] • Counting ($p < .01$) [No exposure = 5.7, Low exposure = 6.2, High exposure = 7.0] • Arithmetic (not significant) 3) Cognitive skills ($p < .001$) [No exposure = 10.6, Low exposure = 11.5, High exposure = 13.2]

Result (1) Use television to help Indonesian children ages 3–6 learn basic skills that help prepare them for entry into primary school

Indicators[1]	Method	2009 (10/1/2008–9/30/2009)	
		Target	Actual
5) Health and safety, including: • Increased knowledge of health behaviors (e.g., healthy foods) • Increased knowledge of personal safety 6) Social development, including: • Increased likelihood of using pro-social reasoning (i.e., explanations that appeal to friendship, cooperation, helping, etc.) to judge social scenarios • Increased likelihood of proposing pro-social means (e.g., sharing, helping, turn taking) to resolve conflicts • Increased understanding of the idea of "gotong royong" • Increased likelihood to express inclusiveness toward children of another ethnicity or religion			4) Environmental awareness ($p < .01$) [No exposure = 7.1, Low exposure = 6.9, High exposure = 8.4] 5) Health and safety: • Body parts (not significant) • Knowledge about general health (not significant) • Knowledge of health practices (not significant) • Knowledge about healthy eating (not significant) • Safety ($p < .01$) [No exposure = 3.6, Low exposure = 4.1, High exposure = 5.4] 6) Social development • Being friends (not significant) • Social development (not significant) • Cultural awareness ($p < .001$) [No exposure = 5.0, Low exposure = 5.2, High exposure = 7.0]

1 Not all indicators and results are included in this excerpt. Indicators pertaining to training, production of episodes, sustainability, and the reach of outreach (school engagement) projects have been excluded.

2 The *p* values presented denote statistically significant differences between children with no exposure and children with high exposure. The statistical tests controlled for the effects of baseline score, child gender, child age, and parent education.

specify the results to be achieved by a given project; the indicators to be used to measure those results; the method for collecting data to support those indicators, and the targeted change to be promoted. Table 2.1, which is an excerpt from the monitoring and evaluation plan for Jalan Sesama (Sesame Street in Indonesia) in 2009, provides an example of the formal articulation of this detail. The table was extracted from a 14-page document that the project team created during the project's development phase to outline the specific data they would collect to measure program impact. The plan covers comprehensive aspects of the project listing what would be delivered (including elements such as key project activities—trainings, seminars, and the like—as well as production and delivery specifics such as the number of TV episodes to be produced). The document also sets targets around primary outcomes, such as the percentage of children in the population to be reached, as well as children's anticipated learning gains in each curriculum area.

Per the table, much of the information about the program's effect was then measured using data from ratings and market studies (Synovate, 2008, 2009, 2010, 2011). These provided information about reach and perception, while studies of educational impact (Borzekowski, 2010; Borzekowski and Henry, 2010) examined children's learning from exposure. (See Chapter 4 for more information on the specific impact of the Indonesian program.) The portion of the plan presented in Table 2.1 lists the indicators, data collection methods, targets, and achievements ("actuals") for 2009, with particular focus on the findings on reach and perceptions of the program. It also codifies data from an experimental study of educational impact that examined six aspects of the program curriculum: literacy, mathematics, cognitive skills, health and safety, environmental awareness, and social development.

Interestingly, while this kind of comprehensive monitoring and evaluation blueprint was, in this case, required by the project's funder (the United States Agency for International Development (USAID) and is built around a template USAID provided), since the beginning Sesame Workshop's projects have included detailed research plans. As explained in Chapter 1, teams build curricular frameworks at the onset of each project that outline the specific educational objectives to be met by content. Commissioned studies of reach and educational impact (the descriptions of which are a core element of this book) have provided insights into the degree to which projects have met targeted outcomes. This rigorous attention to measuring impact, which is increasingly required by international funding organizations (see, for example, USAID, 2010), is relatively new to some organizations working in low- and middle-income countries. It is, however, very familiar to Sesame Workshop, as it is inherent in the production process the organization has employed since its inception (Lesser, 1974).

The following sections further delve into the issues of measurement by unpacking the various facets of our Theory of Change through the lens of the specific educational domains that have been a focus of Sesame Workshop's work in low- and middle- income countries.

Cognitive and Basic Academic Skills

Sesame Workshop's projects in the developing world, most specifically those in Africa, South Asia, Latin America, and the Middle East, have been intentionally designed to support the delivery of high-quality basic education to young children, particularly those from the most disadvantaged backgrounds. There is an increasing body of evidence that suggests that when children are prepared for school, they are more likely to succeed in school and more likely to stay in school (UNICEF, 2012). Thus, preparing children for school experiences has been an important focus of much of Sesame Street's work. Additionally, while much progress has been made since the turn of this century in increasing matriculation, large numbers of children remain out of school, and many who are in school attend institutions that are well below an internationally recognized acceptable standard (United Nations, 2014). Given its reach and effect size (see Chapter 1), Sesame Street has been shown to be a valuable tool for both supporting school preparation and for providing introductory learning experiences for the most vulnerable children (Mares and Pan, 2013).

As elucidated in more detail in other chapters of this book (see, in particular, Chapter 4), in the realm of basic skills most of Sesame Workshop's programming in low- and middle-income countries has aimed to bolster core skills such as literacy, mathematics, science, and problem solving. Accordingly, some of the strongest findings with respect to Sesame Street's impact in these countries have emerged within this curricular realm. Interestingly, this is a pattern noted in early studies of Sesame Street domestically and in particular in a re-analysis of the Educational Testing Service (Ball and Bogatz, 1970; Bogatz and Ball, 1971) studies of the first seasons of Sesame Street. Cook et al. (1975) used a more conservative statistical technique to analyze the data than was employed in the original studies. Their secondary analysis demonstrated the strongest findings in areas they referred to as "letter," "number," and "relationship" skills (p. 238).

Similarly, several studies of international co-productions, such as those from Portugal (Brederode-Santos, 1993), Egypt (Rimal et al., 2013), India (Gyan-vriksh Technologies, 2009a, 2009b), Indonesia (Borzekowski and Henry, 2010), Mexico (Diaz-Guerrero and Holtzman 1974; Diaz-Guerrero et al., 1976), Turkey (Sahin, 1992), and Bangladesh (ACPR, 2008) also showed the strongest impact in academic skills and literacy and numeracy. The two latter studies, from Turkey and Bangladesh, are especially notable in that they both found an advantage of exposure to Sesame Street that is equivalent to as much as a year of learning (Sahin, 1992; ACPR, 2008). Impressively, these studies—which used pre-post exposure designs—examined large samples (1,166 children in the case of Turkey and over 6,000 in Bangladesh), heightening their representative applicability to the population at large.

It is difficult, however, to disentangle the reason for the strength of these two curricular areas (literacy/numeracy) over others. It could be due to the fact that literacy and math goals have greater representation within the Sesame Street programs studied, and children were, therefore, exposed to more related content. It is also plausible that researchers are better able to measure (and, therefore, more likely to measure) skill and incremental levels of progress within these, rather than other, domains. Additionally, in many LMICs (such as, for example, Bangladesh) children's alternative access to learning is more limited and the potency of Sesame Street is potentially elevated because it provides novel learning opportunities.

Most likely, the strength of the findings in literacy and math are due to some combination of the above factors. When seen in light of other curricular areas, the point about ease of measurement surfaces as particularly noteworthy. In countries using alphabetic languages, for example, knowledge of the alphabet and the ability to decode are typically included as components of a given Sesame Street project's curricular framework. Researchers use a combination of relatively straightforward strategies to test this knowledge that includes such elements as asking children to recite the alphabet, identify names and sounds of letters, point to items that start with the sound of a given letter, and even read and write simple words. Similarly, testing numeric knowledge is relatively clear-cut. Researchers show children quantities of items and ask them to count "how much" or describe "how many." In this way, in both the literacy and numeracy domains, researchers are able to test aspects of learning that are closely linked to the content presented on Sesame Street. Along with the fact that most episodes of most co-productions include some segments focusing on math and literacy, researchers may have a more precise "fix" on children's skill level in these areas and its connection to the Sesame Street intervention which is more refined than in other curricular domains.

Health and Wellbeing

It is commonly accepted in the social change literature that increases in knowledge are generally easier to promote than alterations in behavior (Aboud, 2009). It is perhaps not surprising that the impact of Sesame Workshop's health content has been strongest in the arena of transformation of knowledge. Multiple studies of international co-productions have tracked change in a range of health-related topics, including general health knowledge and practices (UNICEF, 1996; Consultores en Investigación y Comunicación, S.C., 2009; Céspedes et al., 2012), HIV/AIDS (Khulisa Management Services, 2005; Schierhout, 2005; Borzekowski and Macha, 2010), and malaria (Borzekowski and Macha, 2010). But, while providing evidence of positive influence on knowledge and attitudes, the earlier studies shed less light on Sesame Street's effect on behavior. Most studies of behavior change rely on the self-report of practices, an admittedly fallible test of learning. However, given that the ultimate purpose of these health initiatives is to promote the practical adaption of healthier habits, a handful of more recent studies have begun to use designs that more reliably capture data on changes in routines and habits in addition to knowledge and attitudes.

One notable attempt examined the impact of Alam Simsim ("Sesame World" in Arabic), the Egyptian Sesame Street program. The study is particularly interesting in that it relates to multiple levels of our Theory of Change. Researchers (SPAAC, 2004b) incorporated home observation into a more traditional interview survey study of the impact of the project's community health program. (More detail on this study is presented in Chapters 5 and 6.) A cultural anthropologist conducted a series of in-home visits before and after the multi-week health education initiative in two communities (Cairo and Beni Seuf). She visited the homes of five families who had participated in the Sesame Street community program—an intervention that emphasized basic health practices—and observed marked changes in the habits of the families who had been exposed to the program. Her observations paralleled data from the accompanying pre-post exposure survey of 300 parents/caregivers and 200 children. The survey compared responses from an experimental group (who had participated in the intervention) with that of a control group who had not been exposed. Results showed changes in knowledge of hygiene practices and increased knowledge of vaccination that were attributable to the Sesame Street program. There was also some evidence of positive change in nutrition practices with the families in the experimental group more likely to eat fresh fruits and vegetables and encourage children to drink more milk.

Findings from the quantitative survey and qualitative observations of household practices complemented each other. While the former presented a good measure of knowledge gained, the in-depth observations, while conducted in only five households, provided insight into the behavioral application of Sesame Street's programming messages. Notably, while participants gained knowledge from the exposure, for many, their ability to put into practice what they knew was restricted by practical realities including financial constraints. While participants learned of the benefit of good oral hygiene, improved nutrition, and other health habits, the cost of practicalities—such as toothbrushes and toothpaste, having separate towels for each member of the household, regular visits to the doctor, and buying fresh fruits/vegetables and milk—was a barrier for many of the individuals and families studied. Interestingly, the observations highlighted some of the creative ways people put some of what they learned into practice, despite the cost constraints. One mother, for example, who reported understanding the importance of having separate towels for each of her children, cut up an old nightgown to provide individual towels for different family members. Yet, while such innovation was inspired by personal creativity, for others, it was evident that there was a level of frustration in having knowledge that could not be practically implemented.

Findings that reflect the reality on the ground (and in this case, the inability of people to put knowledge into practice due to a lack of resources) are extremely important for an initiative such as Sesame Street. Our intention is to provide knowledge that can help families improve living conditions. A central purpose of the research is to examine effectiveness and use the lessons learned to enhance engagement in the future. The information gleaned from research, while it can be humbling in that it highlights an arena of less success, has helped Sesame Workshop to improve content-development approaches, not only in the given country where research has taken place, but also elsewhere. In the case of Egypt, the results highlighted a need for refinements in the messaging of future initiatives and a drive toward orienting content to provide cost-effective, practically obtainable ways to implement recommended health practices. While it is always our hope that our data will demonstrate positive change, part of the success (and longevity) of Sesame Street has grown from our ability to use the information we gain from research constructively to improve the overall quality of our content in the future.

The SPAAC household observation study in Egypt was particularly important in that it broke new ground in the way Sesame Workshop assessed impact in LMIC countries; it was the first attempt to systematically codify observed behavioral change as a result of an international Sesame Street health initiative. The research included a great deal of detail about the daily living situations of the families observed. Despite its limited scale (the inclusion of only a handful of families) and other concerns (such as a potential bias in that all the families observed had participated in the intervention and there was, therefore, no true comparison group), the study showed that gaining in-depth information about even a few people can greatly improve the understanding of the practical adaption of learning from a Sesame Street intervention.

The SPAAC study also underscores the value of qualitative approaches in helping to understand the effects of Sesame Street programming on behavior. Similarly, a study of Sisimpur, the Sesame Street project in Bangladesh, provides insights, in this case, into the benefit of an in-depth interview methodology (Kibria and Jain, 2009). While this study was dependent on self-report, rather than observed behavioral change, the richness of descriptions are informative. One mother's explanation illustrates the way the program's health messaging was internalized:

> Sisimpur shows a lot of things that we should know about. Suppose the child has used the toilet and then s/he sits down to eat without washing up. This is not right. Because if you do toilet in an open area then dirt can spread. In Sisimpur, it shows one child telling another child, "Look, the child's mother has given him lunch without making him wash his hands first. The child will get sick, it is harmful for him." Sisimpur also shows that it's important for children to eat red spinach. Now I try to give this to my children and they willingly eat it.
>
> Kibria and Jain, 2009, 65

To overcome the limitations of relying solely on self-report of behavioral change (the most common way the studies have assessed behavior) a more recent study (Céspedes et al., 2012) conducted in Colombia took a different tact. Focusing on Level 3 (community) of our Theory of Change, it employed a randomized experimental design that included pre-post intervention tests of children (and caregivers) who had and had not participated in a community health educational program that utilized Plaza Sésamo (Sesame Workshop's Latin American co-production) content. The research incorporated biological indicators such as body mass index and height and weight measures to evaluate changes in nutrition and other health status markers. Results show a positive effect of the Sesame Street programming on health knowledge, attitudes, and behaviors. Importantly, the authors note that the effectiveness of the intervention was linked to the high level of participation and motivation of the educational community in which it was implemented (an aspect that might be difficult to duplicate in other contexts and within a larger scale), which links back to the importance of an enabling context and supportive adults in our Theory of Change. The team plans to conduct further research to verify whether the program effects hold over longer periods of time (the initial study took place over an 18-month period), whether effects are positively associated with anthropometric and biological markers of disease, and whether there are practical ways to bring the program to scale (J. Baxter, personal communication, October 8, 2014).

Mutual Respect and Understanding

Evaluating the impact of Sesame Workshop programming in the pro-social realm is arguably even more challenging than studying cognitive and health skills. Projects designed to promote respect and understanding across group divides, which fall into the pro-social domain, are particularly difficult to assess because they involve discerning not only *how* to measure the curricular construct, but *what* to measure. In this realm, the impact indicators and gauges of success can, at least on the surface, seem less tangible and more abstract than those associated with other educational domains. Yet, researchers have made progress in codifying them and from such categorization have begun to develop usable instruments to track changes in associated attitudes, skills, and behaviors (e.g., Aboud, 2003; Tredoux et al., 2009).

Sesame Workshop's projects work to achieve mutual respect and understanding goals by providing content that helps children from oppositional groups learn about each other (see Chapter 7 for more detail). Our orientation has been based on what others have articulated as a "culture of peace" theory (Babbitt et al., 2013) focused on fostering a paradigmatic shift from a violent orientation ("culture of war") to envisioning a sustained transformation of attitudes and normative engagement.

But measuring the impact of such efforts is not easy. In engaging in Sesame Street co-productions over the years, we have begun to codify and better define what peace education and building respect and understanding means in an early childhood context. At the core of this work are theories of the origin of prejudice and stereotypes in young children (see, for example, Allport, 1954/1979; Aboud, 2003). Children make meaning of the world through categorization. In fact, as educators in any curricular domain, a thrust of our work is helping children to make distinctions that enable them to differentiate characteristics. Children learn concepts such as "high" and "low," "loud" and "soft," and "dark" and "light" by discerning variation. If we didn't categorize, it would be very difficult to communicate and make sense of the world.Yet, the important function of categorizing and labeling is sometimes lost in the discussions of stereotypes. Labels and classifications are not inherently bad or good, but they are potentially problematic when they become extended and take on negative potency and develop into stereotyped knowledge.

Sesame Workshop promotes respect and understanding by applying the same process we have used to develop curricular messaging in other content areas. Child development, education, and other specialists have helped production teams to identify the educational objectives associated with building children's skills. As a point of departure, we have enlisted an approach (again inspired by ecological systems theory; Bronfenbrenner and Morris, 1998) that builds from the child's awareness of self and then extends to an understanding of the lives of others and then to communities and infrastructures and the interdependence of humankind (Cole et al., 2008). This tri-level orientation, that is, learning about self, others, and the interdependences of communities, has provided a framework for measuring the impact of Sesame Workshop's mutual respect and understanding programs at the level of the child (Level 1 of our Theory of Change). Having such a rubric has been particularly helpful given the skepticism of many about the ability to effectively measure the effects of these programs as it has taken us closer to defining the building blocks of peace education in a fashion similar to those defined for other content areas, such as literacy and math.

While there is common agreement that media have the power to persuade (and advertisers have enlisted this knowledge for generations), the negative effects of media are more readily accepted than the positive.The general public is quicker to see that media can distort and convey inaccurate information than acknowledge that it can work toward positive influence.When examined more specifically from the perspective of peace initiatives, it is media's ability to bring groups together by building common ground, providing powerful images and stories that can humanize the face of "other," and building empathy and understanding of different perspectives, can be harder to recognize than media's association with violence and polarization. Part of the resistance to believing in media's positive impact stems from the fact that measuring the effect of something as ethereal as peace building is challenging.The descriptors of peace are more abstract conceptually than those of war.Words like "conflict," "violence," and "aggression" are more easily accessed in our cultural lexicon than are the components of peace, such as "harmony" and "respect," which are more difficult to concretize.Yet, Sesame Workshop and others working in the field are beginning to make headway on how to study this concept.

Studying program effects on peace-building media, as with other curricular areas, typically begins with analyses of the media content presented. For example, examining a media effort to promote literacy attainment might start by determining the desired outcome—in this case, being able to read and write. Researchers would then break down the skills involved in learning to read and write; identify the development trajectory for gaining those skills; examine children's level of attainment on that trajectory, and study the relationship between that proficiency and exposure to the media intervention. For literacy, while educators and academics may dispute specifics, and there are different theories associated with the details, there is a shared sense of the basic components which include the ability to decode words, receptive and productive vocabulary, and text comprehension. Furthermore, researchers have developed (and continue to develop) various standardized (and other) tests to gauge reading and writing levels. Children's proficiency can then be linked to the degree of exposure to a given media intervention to determine the overall effectiveness of the intervention.

Similarly, in the realm of peace building and building respect and understanding across group divides, while theories and approaches are evolving, there is a level of common agreement that the components of peace building, at least to some extent, involve lessened polarization and moving from violence to positive exchanges between oppositional groups. Translated into Sesame Street programming, this means investigating the effectiveness of content designed to build children's self-esteem and pride in their own culture (self), gain an understanding of similarities and respect for differences (other), and build a sense of responsibility to and the linkages between a child's local and global communities (interdependence). As elucidated in more detail in Chapter 7, researchers examining the impact of Sesame Street programming in this content arena have developed a range of quantitative and qualitative tools to measure these curricular aspects. The studies highlight some of the challenges of gaining information about elements such as changes in self-esteem, pride in culture, respect for difference, and awareness of the interconnectedness of humankind.

In Israel and Palestine, Cole et al. (2003) used the Social Judgment Instrument (Fox et al., 1993; Brenick et al., 2007) to examine the educational impact of Rechov Sumsum/Shara'a Simsim, a joint Palestinian/Israeli project that resulted in Hebrew (Rechov Sumsum) and Arabic (Shara'a Simsim) versions of the program. The study gauged Palestinian and Israeli children's perceptions of each other as well as changes in their knowledge of each other's culture, through a series of questions that prompted them to tell researchers what they knew about each other and to solve social dilemmas involving interactions between children of the different groups. The questions presented child-appropriate scenarios, such as which of two children should play on a swing if there is only one. Children's responses were then coded with respect to their positive, negative, and neutral orientations to the "other." The questionnaire yielded information about children's moral reasoning and about Israeli and Palestinians' perceptions and knowledge of the "other" before and after broadcast of the series.

Connolly and colleagues' (Connolly et al., 2008; Larkin et al. 2009) studies of effects of exposure to Sesame Tree in Northern Ireland build on the Cole et al.

(2003) study as well as Connolly's earlier work examining cross-group perceptions of young Protestant and Catholic children living in Northern Ireland (Connolly et al., 2002). The researchers employed an interview protocol that was similar to that used in the study done in the Middle East. Differences in the production process for Sesame Tree in Northern Ireland versus that of the Rechov Sumsum/ Shara'a Simsim project allowed Connolly and his associates greater access to the program content as it was being finalized and they were, therefore, able to develop questionnaires that more directly reflected program content than had been the case in the Israeli/Palestinian study. To assess children's knowledge and perceptions, the researchers used scenarios that were derived from content presented on the screen, testing aspects such as children's willingness to be inclusive of others from a different background, participating in their own and the other group's cultural events, and seeing people from different groups as being similar or different.

Fluent Research's (2008) work advanced the study of program content in this curricular area in a different way. Their use of an index that factored responses from various related questions assessing children's perceptions and knowledge of each other included information on the reliability of their measure (using, for example, statistical tests such as Cronbach's alpha, to evaluate the internal consistency of the index).

All of this is to say that, across the progression of studies, beginning with the use of Fox et al's (1993) Social Judgment Instrument for the study of Rechov Sumsum/Shara'a Simsim, researchers have begun to hone the way the Sesame Street's mutual respect and understanding concept is measured. Yet there is still much work to do. While the Social Judgment Instrument does a good job of evaluating children's moral reasoning, the skills and attitudes that the instrument targets were only indirectly linked to program content were, therefore, less successful at assessing children's learning from the program. Fluent Research (2008), Connolly et al. (2008), Larkin et al. (2009), and others have advanced the measurement further, but we are still only at incipient stages.

This brings into focus a key aspect of research in this realm: the more dissimilar the program content is to the measures used to evaluate it (i.e., the knowledge, attitudes, and behaviors assessed by the instrument), the less likely researchers will find effects (Fisch, 2004). While this may seem an obvious point, in a practical realm it can be more difficult than one might think to link a research measure directly to program content. Part of the issue in this case is a conundrum that confronts many researchers studying the effects of Sesame Street programming. There is tension (mostly due to timing) between the need to conduct baseline data collection prior to the airing of a production and the need to develop instruments that directly measure the content based on what is actually broadcast. Because the actual content of the series is not completely known until it is produced, developing instruments to measure program content for a baseline measure is a challenge, particularly since producers are motivated to make the window between completion of production and broadcast as narrow as possible.

In the case of Rechov Sumsum/Shara'a Simsim and some other Sesame Street projects, researchers developed the research instruments as program content was developed; while they had access to the production plan, curricular materials, and other resources that provided insights into the general content of the programming, they didn't have access to the specifics of the completed material prior to collection of the baseline (pre-exposure) data. In other curricular areas (literacy, math, and health, for example) this has proven less critical as the specific content tested is more easily generalized to an experimental setting. One of the lessons learned from our various studies is that it is essential that the instruments used to measure learning map as directly as possible to specific lessons presented on the screen. This means that research is the most effective when production scheduling accommodates the need to develop research measurement tools (questionnaires, observation protocols, etc.) prior to baseline data collection.

We have gleaned other valuable insights about studying the effects of these programs from the body of studies as a whole (see Chapter 7). The pattern of findings—which show moderate effects of the programming (with impact generally the strongest for the least disenfranchised groups)—demonstrates that there is value in providing content of this nature, but that there is more work to be done both in terms of how we deliver the messaging (particularly to the most marginalized groups) and how we study it. As Aboud et al. (2012) note in their analysis of different programs—including media programs designed to promote social inclusion—there is a great need for research that uses more robust research designs. They advocate, in particular, including more randomized trials, which are clearly needed, as is the need to marry qualitative and quantitative methodologies to gain a fuller picture (in a fashion similar to what we have begun doing in other curricular arenas).

As Sesame Street has refined its study designs in this arena, it has benefited from the work of others, including the study of initiatives such as the Peace Initiative Institute's animation series in Northern Ireland (Connolly et al., 2006) and Search for Common Ground's work (Brusset and Otto, 2004; PARC, 2010). Across these various studies, as with the Sesame Street data, while the nuances of the findings are mixed, there is enough evidence of positive change (albeit often only small effect sizes) to see that this kind of programming holds promise as an effective tool. Further, the research processes, while admittedly still in nascent stages, are becoming increasingly more sophisticated and robust. One limit to all these studies is that none have captured long-term effects. Additionally, to measure abstract concepts, such as a shared common humanity and interdependence, we have used formulations such as looking at knowledge of a child's own and other groups' daily lives, understanding of similarities and differences, readiness to engage with others, and willingness to share limited resources, but there are many questions about whether the instruments used are truly measuring their intended constructs, how the attitudes measured translate into real-world behaviors, and to what degree the elements tested are truly linked to long-term positive change.

In sum, future research examining mutual respect and understanding programming needs to focus on gaining a better understanding of the long-term effects; building better measures to detect more refined gradient changes in attitudes, knowledge, and perception; and employing more robust research designs, including randomized controlled designs and more comprehensive qualitative assessment.

Cultural Relevance

Level 4 of our Theory of Change is focused on a key element of Sesame Street's international work: the creation of culturally relevant content developed by local production teams. Given the evidence that children's learning is greatly facilitated by educational materials and teaching practices that are relevant to the lifestyles and home and community environments in which they live (Myers, 1992, 121), it is reasonable to attribute much of the success of the company's international work to its commitment to cultural relevance. Many early childhood development efforts originating from higher-income countries in the West have been criticized for being based on concepts, values, and orientations—such as a focus on individualism and the nuclear family—that are inconsistent with the norms and traditions of different locales, communities, and groups. Such efforts have been viewed in a negative light and deemed culturally imperialistic (Penn, 2005). As cultural relevance has been a point of distinction for Sesame Workshop's international work, it has been critical to attempt to measure—both informally as well as through formalized research processes—the degree to which programming is perceived as locally relevant.

But it is difficult to discern what is truly meant by cultural relevance. At the most basic level, it can be viewed as the level of acceptance of the program by the general public. One informal indicator is the degree to which Sesame Street programming enters the popular ethos through culturally specific messages and images. For example, political cartoons of several countries have over the years featured local Muppet characters. Additionally, a few countries such as the Netherlands and Germany have issued postage stamps using Sesame Street characters. The Netherlands stamps included both a stamp with classic American characters (Bert and Ernie) as well as several local Dutch characters (Plate 2.1).

In addition to these informal indicators of positive cultural acceptance of the program, Sesame Workshop also conducts studies of audiences' perceptions of the program. This is typically done through national surveys of adult caregivers (parents), who are asked to rate the project on a range of attributes, including cultural relevance (e.g., the degree to which a project looks and feels like a local production and aligns with the parent's values and beliefs). While these self-reported perceptions have some methodological limitations, they can be especially useful when applied in concert with other measures or against data measuring other programs.

Furthermore, a few researchers have devised formalized studies to examine the cultural relevance of Sesame Street co-productions. Li and Li's (2002) study of Zhima Jie, the Chinese adaptation of Sesame Street, grew from attention in research pointing to differences in Asian and Western children's learning and achievement (Biggs, 1996) and its linkages to Chinese people's internalization of Confucian values (Li, 2001, 2002). The study confirmed the researcher's hypothesis that Chinese preschool children would show signs of what is known as "heart and mind for wanting to learn" (hao-xue-xin), which the researchers explain is a native Chinese term used to describe the desire to learn. Further, the study linked the expression of hao-xue-xin back to Zhima Jie's educational framework and a specific curricular aim (i.e., the desire for books and learning).

Kibria and Jain (2009) conducted the most comprehensive study of cultural impact to date. Their study of Sisimpur in Bangladesh employs a variety of qualitative techniques including household observation, individual interviews, and focus groups. The researchers collected data in two phases (beginning in 2005 prior to the broadcast of Sisimpur and then again in 2006 after the program had aired for several months) with a sample that included varied communities: urban, semi-urban, rural with different socio-economic profiles, and a variety of types of respondent: children, parents, teachers, and community leaders.

The study's observational component illuminated the ways children and families engage with Sesame Street. Just as the previously mentioned Egyptian ethnographic study (SPAAC, 2004b) uncovered important limits in the ways individuals and families were able to apply learning, Kibria and Jain (Kibria, 2006; Kibria and Jain, 2009) shed light on something even more basic: practical implications of the limited access to the broadcast. The researchers learned, for example, that many of the children were dependent on the kindness of neighbors who had televisions in order to watch the series; additionally, the unreliability of electricity in communities surfaced as a factor for many children who worried that there would be an outage during the broadcast time (Kibria, 2006). Aware of this issue prior to the Kibria study, Sesame Workshop had worked with Save the Children to implement an innovative community viewing program that brought the series to a limited number of rural communities using rickshaws outfitted with television monitors and generators (Plate 2.2). The benefit of this program was also something captured in the Kibria study, as evidenced in this quote from one of the teachers they interviewed: "The van came here last week and I watched Sisimpur that entire week. Almost 300 people came to see it. I have never seen anything like it. We have become a lot more knowledgeable" (2006, 12).

The research also suggested that Sisimpur was beginning to shift prevailing attitudes toward early childhood education. The dominant attitude toward early childhood was one of "natural growth" rather than purposefully developing knowledge and skills that can help prepare children for the future. Education was often seen as a process of rote memorization rather than engaged, joyful learning (Kibria, 2005). Researchers noted a shift in these attitudes a year after Sisimpur's broadcast. Teachers reported that the series inspired them to be more creative in their teaching; some incorporated songs from the show in their engagement with their students; others modeled the live-action films that showed clever ways to re-use discarded materials. Some educators also felt that children were more prepared with basic literacy and math skills because they watched Sisimpur, and parents were more likely to think about parenting as involving active interactions with children than before (Kibria, 2006). Such wide-ranging effects were not necessarily planned or intentional; that they can emanate from a media project speaks to the powerful ripples that Sesame Street can create. It is also worth noting that such ripple effects—unlike assessments of learning—are difficult to quantify, which underscores the value of qualitative methods for documenting and understanding such impact.

Measuring Exposure and Its Relationship to Educational Impact

While reliably measuring outcome variables associated with educational impact is critical, the quality of evaluations of Sesame Street also depends on researchers' ability to measure exposure to the intervention (whether via TV, radio, print, or other platforms, separately or in combination). Measuring exposure or viewership is important in and of itself (the program cannot have an impact if it is not reaching its target audience) and as a way to discern the linkage between exposure and children's learning (the ultimate test of program impact).

But measuring exposure to a media program with the reach of Sesame Street is challenging. Some of the difficulties have to do with an issue, as Lesser (1974, 222) explains, that plagued even the earliest studies of Sesame Street: the popularity of the program and the universality of its access has made it difficult for researchers to find unexposed (or "control") groups that enable clear comparison of children who have been exposed with those who have not. A few international studies, most notably the study of the Russian Ulitsa Sezam, had an advantage of examining a program that was broadcast only in specific regions before airing nationally. This enabled an experimental study of the program in a "media-dark" region. Researchers randomly assigned schools in Irkutsk (a city in Siberia that did not initially receive the broadcast of the program) to either an intervention group, who regularly viewed half-hour episodes in their school classrooms, or a control group who saw a series of animated fairy tales (that had pro-social educational messages). Analysis of the performance (before and after a five-month period of exposure) on tests of literacy, math, and pro-social skills demonstrated that the Sesame Street viewers on average gained the curricular skills at a faster rate than their non-viewing peers (Ulitsa Sezam Research and Content Team, 1999; Cole et al., 2001).

Most research, however, has been conducted in places where the television broadcast has been either accessible by a broad sector of the population (as was the case in the United States) and/or the accessibility of the program is not easily determined given infrastructure and other issues (such as lack of electricity) that make it difficult to discern who is and isn't watching. (This has been typical of many of the low- and middle-income countries where Sesame Workshop has productions.) Different methods are used to measure children's media use (see Vandewater and Lee, 2009, for a full review) but each has their strengths and challenges. The challenges can be especially acute in low-resource or low-literacy contexts.

Adult (generally parent and/or caregiver) reports of child viewing is one frequently used approach. Parents/caregivers may be asked to keep viewing diaries (as was the case for Anderson et al., 2001) where they record information such as when the child was watching TV, what program (or channel) he/she was watching, and with whom he/she was watching. Other studies asked parents/caregivers simple questions regarding whether and how much their children were currently watching, or used to watch, Sesame Street (see Cohen and Francis, 1999). Such strategies have multiple pitfalls. Parents and other adults often lack accurate information (and/or report inaccurate information) about children's viewing habits (Vandewater and Lee, 2009) and may not provide reliable estimates of viewing time or frequency. Additionally, methods that require careful record keeping, such as viewing diaries (which require time, effort, and familiarity with recording information on paper) can be very burdensome for adults.

For researchers whose primary interest has been to assess educational impact, rather than viewership frequency per se, some have opted to solve the exposure issue using various research design strategies. A study of Susam Sokagi, the Turkish Sesame Street, employed a pre-post exposure design that enabled the researchers to examine learning from naturalistic exposure to the program. Researchers examined a "study" group (that researchers tested before and after a six-month broadcast period) and a "comparison" group (that was only tested once to factor out the effects of maturation and re-test administration). The researchers grouped cohorts of children in the study group on the basis of their ages (within a six-month age span) and tested their skill level prior to and after a six-month broadcast period. They then compared the performance of matched aged cohorts within this group before and after the exposure period. For example, they compared the average performance of children who were age four to four-and-a-half years prior to broadcast with those who were four to four-and-a-half years after the broadcast period. In this way, the researchers compared the skill level of children of the same age before and after the program aired analyzing the difference in "expected" and "obtained" scores on the test battery. They then analyzed the findings with respect to viewing frequency (measured by mother and child reports of viewing frequency and a measure of children's character recognition). Analysis revealed (taking into account maturation and repeated testing effects as examined through the "comparison" group data) that children had gained, on average, a year of competence with respect to the various curricular skills tested. That is to say, four-year-olds at post-broadcast were performing at the same levels as the five-year-olds prior to Sesame Street; four-and-a-half-year-olds the same level as five-and-a-half-year-olds, and so on.

Another approach has been to control the frequency of viewing so that the amount of exposure is easily measured. Using an experimental design, children are assigned to either a viewing or non-viewing group, and researchers administer viewing sessions (either directly or with the help of teachers in classrooms) at a pre-determined frequency. Evaluations in China (Hsueh et al., 2012) and Israel (Fisch and Oppenheimer, 2012), for example, have used this approach. Other researchers have varied the amount of exposure to better understand the "dosage" necessary to make a difference in learning. In a study in Indonesia, researchers randomly assigned children to different exposure groups (a "high exposure" group watched three to four times a week; a "low exposure" group watched once a week, and a "no exposure" group did not watch) and assessed their knowledge before and after viewing (Borzekowski and Henry, 2010). Interestingly, they found that children in the "high exposure" group—but not the "low exposure" group—performed better than those in the "no exposure" group in several outcomes tested, suggesting that regular viewing is important for learning.

Beginning with the earliest studies of Sesame Street, "encourage to view" strategies (Ball and Bogatz, 1970; Bogatz and Ball, 1971) have been one way to handle the exposure issue. Fluent Research (2008) employed such a strategy in their study of the Sesame Street program in Kosovo. They randomly assigned 536 children, aged five and six years, to either an intervention group who were encouraged to view the program or a control group who were asked not to view. Caregivers of children in the intervention group were asked to have their children view the program at least twice a week for six weeks in their homes, whereas caregivers of children in the control group were asked to prevent their children from viewing during the experimental period. While there are limits to this approach as well, its advantage is that the study design provided a way to measure learning from exposure to the program in children's home settings (rather than in an experimental viewing setting such as a classroom).

Research designs that either manipulate or encourage exposure have multiple limitations including the possibility of "corruption" or "contamination" of the control group. Children from the exposure group may share their experience with those in the control group and/or control-group children may inadvertently have access to content that is broadcast. Because it involves an experimental manipulation, the data do not answer the question of what children learn from natural exposure.

Several researchers have worked to solve the exposure issue by devising alternative measures of exposure to increase the precision of the measurement. One approach, similar to that used in the Turkish study, is to use a combination of character recognition and reported viewing frequency to assess children's exposure. This is a technique employed by Rimal and colleagues (2013) in their study of the Egyptian Alam Simsim, which focused on the validity of using character identification as a measure and concluded it was a reliable and recommended method for measuring exposure.

Borzekowski and colleagues (Borzekowski, 2010; Borzekowski and Macha, 2010) take this a step further by capturing not only what a child has been exposed to but also what they remember. They call this measure "receptivity." In one-to-one interviews, researchers present children with a page of character photos: some from the local Sesame Street program, representing familiar and less familiar characters. Researchers ask children to name all the characters on the page (rather than point to a character that the researcher names). This approach avoids the potential that the child may select the correct response by chance; a child can only provide a correct response if he or she is knowledgeable about presented material, even if material was learned indirectly.

To address the critique that receptivity simply distinguishes children who are good at verbal labeling or at remembering media characters from those who are not, this approach requires interviewers to also ask children to name the characters representing generic (non-Sesame Street) media programs. This results in a variable called "general media receptivity." In statistical analyses predicting learning outcomes, the researcher includes both the variables "Sesame Street receptivity" (as the measure of exposure to Sesame Street) and "general media receptivity" (to control for both the child's ability to name characters and general media exposure). Analyses can then demonstrate if exposure to Sesame Street is a significant predictor of learning outcomes, above and beyond exposure to other programs. The researchers have found this to be a simple and straightforward method that is both fun for the child and quick to administer. While receptivity is intuitive and easy to use, further research is needed to validate it, including closely examining its associations with actual exposure to media content, children's cognitive abilities and learning outcomes, and other measures of exposure.

Implications for Future Research

Measuring the effects of Sesame Street's impact in LMICs is a challenge that is at once encouraging and humbling. It is encouraging in that over the years we've made great progress in how effects are studied across a range of domains; yet humbling in the enormous complexity of the task and in the realization of the need for continued efforts to hone our ability to study impact. But if there is a single message that surfaces from the compendium of studies, it is that, as Joan Ganz Cooney (2001) has asserted, "without research, there would be no Sesame Street" (p. xi). The commitment to research is what has guided the company's efforts both domestically and internationally and sustained Sesame Street's capacity as a culturally relevant and effective educational tool both domestically and internationally.

In terms of our ability to examine impact, in the future there is a continued need for robust research. In the literature this is often translated into a call for randomized experimental designs that include comparison groups. Frequently extolled as the "gold standard" of research (Parker, 2010), the approach is valued for its ability to isolate effects related to a specific intervention. Yet, as helpful as experimental studies are, the range of approaches to the study of Sesame Street has shown that there is enormous value in enlisting a compendium of research approaches in studying the effects of Sesame Street programming. While the quantitative methodologies, employed by Céspedes et al. (2012), Borzekowski and Henry (2010), Fluent Research (2008), and Connolly et al. (2008, 2009) have done much to advance the understanding of impact, carefully conceived and executed ethnographic studies such as that of Kibria and Jain (2009) and SPAAC (2004a, 2004b) and have provided information that has particularly enhanced the understanding of the program's impact both in how it is used naturalistically and how learning is applied. Furthermore, the many other qualitative studies which have used focus groups, interviews, and other designs have done much to build our understanding of personal reactions to the programs and ways to enhance their effectiveness within specific contexts.

There is more work to be done to tackle the challenge of measuring exposure but new and better methodologies, such as that proposed by Borzekowski (Borzekowski 2010; Borzekowski and Macha, 2010) are emerging. The advent of new technologies for delivering content also opens a new frontier for research design, data collection, and analysis that has the potential to bolster both the ability to gauge exposure as well as children's learning.

Research efforts would also benefit from greater focus on the reliability of measures and the creation of more standardized approaches to studying effectiveness. Over the years, Sesame Workshop has developed a significant body of questionnaires and other research instruments in various curricular areas that could be used, not only in the study of Sesame Street's impact but more generally, to assess children's learning from other educational programming. The World Bank, UNICEF, UNESCO, the Center for Universal Learning at the Brookings Institution, the Association for Childhood Education International, and other international organizations have done much to develop standardized instruments to assess early childhood programs. While most of these are intended for on-site settings, rather than informal media contact, as the educational objectives are shared, there is much value in greater cross-fertilization of research approaches. As Sesame Workshop's work continues, it is increasingly both contributing to these efforts and benefiting from them as it hones the tools it uses to study program effects. There is, however, more work to be done to standardize these efforts and build tools that can be practically used in a range of contexts, particularly in the least resourced parts of the world.

Sesame Workshop has been a world leader in its commitment to research examining impact of children's media programming in low- and middle-income countries. Into the future, it is critical that this dedication is maintained, as it not only benefits Sesame Workshop's own programming, but has great value to others working in the field. To this end, there is a need for developing networks that more easily share not only findings from various studies (as there are currently good resources such as the Communication Initiative Network[1] for that purpose), but also to exchange research designs, measurement tools, and analytic approaches. A shared, more collective approach, will improve the overall quality of the study of the impact of children's educational media at the level of the child, parents/ families, educators/schools, and the cultural context at large. It will also help researchers avoid "reinventing the wheel" as they develop measures and other resources and, in turn, ultimately enhance the effectiveness of these efforts to reach and teach their intended audiences.

Note

1. See http://www.comminit.com/global/spaces-frontpage.

References

ACPR (2008). *Summary: Sisimpur's reach and educational impact evidence from a national longitudinal survey.* Unpublished manuscript, Associates for Community and Population Research.

Aboud, F.E. (2003). The formation of in-group favoritism and out-group prejudice in young children: Are they distinct attitudes? *Developmental Psychology*, 39(1), 48.

Aboud, F. (2009). Editorial virtual special issue: Health behaviour change. *Social Science and Medicine*, http://www.elsevier.com/wps/find/S06_351.cws_home/SSM_vi_.

Aboud, F.E., Tredoux, C., Tropp, L.R., Brown, C.S., Niens, U., and Noor, N.M. (2012). Interventions to reduce prejudice and enhance inclusion and respect for ethnic differences in early childhood: A systematic review. *Developmental Review*, 32(4), 307–36.

Allport, G.W. (1979/1954). *The nature of prejudice.* Cambridge, MA: Perseus Books.

Anderson, D.R., Huston, A.C., Schmitt, K.L., Linebarger, D.L., and Wright, J.C. (2001). Early childhood television viewing and adolescent behavior: The recontact study. *Monographs of the Society for Research in Child Development*, 66(1, serial no. 264).

Babbitt, E., Chigas, D., and Wilkinson, R. (2013). *Theories and indicators of change briefing paper: Concepts and primers for conflict management and mitigation.* Washington, DC: United States Agency for International Development.

Ball, S. and Bogatz, G.A. (1970). *The first year of Sesame Street: An evaluation.* Princeton, NJ: Educational Testing Service.

Biggs, J.B. (1996). Western misperceptions of the Confucian-heritage learning culture. In D.A. Watkins and J.B. Biggs (eds), *The Chinese learner* (pp. 45–67). Hong Kong: Comparative Research Center.

Bogatz, G.A. and Ball, S. (1971). *The second year of Sesame Street: A continuing evaluation* (Vols I and II). Princeton, NJ: Educational Testing Service.

Borzekowski, D. (2010). *The educational impact of Jalan Sesama: Evidence of children's learning from a longitudinal study.* Unpublished manuscript.

Borzekowski, D. and Henry, H. (2010). The impact of Jalan Sesama on the educational and healthy development of Indonesian preschool children: An experimental study. *International Journal of Behavioral Development*, DOI: 10.1177/0165025410380983.

Borzekowski, D.L.G. and Macha, J.E. (2010). The role of *Kilimani Sesame* in the healthy development of Tanzanian preschool children. *Journal of Applied Developmental Psychology*, 31, 298–305.

Brederode-Santos, M.E. (1993). *Learning from television: The secret of Rua Sésamo* (translation of the Portuguese (1991). *Com a televisão o segredo da Rua Sésamo*. Lisboa: TV Guia Editora). New York: Children's Television Workshop.

Brenick, A., Lee-Kim, J., Killen, M., Fox, N., Raviv, M., and Leavitt, L. (2007). Social judgments in Israeli and Arabic children: Findings from media-based intervention projects. In Dafna Lemish and Maya Götz (eds), *Children and Media in Time of War and Conflict* (pp. 287–308). Cresskill, NJ: Hampton Press.

Bronfenbrenner, U. (1992). *Ecological systems theory*. London: Jessica Kingsley Publishers.

Bronfenbrenner, U. and Morris, P.A. (1998). The ecology of developmental processes. In W. Damon and R.M. Lerner (eds), *Handbook of Child Psychology, Vol. 1: Theoretical Models of Human Development* (5th ed.) (pp. 993–1028). New York: John Wiley and Sons.

Brusset, E. and Otto, R. (2004). Evaluation of Nashe Maalo: Design, implementation, and outcomes of social transformation through the media on behalf of Search for Common Ground. Ohain: Channel Media, https://www.sfcg.org/wp-content/uploads/2014/08/nash2004.pdf.

Céspedes, J., Briceño, G., Farkouh, M.E., Vedanthan, R., Baxter, J., Leal, M., and Fuster, V. (2012). Targeting preschool children to promote cardiovascular health: Cluster randomized trial. *American Journal of Medicine*, 126, 27–35, http://dx.doi.org/10.1016/j.amjmed.2012.04.045.

Cohen, M. and Francis, V. (1999). *Rechov Sumsum/Shara'a Simsim quantitative report*. New York: Applied Research and Consulting.

Cole, C.F., Richman, B.A., and McCann Brown, S.A. (2001). The world of *Sesame Street* research. In S. Fisch and R. Truglio (eds), *'G' is for growing* (pp. 147–79). Mahwah, NJ: Erlbaum.

Cole, C.F., Arafat, C., Tidhar, C., Tafesh, W.Z., Fox, N.A., Killen, M., and Yung, F. (2003). The educational impact of Rechov Sumsum/Shara'a Simsim: A Sesame Street television series to promote respect and understanding among children living in Israel, the West Bank and Gaza. *International Journal of Behavioral Development*, 27(5), 409–27.

Cole, C.F., Labin, D.B., and del Rocio Galarza, M. (2008). Begin with the children: What research on Sesame Street's international co-productions reveals about using media to promote a new more peaceful world. *International Journal of Behavioral Development*, 32(4), 359–65.

Connolly, P., Smith, A., and Kelly, B. (2002). *Too young to notice? The cultural and political awareness of 3–6 year olds in Northern Ireland*. Belfast: Northern Ireland Community Relations Council, http://www.healingthroughremembering.org/images/j_library/lib/Too%20Young%20to%20Notice.pdf.

Connolly, P., Fitzpatrick, S., Gallagher, T., and Harris, P. (2006). Addressing diversity and inclusion in the early years in conflict-affected societies: A case study of the Media Initiative for Children: Northern Ireland. *International Journal of Early Years Education*, 14(3), 263–78.

Connolly, P., Kehoe, S., Larkin, E., and Galanouli, D. (2008). *A cluster randomised controlled trial evaluation of the effects of watching Sesame Tree on young children's attitudes and awareness*. Unpublished manuscript.

Consultores en Investigación y Comunicación, S.C. (2009). *Impact assessment of the community program "Healthy habits for life" in Merida, Yucatan*. Unpublished manuscript.

Cook, T.D., Appleton, H., Conner, R.F., Shaffer, A., Tamkin, G., and Weber, S.J. (1975). *Sesame Street revisited*. New York: Russell Sage.

Cooney, J.G. (1968). *The potential uses of television in preschool children: A report to Carnegie Corporation*. New York: Author.

Cooney, J.G. (2001). *Foreword*. In S. Fisch and R. Truglio (eds), *"G" is for growing: Thirty years of research on children and Sesame Street* (p. xvii). Mahwah, NJ: Erlbaum.

Diaz-Guerrero, R. and Holtzman, W.H. (1974). Learning by televised Plaza Sésamo in Mexico. *Journal of Educational Psychology*, 66(5), 632–43.

Diaz-Guerrero, R., Reyes-Lagunes, I., Witzke, D.B., and Holtzman, W.H. (1976). Plaza Sésamo in Mexico: An evaluation. *Journal of Communication*, 26(2), 145–54.

Fisch, S.M. (2004). *Children's learning from educational television: "Sesame Street" and beyond.* Mahwah, NJ: Lawrence Erlbaum.

Fisch, S. and Oppenheimer, S. (2012). *Rechov Sumsum experimental study: Learning among Jewish preschoolers in Israel.* Unpublished manuscript.

Fluent Research. (2008). *Assessment of Educational Impact of Rruga Sesam and Ulica Sezam in Kosovo: Report of Findings.* Unpublished manuscript.

Fox, N.A., Killen, M., and Leavitt, L. (1993). *Justification coding manual: Recho Sumsum/ Shara'a Simsim.* Unpublished manuscript.

Gyanvriksh Technologies (2009a). *The reach and impact of the Galli Galli Sim Sim television show in India: Midline report of a naturalistic longitudinal study.* Unpublished manuscript.

Gyanvriksh Technologies (2009b). *The reach and impact of the Galli Galli Sim Sim television show in India: Endline report of a naturalistic longitudinal study.* Unpublished manuscript.

Hsueh, Y., Zhou, Z., Su, G., Tian, Y., Sun, X., and Fan, C. (2012). *Big Bird Looks at the World*, Season 1 evaluation report. Unpublished manuscript.

Khulisa Management Services (2005). *Impact assessment of* Takalani Sesame: *Season II programme.* Unpublished manuscript.

Kibria, N. (2005). *Social and cultural impacts of* Sisimpur: *Phase 1 report.* Unpublished manuscript.

Kibria, N. (2006). *Social and cultural impact of* Sisimpur: *Phase 2 report.* Unpublished manuscript.

Kibria, N. and Jain, S. (2009). Cultural impacts of *Sisimpur, Sesame Street*, in Bangladesh: Views of caregivers of children in rural Bangladesh. *Journal of Comparative Family Studies*, 40, 57–75.

Larkin, E., Connolly, C., and Kehoe, S. (2009). A study of the effects of young children's natural exposure to Sesame Tree on their attitudes and awareness. Unpublished manuscript.

Lesser, G.S. (1974). *Children and television: Lessons from Sesame Street.* New York: Vintage Books.

Li, J. (2001). Chinese conceptualization of learning. *Ethos*, 29, 111–37.

Li, J. (2002). A cultural model of learning: Chinese "heart and mind for wanting to learn." *Journal of Cross-Cultural Psychology*, 33(3), 246–67.

Li, J. and Li, J. (2002). "The cow loves to learn": The Hao-Xue-Xin learning model as a reflection of the cultural relevance of *Zhima Jie*, China's *Sesame Street*. *Early Education and Development*, 13, 379–94.

Mares, M.L. and Pan, Z. (2013). Effects of *Sesame Street*: A meta-analysis of children's learning in 15 countries. *Journal of Applied Developmental Psychology*, 34, 140–51, doi: 10.1016/j.appdev.2013.01.001.

Myers, R. (1992). The twelve who survive: Strengthening programmes of early childhood development in the Third World. Paris: UNESCO.

PARC (2010). *Evaluation of "Kilna Bil Hayy" TV program.* Washington, DC: Search for Common Ground, Pan Arab Research Center, https://www.sfcg.org/wp-content/uploads/2014/03/LEB_EV_Feb10_Qualitative-Research-Evaluation-of-Kilna-Bil-Hayy-TV-Program.pdf.

Parker, I. (2010). The poverty lab: Transforming development economics, one experiment at a time. *New Yorker,* 17, 79–89.

Penn, H. (ed.) (2005). *Unequal childhoods: Young children's lives in poor countries.* New York: Routledge.

Rimal, R.N., Figueroa, M.E., and Storey, J.D. (2013). Character recognition as an alternate measure of television exposure among children: Findings from the Alam Simsim program in Egypt. *Journal of Health Communication,* 18(5), 594–609.

Sahin, N. (1992). *Preschoolers' learning from educational television.* Paper presented at the XXVth International Congress on Psychology, July, Brussels.

Schierhout, G. (2005). *Impact assessment of a new programming component on HIV and AIDS.* Unpublished report.

Sesame Workshop (n.d.). *Our mission,* http://www.sesameworkshop.org/about-us/our-mission/.

SPAAC (2004a). *Alam Simsim outreach program impact report.* Social Planning, Analysis and Administration Consultants, unpublished manuscript.

SPAAC (2004b). *The impact of Alam Simsim's health education outreach initiative.* Social Planning, Analysis and Administrative Consultants, http://www.spaac.com/uploads/files/1138287381_Alam_Simsim8_1-.

Synovate (2008). *Reach and perception of* Jalan Sesama *(Wave 1).* Unpublished manuscript.

Synovate (2009). *Reach and perception of* Jalan Sesama *(Wave 2).* Unpublished manuscript.

Synovate (2010). *Reach and perception of* Jalan Sesama *(Wave 3).* Unpublished manuscript.

Synovate (2011). *Reach and perception of* Jalan Sesama *(Wave 4).* Unpublished manuscript.

Tredoux, C.G., Noor, N.M., and de Paulo, L. (2009). Quantitative measures of respect and social inclusion in children: Overview and recommendations. *Effective Education,* 1, 169–86.

Truglio, R. and Fisch, S. (2001). *Introduction.* In S. Fisch and R. Truglio (eds), *"G" is for growing: Thirty years of research on children and Sesame Street* (p. xvii). Mahwah, NJ: Erlbaum.

Ulitsa Sezam Research and Content Team (1999). *Learning from Zeliboba: The educational impact of Ulitsa Sezam.* Unpublished manuscript.

UNICEF (1996). *Executive Summary: Summary assessment of Plaza Sésamo IV: Mexico* (English translation of Spanish, *Sumario ejecutivo: Evaluacion sumativa Plaza Sésamo IV: Mexico*). Unpublished manuscript.

UNICEF (2012) School readiness: A conceptual framework, http://www.unicef.org/earlychildhood/files/Child2Child_ConceptualFramework_FINAL%281%29.pdf.

United Nations (2014). Accelerating action: Global leaders on challenges and opportunities for MDG achievement. *MDG Leadership Report.* New York: United Nations, http://www.mdgleaders.org/wp-content/uploads/2014/09/UN_MDGLeadersReport.pdf.

USAID (2010). *USAID Forward,* http://www.usaid.gov/usaidforward.

Vandewater, E.A. and Lee, S.-J. (2009). Measuring Children's Media Use in the Digital Age: Issues and Challenges. *American Behavioral Scientist,* 52(8), 1152–76, doi:10.1177/0002764209331539.

Weiss, C. (1995). Nothing as practical as good theory: Exploring theory-based evaluation for comprehensive community initiatives for children and families. In J. Connell, A. Kubisch, L. Schorr, and C. Weiss (eds), *New Approaches to Evaluating Community Initiatives.* Washington, DC: Aspen Institute.

PART II

Meeting Children's Educational Needs

3

R IS FOR RESPONSIVE

How Sesame Street Meets the Changing Needs of Children in the United States

Jennifer A. Kotler, Rosemarie T. Truglio, and Jeanette Betancourt

From its inception (in 1969), the mission of Sesame Street has been about meeting the needs of young children and helping them reach their highest potential. Our goal is to provide educational experiences through media to help children grow *smarter* (building their academic skills in science, mathematics, and literacy), *stronger* (both physically and mentally), and *kinder* to others. These school-readiness skills, as well as life lessons, not only prepare children for school, but for the changing needs of our global world. To this end, we have delivered research-based, goal-directed content across a variety of media platforms, including the television show, books, games, mobile apps, and community-engagement initiatives for over 45 years.

The world has changed in this time and as new research and policy emerge about what critical skills are important for child wellbeing and development, we provide specific fresh new content. We respond to the contemporary needs of children through a comprehensive whole child curriculum that is adapted on an annual basis with guidance from external early childhood content and research experts. Throughout the years, therefore, our particular focus shifts depending on what educational gaps need to be addressed by providing children appealing content with the skills and knowledge they need to succeed. In the early 1990s, when racial divides continued to plague American society, Sesame Street built on its history of engendering positive race relationships with a focus on acceptance, mutual respect, and understanding. During that time, four seasons of the program each focused on promoting heightened understanding of a different group: African American, Asian, Latino, and Native American. In the early 2000s, we focused on concerns around the uncertain world in which we lived as a function of the September 11 attacks. In subsequent years the curriculum foci ranged from 21st-century thinking skills and specific academic skills (literacy, mathematics, and science) to our current curriculum focus—self-regulation and executive function skills as foundational cognitive process skills for school readiness. All of these initiatives were dedicated to the whole child—the child's wellbeing across academic, socio-emotional, and physical health.

In this chapter, we describe four recent Sesame Street initiatives that address contemporary critical needs of young children in the United States in order to succeed in the 21st century. In accordance with the Sesame Workshop Model (detailed in the Introduction), the process begins by identifying leading content experts, as well as key distribution partners, and inviting them to participate in a Content Advisory Seminar. These advisors play a key role in identifying the educational goals, recommending key age-appropriate messages for preschoolers, and planning the development of the initiative. The process ensures that our educational messaging employs up-to-date best practices in early childhood education. The four we focus on here are:

- science, technology, engineering, and math (STEM);
- healthy habits for life;
- resiliency; and
- self-regulation and executive function.

Science, Technology, Engineering, and Mathematics

Much has been written about the low performance of the United States in comparison to other high-income countries on assessments of student achievement in math and science (Gonzales et al., 2008; Provasnik et al., 2012). This measured lag and resulting concern that the United States is losing its competitiveness within a global economy prompted efforts such as the launch of President Obama's "Educate to Innovate" campaign to improve the quality and accessibility of science and math education. Most STEM-based initiatives in the United States are aimed at middle or high school-aged children. In contrast, most early childhood programs have limited opportunities to include inquiry-based learning to promote better understanding of STEM concepts (Wheelock College Aspire Institute, 2010). The irony, however, is that the educational benefits of building upon young children's innate sense of awe, wonder, and curiosity about how the world works and introducing STEM education to children at an early age is well documented. Research suggests that an early start in science, for example, provides a solid foundation for long-term school achievement (French et al., 2003; French, 2004; Sackes et al., 2010). Studies also have shown that preschool science activities significantly increase children's creativity and problem-solving skills (Mizraie et al., 2009). In addition, math skills at an early age predict later academic success even more consistently than social skills or reading (Duncan et al., 2007).

Science and mathematics have always been part of the Sesame Street curriculum; however, as educational standards and best practices evolved and the needs of young children changed, we made the necessary adaptions to our curriculum. While children naturally engage in scientific-inquiry behaviors, their proclivity toward science and math learning can become easily displaced as they enter formal learning environments. Because many early childhood educators harbor anxieties about their own lack of science and math knowledge, they may not introduce a broad range of math and science topics or understand how to approach an interdisciplinary STEM curriculum through age-appropriate activities. Furthermore, educators, as well as parents, may underestimate the degree to which children can understand STEM. As a result, they may not capitalize on opportunities for preschoolers to inherently engage in STEM-themed activities, such as engineering by building or designing (e.g., blocks) or investigating properties of matter as they help to cook or bake, do art projects, or play at a water table (Clements and Sarama, 2013).

To this end, our integrated STEM curriculum unified the disciplines of science, technology (e.g., the tools used across disciplines), engineering, and mathematics *through* the scientific processes that underlie STEM learning: 1) observing/questioning, 2) investigating, 3) analyzing/reporting findings, and 4) reflecting on the big idea. Through engaging stories, live-action films, and animations, our characters explored a range of preschool relevant topics that drew upon children's natural curiosity pertaining to the biological and physical world around them. This curriculum was first developed as a science and nature curriculum in 2008 and evolved over the years to guide a four-year STEM initiative (Seasons 40–43).

Season 40

Science and nature education, through the lens of scientific exploration and investigation, provides preschoolers opportunities to experience various habitats, animals, and plants. Through these interactions, children begin to connect to the natural world on a deeper level and grow up to care about the environment because they feel they are a part of, not separate from, the natural world in which they live (Wilson, 1993). Introducing young children to the natural world is the first step towards helping them develop a caring attitude towards the environment and to creating thoughtful stewards of our planet. Many children are deprived of frequent positive experiences with the natural world. Richard Louv (2006) uses the term "de-naturing of childhood" and discusses its impact, citing difficulties such as attention deficits, diminished use of the senses, lack of physical activity (which can lead to higher rates of childhood obesity), and the development of unfounded fears of the natural world.

To help remedy this, key messages for Sesame Street's science and nature curriculum were: 1) nature is fun and interesting, 2) nature needs us and we need nature, 3) nature has a lot to teach us, and 4) nature needs our care and respect. In accordance with Sesame Workshop's production method, before we created the curriculum and developed specific topics and recommendations for storylines, we conducted a baseline study to assess preschoolers' knowledge of the environment, capture the language and vocabulary used among children when discussing nature and the environment, and assess regional differences (rural, urban, and suburban) in children's knowledge (Brooks et al., 2012). We individually interviewed pre-schoolers (n = 419, ages three–five years) and learned the following: 1) children had a difficult time articulating a definition or description of the environment and nature; 2) there were some age differences in knowledge of environmental concepts and vocabulary as expected, but baseline knowledge was extremely limited across the ages; 3) children had a better understanding of some specific topics such as bees and animal tracks, compared to broader topics such as migration and hibernation; 4) children had some knowledge of what "helps" the environment (e.g., pick up litter), but less aware of concepts such as recycling and reuse; 5) surprisingly, there were only some regional differences (with children living in suburban areas being more aware of some topics compared to children living in urban and rural neighborhoods). This research supported our initial belief that young children's knowledge about science and nature was limited and Sesame Street had a role to play.

Based on this research, our overall educational goals were to: increase positive attitudes toward nature; deepen knowledge about the natural world, and encourage behavior that shows respect and care for the environment. Guided by Wilson's (1993) guidelines for providing developmentally appropriate environmental education experiences for young children, our approach was to nurture children's appreciation for nature. Therefore, we portrayed Muppets and children actively involved in their own experiential learning by modeling using their senses to explore and investigate nature in their immediate environments. Moreover, we wanted to empower children by demonstrating what they can do to show appreciation for nature and living things. For example, here is a description of one of our street stories from that season:

> While Elmo is drawing, he looks up and sees a rainbow in the sky! Elmo rushes to show everybody, but when his friend Rosita arrives, the rainbow disappeared. Elmo asks Leela if there is something he can do to bring the rainbow back. Leela offers to draw a picture of a rainbow. Leela can't remember all the colors of the rainbow, but uses the acronym Roy G. Biv to help her remember the colors. Rosita likes the picture, but she wants to see a real rainbow. Elmo gets an idea! What about a rainbow of monsters? Elmo gathers monsters of all different colors; red, orange, yellow, green, blue, indigo, and violet. After many attempts, the monsters finally line up in appropriate order. Rosita enjoys seeing a rainbow of different colored monsters, but still wishes she could see a real rainbow. Abby (our newest female Muppet who is a fairy in training) hears Rosita and recites a magic rhyme to grant Rosita's wish. Poof! Oh no! Instead of making a rainbow appear, raincoats appear on Elmo and Rosita! Abby tries again and again.

Her magic rhyme still doesn't work. Abby makes a rainstorm, instead of a rainbow. Everyone rushes inside, where Gordon makes a rainbow appear using a flashlight, glass of water, and white paper. Afterward, as Elmo and Rosita are playing outside, Rosita looks up and sees something special, a rainbow! Elmo and Rosita sing all about the beautiful rainbow in the sky.

Season 41

In the following season, we continued our focus on connecting preschoolers to nature and the environment, but for this season, placed emphasis on the investigation of science-related topics by posing a question sparked by an observation and then finding out the answer or possible answers. Linking concepts such as what's alive, plants, animals, properties of matter, color and light, and how the body works brings children a richer understanding and awareness of the world around them and may have a secondary benefit of motivating them to become scientists. For example, in one story, preschoolers learn that "everyone is a scientist" as they watch the characters model the scientific process skills and use tools (such as a journal) to collect data.

Seasons 42 and 43

In Season 42, our educational approach was to make connections between the four disciplines of STEM to foster deeper understanding of how things work through an integrated STEM curriculum. In one episode, Elmo and Zoe solved an engineering question: how to design something to keep a rock from sinking. Leela (a human cast member) guided Elmo and Zoe through the scientific inquiry process as they experimented with different designs of and materials for a flotation to hold Zoe's pet rock, Rocco. Along the way, they learn about properties of matter (science), technology (tools needed in the design of a product), engineering (the process of using tools to design a product to solve a problem), and math (measurement).

In addition to stories, animated segments, and live-action films, Murray (the Muppet host on Street Street) did fun experiments based on child-relevant questions on the streets of New York City! The message was: *everyone can be a STEMist by doing experiments with everyday objects at home or outside.* We demonstrated children and adults learning together (with the recurring phrase "let's find out together") using questions such as: How do you design a bridge to hold a lot of weight? How does the design of a kite change the way it moves in the air? How does the design of a toy car change the distance it rolls? To reinforce the message that everyone is a STEMist, we created a STEM-driven show format featuring our character, Super Grover 2.0 who had the special "powers" of observation, investigation, and technology (tools and simple machines used to help solve problems). Super Grover 2.0 not only modeled the scientific inquiry skills that unified the STEM curriculum, but portrayed the important lessons of task persistence and learning from one's mistakes. In addition, to show content, we created a series of digital games to help preschools learn and practice STEM concepts.

Finally, in the fourth year (Season 43), we added the arts as a discipline to explore STEM concepts and transformed the STEM curriculum into a STEAM curriculum. The following story example illustrates how the arts provide an excellent opportunity to learn STEM concepts through child-relevant topics. In this scenario, the topic was ballet.

> Zoe choreographed a special dance, the Dance of the Six Swans, for her and her friends to perform. Snuffy is so excited to participate, as he loves to dance ballet and always dreamed about being lifted into the air. However, because of Snuffy's size and weight, no one could lift him which posed an interesting engineering problem: what can we design to lift Snuffy? The characters explore objects and tools and then design a blueprint to guide their design. After trial and error, Gordan (a human cast member) teaches them about an essential tool (a pulley) for their design to lift Snuffy.

Assessment

To assess children's learning, we conducted three different studies (one from Seasons 40–42) across several years using similar methodology. More than 800 three–five-year-olds from lower- and middle-income households in the US urban northeast and suburban midwest participated. The first study also included a sample of children from the northwest. The children were randomly assigned either to a control group (viewed Sesame Street episodes that featured health and nutrition content in the first two studies and social/emotional content in the third study) or an experimental group (viewed Sesame Street science-related and STEM videos). We collected data in child-care centers where children watched seven 15-minute Sesame Street clips two to three times a week for four weeks for a total of 20 viewings. We tested children's science knowledge before and after the four-week viewing period. We created our own measures for each of the studies as no standardized measure existed publically that assessed children's knowledge of the concepts we addressed and no measures were available to test general STEM knowledge in preschoolers. We instructed teachers not to supplement the video instruction between the pre- and post-tests.

In all three studies, we used free-response and multiple-choice measures to evaluate children's knowledge of the concepts and vocabulary presented in the created episodes. A comparison of pre/post-viewing scores of the experimental and control groups demonstrated learning gains as a result of the Sesame Street STEM programming in Season 40. In particular, there was evidence of improved understanding among the experimental group of several curricular topics, such as pollination, hibernation, and habitats (Brooks et al., 2012).

The second study, based on Season 41, was similar to the first, but focused on different and more challenging scientific concepts. Given the successful results from Season 40, we examined whether Sesame Street content could extend beyond teaching scientific facts into scientific process skills. In addition to free-response and multiple-choice questions, we assessed children's story comprehension. Results were similar, with children in the experimental group scoring significantly higher than children in the control group after watching the videos (Brooks et al., 2011). In fact, children's scores on the free-response questions were 100% greater at post-test for children in the experimental condition.

The concepts presented in Season 42 were the most challenging of all. In these episodes, science, technology, engineering, and math were tightly integrated into relatively complicated scenarios. Even so, the evaluation, the third in the series, indicated that children learned the difficult concepts such as what it means to engineer, observe, investigate, and experiment (Brooks et al., in preparation).

A next phase emerged from the feedback we heard from educators in the Season 40–42 studies who stated they wanted ways to explore this STEM content in their classrooms. With funding from CA Technologies, Bechtel Foundation, and the Heising Simons Foundation, we created Little Discoverers: *Big Fun with Science, Math and More*, a digital destination (desktop and mobile) featuring interactive Sesame Street videos, games, and hands-on activities aimed at inspiring young children and the adults in their lives, to investigate and explore STEM concepts. Designed to be used both in school and at home, *Little Discoverers* provides educators with tools to integrate STEM concepts into their classroom lessons, and gives parents the resources needed to include activities and language in their everyday moments with their children. The program included the following six STEM topics: experiments, sink or float, measurement, force and motion, properties of matter, and engineering.

The Education Development Center (2014) conducted an evaluation of the website and the resources for educators to assess the educational impact of *Little Discoverers* in 30 classrooms over a six-week period. Results suggest that, at the classroom level, more science instruction, activity, and dialog was present in the classrooms that had the *Little Discoverers* content. Children in the experimental group were exposed to more new activities and experiences, were engaged in more academic and scientific conversations, and were doing more science activities in general. Children in the experimental classrooms were more likely to gain exposure in all four STEM topic areas, whereas children in the control conditions were more likely to experience predominantly math activities. In 85% of their visits, when observers were in the classrooms where children received the *Little Discoverers* intervention, they heard target STEM vocabulary words used by teachers and children compared to in 64% of the visits of the control classrooms (Education Development Center, 2014).

In sum, the studies we conducted on children's learning from Sesame Street content about the variety of STEM topics suggest that children gain valuable factual information and STEM language to enable them to express their under-standing and scientific inquiry skills from our content. Furthermore, from the *Little Discoverers* study, we learned that educators can change classroom practices around STEM when given the appropriate support.

Healthy Habits for Life

The childhood obesity rate has tripled in the past 30 years with about one in three children and adolescents in the United States overweight or obese (Ogden et al., 2014). While health, nutrition, physical wellbeing, and hygiene have always been a part of the curriculum, we decided to revisit our health goals (nutrition, physical activity, hygiene, and rest) as the statistics on childhood obesity became more apparent and alarming (Ogden et al., 2002). Starting at a young age is critical because, once established, health behaviors are much harder to change. Therefore, our approach was one of prevention, rather than intervention, and we created age-appropriate messages for preschoolers, as well as the adults in their lives. This company-wide initiative entitled "Healthy Habits for Life" (HHFL) debuted in 2005 (Season 36).

Our first step in developing messages was to assess what children knew about healthy habits and their understanding of what it means to be healthy. We had gained a robust understanding of children's actual physical health and behaviors from the medical community, but located very little information about children's perceptions about being healthy or if they understood the concept of living a healthy life. In a baseline study conducted with over 100 preschoolers (ages three–five), we found that 46% could articulate or approximate what it means to be healthy. Over half of those who did provide an answer focused on food, while the rest in much smaller numbers mentioned exercise, feeling good, or not being sick. Similarly, when asked how someone "gets healthy," 56% of the children could articulate a legitimate response, with nearly all of those who answered giving a food-oriented response. This demonstrated that we needed to take a comprehensive approach to health that went beyond just food.

We also conducted research to assess whether our characters could indeed encourage healthier habits. We assumed that our Muppet characters are power-ful models to encourage healthier choices because children tend to model media characters they like (Lauricella et al., 2011). We had anecdotal data from educators and parents indicating that a beloved Sesame Street character engaged in certain behavior motivated children to emulate that behavior (e.g., "It's often a struggle to get my child to brush his teeth, but if he sees Elmo doing it, he'll do it," explained a mother in one of our research sessions).

In an initial study, we focused on healthy eating. We found that when children were shown fruits and vegetables with Sesame Street character stickers placed on them, compared to the same foods with no stickers, or with stickers with unfa-miliar characters on them, children chose the foods with Sesame Street stickers on them at a much higher rate—and ate more of those foods. (For more detail on our initial studies, please see Kotler et al., 2012.)

With data supporting the effectiveness of our characters in promoting healthy choices, we embarked on a multi-year, multiple platform, content-driven initiative to help young children and the adults in their lives establish an early foundation of healthy habits. We developed a curriculum and a set of messages with the advice of leading experts in the areas of preschool health, nutrition, endocrinology, pediatrics, and physical education. Some of the key messages were: "Eat the colors of the rainbow;" "Eat your colors every day;" "Try new foods;" "There are sometime foods and anytime foods;" "A cookie is a sometime food;" "Eat a healthy breakfast;" "Get up and move your body," and hygiene messages such as wash your hands, brush your teeth, and sneeze in the bend of your elbow. These underlying messages were crafted for children, parents/caregivers, and educators as we know the importance of reaching the adults who have the ultimate decision-making power over children's lifestyles.

The curriculum and key messages drove content creation of a plethora of materials around Healthy Habits for Life including stories, animations, and films for the television show, public service announcements with celebrities and politicians, online educational games, live shows, a traveling exhibit ("*Sesame Street* Presents: The Body"), books, podcasts, and a home DVD. Furthermore, with licensing partners (e.g., Earth's Best and Produce for Better Health), we also branded healthier food options with our characters. (See Cole et al., 2010 and Cohen et al., 2012 for reviews of many of the licensed initiatives around HHFL.)

To make all of the content we produced accessible to child-care providers, we created a bilingual (English/Spanish) *Healthy Habits for Life Child Care Resource Guide* which was funded by Neumors. This comprehensive tool kit, designed to help child-care providers integrate nutrition and physical activity into daily routines, included video with multiple-themed segments and hands-on activities for child-care providers to address the importance of healthy food choices and increased physical activity. The impetus to develop this guide was to address a void in how conversations about healthy habits were typically presented in child-care settings. According to our advisory panel, too often the introduction to nutrition and physical activity was limited to just snack or food times or outdoor time; it was not embedded in other parts of the day or the curriculum. Therefore, we designed the *HHFL Child Care Resource Guide* to engender a holistic orientation to health that is present throughout the day (even as children transition from school to home). The guide provides practical ways to help children become more aware of and respond to the signals their bodies are giving them when they are hungry, as well as ways to help them think more about the fuel their bodies need; it also offers guidance on how to transform family events into healthy food events.

To assess its educational impact, Kidpoint LLC (Andrews and Buettner, 2009) conducted an evaluation of the materials (pre-post with four weeks in between) with child-care providers. The research demonstrated that providers found the materials to be useful, easy to use, and that they filled some specific voids in available resources as indicated in the approach above. Furthermore, they indicated that the materials were extremely valuable and that they would continue to use them in the future. Providers also reported that children were more engaged in discussing nutrition-related topics after participating in the program.

To reach parents with similar HHFL messages, we created a parent kit comprised of a DVD, storybook, and parent guide in English and in Spanish. This kit was designed to be used flexibly and across a variety of contexts (e.g., as a supplement to an existing government health-education initiative). In partnership with the National WIC Association, the organization facilitating the Women Infant and Children (WIC) nutritional program, we distributed our resources to state agencies, which provided our content to WIC recipients in conjunction with other resources that WIC provides. Mothers who received the HHFL kit as part of WIC's nutrition program gained nutritional knowledge and said they were more likely to change their eating and feeding behaviors as compared to their knowledge and attitudes at baseline. For example, they were more likely to know to eat a "rainbow" of different-colored fruits and vegetables, drink lower-fat milk, and to eat more fruits, vegetables, and whole grains. Mothers eagerly embraced the kit's messages about nutrition and enjoyed using Sesame Street language, such as a "sometime food" (cookie) and an "anytime food" (apple), to motivate their children to make better choices (Ritchie et al., 2010).

Food for Thought

As results came through from some of the studies on HHFL, it became clear that preparing and eating healthy meals was not just about knowledge and preferences. In fact, although the resources were helpful and parents and educators felt it would help change their behavior, the content did not mention how to balance healthy habits on a limited budget and/or with limited access to healthy foods. Therefore, the HHFL initiative evolved once again to include an additional kit (*Food for Thought*) and a prime-time special (*Growing Hope against Hunger*), which was broadcast on PBS.

The main goal of *Food for Thought* was to give families in economically stressed circumstances skills that enable them to manage and provide for their households' nutrition needs. The materials are intended to help families nurture their children's overall development through sound nutrition—even in the face of tough economic conditions. Concrete directives, such as freezing leftovers, looking for sales, and tapping into community resources are just some of the simple tips provided to help families stretch their budgets while inculcating healthy eating habits. The kit provided not just education, but also much-needed emotional support, helping families cope with the stresses and challenges that come with limited access to food. The kit also was designed to help reduce the stigma and embarrassment associated with hunger.

To assess the effectiveness of the content, we commissioned Field Research Corporation to conduct a randomized control trial study, including over 500 caregivers (mothers, fathers, and grandmothers) with moderate to high indicators of food insecurity. After four weeks of using the content in the kit, the caregivers had better attitudes and strategies about maintaining healthy habits on a limited budget than those in a business-as-usual control group. For example, participants were more likely to seek information and assistance from others—friends, family, and outside agencies—on how to cope with food insecurity. They were also more likely to take steps to save money on food and to engage in practices to promote healthier eating in the family, such as involving children in shopping and in food preparation (Cohen et al., 2012).

Through our continued family- and community-engagement efforts, television episodes, and other initiatives, we are working toward making healthy habits an aspect of every family's life. Our research has shown that these topics are relevant to providers, impactful on children, and useful to parents, grandparents, and other caregivers. Although we cannot directly link the effect of our own initiatives to the recent decline in childhood obesity rates in the past few years (Ogden et al., 2014), we believe that we are part of the collective effort of a variety of organizations, businesses, schools, and governmental policies that have helped improve the health of children in the United States.

Resiliency

Sesame Workshop has always been at the forefront of creating resources that help families cope with difficult times and situations. We have not shied away from challenging topics. For example, we addressed death in 1982 when the actor who played a leading human character, Mr. Hooper, died. We address sensitive topics by having our human cast and Muppet characters model for parents, caregivers, and children the language and strategies needed to talk about and cope with the situation (Fisch and Truglio, 2001). The past decade has brought a range of concerns: terrorist attacks, greater deployment overseas for military personnel, growing economic inequality, high divorce rates, elevated incarceration rates, and general increased stress on the family. Sesame Workshop, through various initiatives, has worked to help families cope with the challenges of modern life. Rather than applying a deficit model, our content helps individuals build upon and connect to their inner strengths. Through the promotion of good communication as a key element of our approach, we help parents and caregivers engage with their children using developmentally appropriate tactics and activities that can be applied to simple everyday moments and routines. We provide tips and strategies through a range of content experiences across media platforms (television, podcasts, apps, games), as well as through community-engagement materials, designed to meet the needs of a specific targeted audience dealing with a particular challenge (e.g., news events and natural and man-made tragedies, military deployment, divorce, incarceration, and death).

Our dedicated efforts in building resiliency skills in young children began in the aftermath of the September 11 attacks when we were in Season 33 production. Sesame Workshop created four new Sesame Street episodes, each dealing with a specific issue that some children were facing as a result of the events: exclusion, fear, bullying, and loss. Evaluations of these episodes showed that children understood the messages and developed new coping strategies (including how to express their thoughts and feelings using the language modeled by the characters) around loss and exclusion (Truglio et al., 2005).

These episodes were then re-purposed and complemented by educational outreach materials developed for parents and caregivers who observed the events of the 9/11 attack, but were not directly impacted by the loss or injury of a loved one. In partnership with Project Liberty (through the New York State Office of Mental Health), we developed an outreach kit called *You Can Ask!* for parents and caregivers of three to eight-year-olds to help guide their children through stressful situations. The kit included video and print materials developed in English, Spanish, and Mandarin (given that New York City's Chinatown is in close proximity to the World Trade Towers). While the content was specifically created as a response to the September 11 attack, it did not directly name any particular event and could be applied to a variety of unexpected and stressful scenarios.

To evaluate impact, researchers interviewed 207 mothers (in the tri-state area around New York City) by phone two weeks after they received the *You Can Ask!* materials and then again four weeks later. About two thirds of parents (63% of parents of children three–five years old and 72% of parents of six–eight-year-olds) said that *You Can Ask!* made them more comfortable helping their children cope with stress. More than 90% of children, as reported by their parents, understood the messages in the video, and had highly positive reactions. Furthermore, families reported better coping strategies six weeks after using *You Can Ask!* materials, noting such factors as being more likely to talk to children about things that were bothering them and encouraging their children to ask questions and express themselves. Similarly, parents reported that their children felt less stressed after the family used the *You Can Ask!* materials after six weeks (Russell Research, 2006).

Our *Talk Listen Connect* program enlisted the magic of Sesame Street's Muppets and human cast to support military families, a targeted group with special needs that have emerged from the increase in troop deployment. In fact, approximately 2.5 million service members have been deployed to Iraq and Afghanistan starting in 2001 (O'Connell et al., 2014). Sesame Workshop created three different initiatives under the umbrella *Talk Listen Connect* to support challenges faced by military families with young children. Prior to Sesame Workshop's involvement, most programs supporting military families were geared to school-age children rather than young children. Furthermore, there were few resources that offered suggestions about preparing for frequent life transitions and changing life situations.

Talk Listen Connect includes three multimedia kits that help military families with preschool-aged children cope with different aspects of a parent's military service: a parent's deployment (*TLC I*), reconnection when the parent returns home (*TLC II: Homecomings and Changes*), which also includes a focus on the return of a parent who has changed because of a combat-related injury, and a third kit (*TLC III: When Families Grieve*) designed to help families with young children whose loved one has died. This latter kit was designed to be relevant to both military and non-military families. All of the kits were bilingual (English and Spanish). Across all kits, the goals were to help build a sense of stability by providing age-appropriate strategies for parents to use with small children. Furthermore, the goals were intended to help children feel a sense of security, safety, and love from those who care for them. All of the kits included videos, magazines, and posters.

In each of these cases, real children and adults (not actors) from military families were featured on the set of Sesame Street, talking with our characters or filmed in their homes portraying the challenges they faced as a family. They described how they were feeling and the adults served to model appropriate strategies for encouraging children (including Muppet children) to express themselves even if those feelings were confusing, negative, and seemed immature.

Commissioned studies evaluating the effectiveness of the deployment kit (*TLC I*) showed that parents were more comfortable helping their children handle deployment, stay connected, and become better prepared to handle future deployments (Russell Research, 2006; Cohen et al., 2014). Additionally, parents reported that the resources helped them transition better and feel more comfortable when the service members returned home after deployment compared to a control group who had received a "healthy habits kit" (rather than the deployment kit) (Military Families Research Institute, 2009). Similarly, parents/caregivers who had a service member return with a visible or invisible combat-related injury and used the *Changes* kit (*TLC II*) were significantly more likely than the control group to prepare and explain the injury and its consequences to their children. The resources helped parents to ease their children's anxiety, confusion, and fear by talking about what had happened and recommending ways to connect with the injured parent, resulting in less chaotic and tension-filled households. Overall, parents and their children had fewer feelings of loneliness and social isolation after using the kit (Military Families Research Institute, 2009).

Finally, an evaluation of the effectiveness of *TLC III: When Families Grieve* showed that both military and non-military families who received the kit were significantly more likely than a control group, who received an alternative Sesame Street kit, to report that the materials had a positive impact on their child's coping with the death of a parent, while also having a positive impact on how the remaining spouse coped with his/her own grief (Uniformed Services University of the Health Sciences, 2011).

Collectively, the evaluations demonstrate the effectiveness of providing materials to families who are dealing with serious transitions and breaks in routines. The materials helped caregivers discuss important changes with their children while teaching them to maintain routines, and provided a sense of security despite enormous stress and transition. Furthermore, the materials helped parents feel better about their roles, and gave them valuable information and the language for how to interact with their children around these important topics (Topp et al., 2013). The results demonstrate the power of the Muppets and the Sesame Workshop Model in helping parents and children through potentially harrowing times.

The success of our September 11 and military and non-military families' initiatives, as well as research about stress and its influence on children, led us to develop additional resources to help cope with typical everyday challenges and big, life-changing challenges that children experience. *Little Children, Big Challenges* is a multiyear, bilingual (English/Spanish) initiative that provides tools to help parents, caregivers, and educators use positive routines to foster young children's resilience on a daily basis. This initiative is designed to help children cope with everyday challenges by giving them practical skills and strategies for trying new things, learning from mistakes, making new friends, resolving conflicts positively, overcoming the "bedtime blues," and understanding their own abilities. In addition to helping children conquer day-to-day challenges, *Little Children, Big Challenges* also tackles more serious issues and transitions, such as bullying and coping with parental divorce and incarceration. With over a third of children in the United States living with a single parent (Vespa et al., 2013), and with about 2.7 million children having an incarcerated parent (Glaze and Maruschak, 2008), these initiatives are particularly timely. Preliminary results of studies being conducted by Rutgers University researchers suggest that the content has impressive effects on improving wellbeing in all three areas being tested (divorce, incarceration and resiliency.)

Self-Regulation and Executive Function

In recent years, the importance of self-regulation (the ability to control one's thoughts, actions, and emotions) and the executive function skills needed to self-regulate has garnered new attention as a critical component of school readiness (Bailey and Jones, 2013). Skills such as recognizing and regulating emotions, impulse control (self-restraint), frustration tolerance, task persistence, exerting self-control (delayed gratification), working memory, focused attention, cognitive flexibility (attention set-shifting), planning, and performance monitoring are essential for socio-emotional competence and academic success (Greenburg,

2006; Bierman and Torres, in press). In fact, self-regulation/executive function is often a better predictor of a child's academic success in reading and math than a child's IQ (Blair and Razza, 2007).

Despite the evidence of the importance of self-regulation, kindergarten teachers report that over half their students start school lacking good self-regulation/executive function abilities such as following directions, staying on task with focused attention, and regulating their emotions using concrete strategies for calming down (Rimm-Kaufman et al., 2000). This interferes with learning because children cannot process information if they are not focused (Lin et al., 2003) and these children are often disruptive to the other children, diverting the teacher's attention and reducing learning opportunities of the whole class. It is also common that children who act out and misbehave socially receive less instruction and are less well liked by their peers. In the short term, poor self-regulation affects school readiness; in the long term, underdeveloped self-regulation skills are linked with aggression, low academic achievement, delinquency, and higher drop-out rates (Raver, 2002).

Fortunately, self-regulation and the underlying cognitive skills (executive function) can be taught during preschool years. The capacity to learn executive function skills begins shortly after birth, with the most rapid stage of development occurring from three to five years old (Center on the Developing Child at Harvard University, 2011; Zelazo et al., 2013).

Guided by content experts through a series of advisory seminars, beginning in the spring of 2011, we focused on how Sesame Street's engaging Muppet and human cast could model strategies to foster self-regulation and executive function skills. Throughout Seasons 43 and 45 (2012–15), we developed show content and digital games that required children to self-regulate and use their executive skills as they navigated a variety of interactive situations (Truglio et al., 2014). As we had used our character, Super Grover 2.0, as a role model for STEM education, Cookie Monster was selected to learn self-control and model self-regulation strategies to build executive function skills. In an initial episode, Cookie Monster needed to exercise self-control during a cookie club's taste testing. To pass the club's initiation, Cookie first had to look at a cookie, then smell the cookie, and finally take a nibble (thus the taste test) without gobbling up the whole cookie. Chris, an adult human cast member, modeled several self-control strategies, such as pretending the cookie is something else (like a yo-yo), or smelling something "stinky" to distract himself from the delicious-smelling cookie. Not surprisingly, Cookie Monster had several failed attempts before finding the strategy that worked best for him. Throughout the segment, he used self-talk to remind him of the ultimate reward (becoming a member of the club) and not get distracted by the reward of eating a single cookie. In another segment, *All Good Things Come to Those Who Wait*, Cookie Monster practiced his self-regulation strategies in a delayed gratification game (based on Dr. Walter Mischel's marshmallow paradigm) by Guy Smiley (see Mischel, 2014).

Dr. Deborah Linebarger at the University of Iowa has conducted an evaluation of our self-regulation/executive function videos, including the effects of a single viewing of the aforementioned Cookie Monster clip. Results indicate that in just a single viewing of this clip, children are able to delay eating the treat for almost four minutes longer than those who see an alternative clip unrelated to self-regulation (Linebarger and Gatewood, 2014).

To illustrate how self-regulation and executive function skills are critical to learning outcomes (Seasons 44–45), Cookie Monster was chosen once again to star in a new re-occurring format, Cookie's Crumby Pictures, which parodies the coming attractions of popular movies. In these segments, Cookie Monster learned and modeled strategies for building skills, such as working memory, flexible thinking, focused attention, self-control, task persistence, and planning. He learned the language of self-regulation (e.g., strategy, plan, rules, direction, practice, persist, remember, listen, stop and think, pay attention, wait, and self-control) and the importance of self-talk as a strategy. (See Figure 3.1 for a list of self-regulation and executive function skills.) Through our formative research process, we learned that talking about these strategies wasn't sufficient and children needed characters to use non-verbal gestures, such as putting a hand out as a stop sign, pointing to their temple, hugging their body, and using focus goggles (putting their hands around their eyes and pretending they are goggles) to grasp strategies such as Stop and Think, Remember, Body Calm, and Focus.

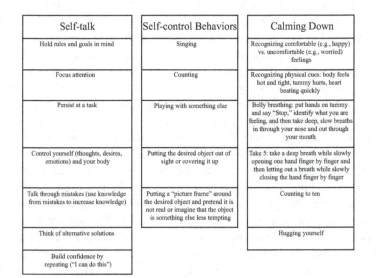

Self-talk	Self-control Behaviors	Calming Down
Hold rules and goals in mind	Singing	Recognizing comfortable (e.g., happy) vs. uncomfortable (e.g., worried) feelings
Focus attention	Counting	Recognizing physical cues: body feels hot and tight, tummy hurts, heart beating quickly
Persist at a task	Playing with something else	Belly breathing: put hands on tummy and say "Stop," identify what you are feeling, and then take deep, slow breaths in through your nose and out through your mouth
Control yourself (thoughts, desires, emotions) and your body	Putting the desired object out of sight or covering it up	Take 5: take a deep breath while slowly opening one hand finger by finger and then letting out a breath while slowly closing the hand finger by finger
Talk through mistakes (use knowledge from mistakes to increase knowledge)	Putting a "picture frame" around the desired object and pretend it is not real or imagine that the object is something else less tempting	Counting to ten
Think of alternative solutions		Hugging yourself
Build confidence by repeating ("I can do this")		

FIGURE 3.1 Self-regulation and executive function strategies

Future Directions for Sesame Workshop in the United States

The initiatives highlighted here demonstrate Sesame Street's commitment to serving the unmet needs of children by providing content and tools directly to children and to the adults in their lives. We remain committed to our mission to help children grow smarter, stronger, and kinder. We will continue to evaluate the state of children's wellbeing on an annual basis and develop projects on issues where educational media can play a role.

While our mission has not changed over the years, what has changed is the children's media landscape. Not only are children watching television, they are playing games on the computer, using mobile phones to play games, and using tablets to create art projects. While many of the initiatives covered here have interactive content (e.g., websites, apps, games) the research on the learning gains from digital experience is just emerging (Shore, 2008).

Several recent short-term studies conducted on basic math and literacy skills demonstrated that children do learn from Sesame Street's digital content. In a study on our Elmo Loves 123s math app, researchers found that children with initially low math skills scored higher on a post-test compared to a control group (Borland, 2014). In another study, children learned new vocabulary words from an app designed to recognize print in a child's environment (Brooks and Moon, 2013). Our goal is to create more multi-platform initiatives and evaluations across a range of school-readiness outcomes in the upcoming years.

Another factor that has changed dramatically is the number of children who are not at home during the day to watch Sesame Street on broadcast television. Today about 60% (Laughlin, 2011) of preschoolers are in some sort of formal/structured preschool program compared to 25% in the late 1960s. To address the implications of these changing statistics, we are strategizing ways to create, package, and deliver content to help educators and family child-care providers educate and prepare young children for kindergarten. Program components consist of professional development materials for the teachers, child-facing content, and materials to connect parents to the learning in the classroom and how they can extend the learning at home. Currently we have several pilot projects in collaboration with different curriculum providers. Preliminary data from educators and parents indicate that they see Sesame Street content as a great way to support and extend the educational lessons in the classroom and at home.

The examples presented in this chapter, outlining our response to critical contemporary issues, highlight the ways in which Sesame Workshop stays true to its process and continually works to meet the critical educational needs of the country's young children. For over 45 years, Sesame Workshop has dedicated its characters, creativity, and heart to improving the lives of children with a particular focus on disadvantaged children. The Workshop continually seeks input from child-development experts, educators, psychologists, policymakers, and innovative entrepreneurs. The most important input we receive, however, is from children. Whether it is with their voices, their gestures, or the expressions on their faces, they are the ones who lead our work. As Joan Ganz Cooney, co-founder of Sesame Workshop, stated from the inception of Sesame Street, "the children are our true experts guiding every step of content creation."

References

Andrews, D. and Buettner, C. (2009). *Healthy habits for life: Child care resource kit evaluation report.* Unpublished Report, KidPoint LLC.

Bailey, R. and Jones, S.M. (2013). *An applied developmental model for social-emotional and self-regulation-related skills from birth to 3rd grade.* Invited presentation for the National Governors Association Center for Best Practices Policy Academy, "Building a Foundation for Student Success: State Strategies to Improve Learning Outcomes from Early Childhood through 3rd Grade," Salt Lake City, UT.

Bierman, K. and Torres, M. (in press). Promoting the development of executive functions through early education and prevention program. In J.A. Griffin, L.S. Freund, and P. McCardle (eds), *Executive function in preschool age children: Integrating measurement, neurodevelopment and translational research.* Washington, DC: American Psychological Association.

Blair, C. and Razza, R.P. (2007). Relating effortful control, executive function, and false belief understanding to emerging math and literacy ability in kindergarten. *Child Development*, 78(2), 647–63.

Borland, J. (2014). *The potential of play: Outcomes of preschoolers playing Elmo Loves ABCs and Elmo Loves 123s.* San Francisco, CA: Rockman.

Brooks, M.K. and Moon, M.J. (2013). *Children's learning from mobile devices: The case of Big Bird's words.* Unpublished presentation, Sesame Workshop.

Brooks, M.K., Kotler, J.A., Gartner, T., and Truglio, R.T. (2011). *The influence of Sesame Street on children's knowledge of STEM concepts.* Presented at the Annual Meeting of the International Communications, Boston, MA.

Brooks, M.K., Kotler, J.A., Gartner, T., and Truglio, R.T. (2012). The words on the street are nature and science: An evaluation of Sesame Street's curriculum. Paper presented at the annual meeting of the International Communication Association, May, Phoenix, AZ.

Brooks, M.K., Kotler, J.A., Truglio, R.T., Moon, M., and Wong, C. (in preparation). *STEM across three seasons of Sesame Street.*

Center on the Developing Child at Harvard University (2011). *Building the brain's "air traffic control" system: How early experiences shape the development of executive function.* Working paper no. 11, www.developingchild.harvard.edu.

Clements, D.H. and Sarama, J. (2013). Rethinking early mathematics: What is research-based curriculum for young children? In L.D. English and J.T. Mulligan (eds), *Reconceptualizing early mathematics learning* (pp. 121–47). Dordrecht: Springer.

Cohen, D., Truglio, R.T., Kotler, J.A., and Betancourt, J. (2012). Interventions for low-income families: Sesame Workshop's Educational Outreach and the Healthy Habits for Life initiative. In V. Maholmes and R. Kings (eds), *The Oxford Handbook of Poverty and Child Development.* New York: Oxford University Press.

Cohen, D., Betancourt, J.A. and Kotler, J.A. (2014). Sesame Workshop's Talk, Listen, Connect: A multiple media resource to benefit military families with young children. In A. Jordan and D. Romer (eds), *Media and the well-being of children and adolescents*. Oxford: Oxford University Press.

Cole, C.F., Kotler, J.A., and Pai, S. (2010). "Happy Healthy Muppets": A look at Sesame Workshop's health initiatives around the world. In P.A. Gaist (ed.), *Igniting the power of community: The role of CBOs and NGOs in global public health*. New York: Springer.

Duncan, G.J., Dowsett, C.J., Claessens, A., Magnuson, K., Huston, A.C., Klebanov, P., Pagani, L., Feinstein, L., Engel, M., Gunn, J.B., Sexton, H., Duckworth, K., and Japel, C. (2007). School readiness and later achievement. *Developmental Psychology*, 43(6), 1428–46.

Education Development Center (2014). *Sesame Street Little Discoverers PreK STEM program evaluation*. New York: Education Development Center's Center for Children and Technology.

Fisch, S.M. and Truglio, R.T. (2001). *"G" is for growing*. Mahwah, NJ: Lawrence Erlbaum Associates.

French, L. (2004). Science as the center of a coherent, integrated early childhood curriculum. *Early Childhood Research Quarterly*, 19, 138–49.

French, L., Conezio, K., and Boynton, M. (2003) Using science as the hub of an integrated early childhood curriculum: The ScienceStart! curriculum. In *Proceedings of the symposium in honor of Lilian G. Katz* (pp. 303–12). Champaign, IL: ERIC.

Glaze, L. and Maruschak, L. (2008). *Parents in prison and their minor children*. Bureau of Justice Statistics special report NCJ 22984 (pp. 1–25), http://bjs.ojp.usdoj.gov/index.cfm?ty=pbdetail&iid=823.

Gonzales, P., Williams, T., Jocelyn, L., Roey, S., Kastberg, D., and Brenwald, S. (2008). *Highlights from TIMSS 2007: mathematics and science achievement of U.S. fourth- and eighth-grade students in an international context*, NCES 2009–001 revised. Washington, DC: National Center for Education Statistics, Institute of Education Sciences, US Department of Education.

Greenburg, M.T. (2006). Preventive interventions and their interface with neuroscience. *Annals of the New York Academy of Sciences*, 1094, 139–50.

Kotler, J.A., Schiffman, J.M., and Hanson, K.G. (2012). The influence of media characters on children's food choices. *Journal of Health Communication: International Perspectives*, 17, 886–98, Doi:10.1080/10810730.2011.650822.

Laughlin, L. (2011) Who's minding the kids? Child care arrangements. *Household Economic Studies*, Spring. Washington, DC: US Census Bureau.

Lauricella, A.R., Gola, A.H., Calvert, S.L. (2011). Toddlers' learning from socially meaningful video characters. *Media Psychology*, 14, 216–32.

Lin, H.-L., Lawrence, F.R., and Gorrell, J. (2003). Kindergarten teachers' views of children's readiness for school. *Early Childhood Research Quarterly*, *18*(2), 225–37.

Linebarger, D. & Gatewood, R. (2014). *Lessons from Cookie Monster*. Poster presentation at the London International Conference on Education, London, UK.

Louv, R. (2006). Last child in the woods: *Saving our children from nature-deficit disorder*. Chapel Hill, NC: Algonquin Books.

Military Families Research Institute (2009). Findings from the *Talk, Listen, Connect* (TLC II: D) kit evaluation: Findings from the *Talk, Listen, Connect* (TLC II: Changes) kit evaluation. West Lafayette, IN: Military Families Research Institute.

Mischel, W. (2014). *The marshmallow testing: Mastering self-control*. New York: Little, Brown.

Mizraie, A., Hamidi, F., and Anaraki, A. (2009). A study on the effect of science activities on fostering creativity in preschool children. *Journal of Turkish Science Education*, 6(3), 81–90.

O'Connell, C., Wenger, J., and Hansen, M.L. (2014). *Measuring and retaining the U.S. Army's deployment experience*. Washington, DC: Rand Corporation, http://www.rand.org/pubs/research_reports/RR570.html.

Ogden, C.L., Flegal, K.M., Carroll, M.D., and Johnson, C.L. (2002). Prevalence and trends in overweight among US children and adolescents, 1999–2000. *Journal of the American Medical Association*, 288(14), 1728–32.

Ogden, C.L., Carroll, M.D., Kit, B. K, and Flegal, K.M. (2014) Prevalence of childhood and adult obesity in the United States, 2011–2012. *Journal of the American Medical Association*, 311(8), 806–14.

Provasnik, S., Kastberg, D., Ferraro, D., Lemanski, N., Roey, S., and Jenkins, F. (2012). *Highlights from TIMSS 2011: mathematics and science achievement of U.S. fourth- and eighth-grade students in an international context*, NCES 2013–009 revised. Washington, DC: National Center for Education Statistics, Institute of Education Sciences, US Department of Education.

Raver, C.C. (2002). Emotions matter: Making the case for the role of young children's emotional development for early school readiness. *Social Policy Report*, 16(3), 3–24.

Rimm-Kaufman, S.E., Pianta, R.C., and Cox, M.J. (2000). Teachers' judgments of problems in the transition to kindergarten. *Early Childhood Research Quarterly*, 15(2), 147–66.

Ritchie, L.D., Whaley, S.E., Spector, P., Gomez, J., and Crawford, P.B. (2010). Favorable impact of nutrition education on California WIC families. *Journal of Nutrition Education and Behavior*, 42(3), 2–10.

Russell Research (2006). Findings from the *Talk, Listen, Connect* kit evaluation. East Rutherford, NJ: Russell Research.

Sackes, M., Trundle, K.C., Bell, R.L., and O'Connell, A.A. (2010). The influence of early science experience in kindergarten on children's immediate and later science achievement: Evidence from the early childhood longitudinal study. *Journal of Research in Science Teaching*, 48(2), 217–35.

Shore, R. (2008). The power of Pow! Wham!: Children, digital media and our nation's future: Three challenges for the coming decade. New York: Joan Ganz Cooney Center at Sesame Workshop.

Topp, D., Cardin, J.F., Walker, D.I., and MacDermid Wadsworth, S. (2013). The Impact of "Talk, Listen, Connect:" evaluation overview of Sesame Workshop kits for military families with young children. West Lafayette, IN: Military Family Research Institute at Purdue University.

Truglio, R.T., Kotler, J.A., Cohen, D.I., and Housley-Juster, A. (2005). Modeling life skills on *Sesame Street*. *Televizion*, 18, 15–19.

Truglio, R.T., Stefano, A.Z., and Sanders, J.S. (2014). *Sesame Street* puts self-regulation skills at the core of school readiness. *Zero to Three*, 35(2), 24.

Uniformed Services University of the Health Sciences (2011). *Talk, Listen, Connect (TLC-III) kit evaluation findings*. Unpublished manuscript, Uniformed Services University of the Health Sciences: Center for the Study of Traumatic Stress, Bethesda, MD.

Vespa, J., Lewis, J.M. and Kreider, J.M. (2013). America's families and living arrangements: 2012. *Current Population Reports* (pp. 20–570). Washington, DC: US Census
Bureau.

Wheelock College Aspire Institute (2010). Foundation for the future: Strengthening
STEM education in the early years. Boston, MA: Wheelock College Aspire Institute.

Wilson, R.A. (1993). *Fostering a sense of wonder during the early years.* Columbus, OH:
Greyden Press.

Zelazo, P.D., Anderson, J.E., Richler, J., Wallner-Allen, K., Beaumont, J.L., and
Weintraub, S. (2013). NIH Toolbox Cognition Battery (NIHTB-CB): Measuring
executive function and attention. *Monographs of the Society for Research in Child Development*, 78 (4, 309), 16–33.

4

HOW SESAME WORKSHOP PROMOTES EARLY CHILDHOOD EDUCATION AROUND THE WORLD

June H. Lee, Yeh Hsueh, Muhammad Zuhdi, Shantimoy Chakma, Sayed Farhad Hashimi, and Lilith Dollard

Currently, nine out of ten children in the world are born in a low- or middle-income country. Compared to their counterparts in higher-income countries, these children are more likely to live in poverty, less likely to receive early childhood education, more likely to be stunted, and less likely to live beyond age five (Engle et al., 2013). At the same time, marked variations exist within countries, drawn along the lines of socio-economic status and poverty, gender, ethnicity, urbanicity, and other factors. For example, across countries, children in the top quintile of income were more than twice as likely to be in preschool as those in the bottom quintile (Engle et al., 2011). Although protective and risk factors jointly operate in a child's life to shape her outcomes, risk factors tend to co-occur to perpetuate a cycle of malnutrition, poor stimulation, early delayed cognitive development, poor school performance, and poverty. Moreover, deficits that occur early in life can accumulate and become more pronounced over time (Nadeau et al., 2011). Correspondingly, early intervention is more effective than remedial interventions; the latter also become more expensive the longer a society waits to intervene (Heckman, 2008).

This chapter describes the unique role that Sesame Workshop plays in a movement to enhance informal education quality and access, especially for children who otherwise have limited or no access. Many of our international projects occupy the intersection of early childhood education, media, and international development. Through broadcast and community-engagement initiatives, we often succeed in delivering content to children in marginalized communities. As an example, the chapter focuses on our work in several Asian countries, although we have achieved similar impact in other parts of the world.

The Importance of Early Childhood Education

The accumulated evidence on the importance and efficacy of early childhood education has been robust and compelling. All children, whether they live in high- or low-income countries, benefit from early childhood education. More importantly, children in greater need often benefit the most (Aboud, 2006; Engle et al., 2011; Heckman, 2008). A recent review that integrates research on 84 early childhood education programs in the United States concluded that children gain about a third of a year of additional learning in language, reading, and math skills from early childhood education programs (Yoshikawa et al., 2013). Benefits can also extend to non-academic domains such as socio-emotional outcomes (Heckman et al., 2012) and health (Currie and Thomas, 1995; Ludwig and Miller, 2007). Early childhood education is an investment that yields great returns; estimates in the United States range from a return of $2.50 to $7 or more per dollar invested (Yoshikawa et al., 2013).

Assessments in low- and middle-income countries have yielded similar findings. A set of estimates concluded that increasing preschool enrollment to 25% or 50% in all middle- and low-income countries would yield a return of $6.4 to $17.6 per dollar invested (in terms of future labor market productivity; Engle et al., 2011). Data from Brazil and Guatemala indicated that an increase of one standard deviation in preschool cognitive skills is linked to up to more than one grade of additional schooling; preschool education also adds increases of 5–10% in lifetime income (Engle et al., 2007).

Beyond the economic benefits of early childhood education are other important arguments, especially in recognizing children as a special and important group, as "intrinsically valuable humans, important in their own right and deserving of services" (Britto et al., 2013, 66). Key international conventions and declarations—notably, Education for All and the International Convention on the Rights of the Child—pay specific attention to the unique rights of the child and view education through a human rights framework. Members of the international community have expressed a commitment to achieving Education for All and the six goals outlined therein (UNESCO, 2000), the first of which addresses the need to expand early childhood care and education. Underscoring each of the goals is the understanding that quality education is a human right, which in turn is informed by the principles of universality, interdependence on other rights, equality and non-discrimination, participation, and empowerment. Yet an estimated 200 million children under the age of five in developing countries are not living up to their full developmental potential (Grantham-McGregor et al., 2007). Still, many countries have yet to articulate a national early childhood development policy (Britto et al., 2013). At the current rate of progress, the world will not reach the Millennium Development Goal of universal primary education in 2015 (United Nations, 2013).

Media as an Educational Tool

Against this backdrop of benefits and challenges to early childhood education, we are witnessing a burgeoning availability of media for young children around the world. Traditional mass media technologies have become prevalent. Access to television continues to grow even in low-income countries, and children's television programs have crossed international boundaries, especially with the increasing availability of cable and satellite television. At the same time, new technologies hold the promise for education and engagement and in some instances are leapfrogging over traditional technologies in terms of mass access (Fong, 2009). Mobile devices such as smartphones are one such example.

In the context of low early childhood education access and high media penetration, Sesame Workshop plays a unique role in providing opportunities for informal early education. This chapter describes the ways in which our global projects have forwarded early childhood education using examples from four specific projects: Afghanistan, Bangladesh, China, and Indonesia. It describes how our carefully considered characters and content, as well as our approach, help to build children's academic readiness. Finally, we review recent research that documents our impact in these areas.

Forwarding Early Childhood Education and Building the Foundations for School Readiness

Although Sesame Street is best known as a television series, we engage broadly on issues around early childhood education in many countries. Sesame Street directly supports the goals of Education for All by making high-quality educational content available and accessible through multiple media outlets, particularly for children in need. We also elevate awareness of the importance of early development by engaging with government ministries, policymakers, and non-government organizations (NGOs) that provide early childhood services to families and young children. Complementary partnerships are often forged with organizations who reach families and whose mission is aligned with Sesame Workshop's; in such cases, our high-quality content naturally strengthens partners' capacity to serve our target audience.

Just as fostering basic academic skills has been the cornerstone of Sesame Street domestically, the same sensibilities have framed the international content. When it was first conceived in 1969, the Children's Television Workshop (as Sesame Workshop was then known) had a simple but formidable mission: to use television to help children, especially boys and girls from low-income families, gain the skills needed for school entry. Sesame Street aimed to have a transformative effect and aspired to be an equalizer by helping to provide children from low-income homes with the same preparation as their peers from wealthier households.

Sesame Street co-productions may vary substantially in their educational orientation, but school-readiness skills[1] such as literacy, math, and cognitive skills are at the core of virtually every project. These educational objectives are articulated in the program's *Statement of Educational Objectives* (or "curriculum"). While symbol systems differ across languages, every series aims to impart the foundational skills for literacy and math, including the alphabetic principle, decoding, vocabulary, number identification, and counting. Exposure to these foundational skills is especially important for children who live in home environments that do not have rich educational resources or regular exposure to print.

An educational television program faces unique challenges in offering content on literacy and math. Unlike a formal educational setting, where lessons progress in a prescribed order according to a scope and sequence, in television, producers and educators cannot make any assumptions about the child's prior knowledge or sustained viewing. A child can come to the series at any point during the season; she may have seen any number of episodes or none of them. Thus, the project has to address these skills in ways that have both breadth and depth. A single episode can contain segments in a given domain that vary in difficulty. For example, for a child who already knows the numerals 1 to 20 but does not yet know how to add, a segment where characters try to find the number 9 will reinforce his existing knowledge and provide an additional opportunity for mastery, while a segment on partitioning (expressing a number as the sum of other numbers) will offer new information that requires him to build on his existing math skills.

In many countries, Sesame Street co-productions provide a means of supplementing existing early childhood education initiatives with media (usually television) content. Our projects in Bangladesh and Indonesia have been particularly successful in this regard; they share many similarities but each one has aspects that are unique, and this chapter will describe them in greater detail. The chapter also describes our project in China, which was also created to support early education, but with a focus on process and inquiry skills that are important for young children's learning. Finally, we discuss our project in Afghanistan, which has a special emphasis on girls' education.

Bangladesh

Sisimpur—the Bangladeshi co-production of Sesame Street—has had a strong presence in Bangladesh since its debut in 2005. Funded by the United States Agency for International Development (USAID), Sisimpur was seen as a means of reaching children with informal early childhood content through television, a vision that holds particular promise in a country where only about one in four children (27%) are enrolled in pre-primary education (UNICEF, 2014). In 2004, the Sisimpur team convened the inaugural educational content seminar for the project, where 17 Bangladeshi advisors with a wide range of expertise came together to discuss the program's educational objectives. What emerged from that meeting was a comprehensive statement of educational objectives (or "curriculum") with wide-ranging goals that reflected a whole-child approach. Among these goals, academic-readiness skills were a focal point for several seasons of production. In Season 5, the series specifically highlighted literacy; in Season 6, numeracy and math skills were the focus; and the importance of science and science-mindedness was underscored in Season 7.

There were several innovative efforts to create a distinctively Bangladeshi project with Sisimpur. Special Muppet characters were, of course, one such approach. The content in each season of television production was delivered through furry, culturally relevant, and locally created Muppets. Halum is a Bengal tiger who loves to eat fish and vegetables and cares about the environment; Tuktuki is a six-year-old girl from an underprivileged family who goes to school and loves to learn new things every day; Ikri Mikri is a three-year-old monster who loves to ask questions and has a rich imagination; and Shiku is a six-year-old jackal and "scientist-in-training" who likes to invent things. These Muppet characters are not only beloved by children; they also serve as role models for learning. In addition to Muppets, Sisimpur also incorporated traditional Bangladeshi marionettes (designed and crafted by well-known Bangladeshi artist Mustafa Monwar) in the series through a special format called *Ikri's World*, where Ikri enters her imaginary world when adult human characters read a story. That a Sesame Street series included a kind of puppetry that was different from Muppets was unique to the project, and was testament to the importance that the team placed on the country's rich tradition of puppetry as a source of teaching and entertainment, especially in rural areas. In another "first" for Sesame Street co-productions, the creative team in both Bangladesh and New York saw great value in storytelling from teenagers' perspectives, and project trained youth from rural Bangladesh to create live-action films for the series (see Cole et al., 2007, for a detailed description of this initiative).

In a context where much of the formal education system still relies on rote learning, Sisimpur's approach—which emphasizes joyful learning, reading, using all of one's senses to learn about the world, questioning, observing, and task persistence—is a departure from traditional pedagogy. It aims to build skills and attitudes in children that will prepare them for success in school and in life.

The production and education teams have created many formats that address school-readiness skills and make learning fun, engaging, and meaningful. In addition to literacy segments that address Bangla letters, letter sounds, and letter-word associations, special formats were created to speak to the unique aspects of the language. For example, out of 50 Bangla letters, there are 26 confusable vowels and consonants—letters that look virtually identical except for a line or dot and are thus easily confusable for younger children. To familiarize children with these letters, the team created a special animated format called "Eraser and Pencil". Pencil writes a confusable letter; the Eraser erases a line or dot from the letter, turning it into another letter. True to Sesame Street's research model, the team tested the format to ensure that the animated characters were appealing and that the approach of showing confusable letters was effective with young children in both urban and rural areas.

Sisimpur is distinctive in the world of children's television in Bangladesh, marked by a unique blend of education, entertainment, and pro-social messages as well as a deeply child-focused approach. The show empowers children, especially by allowing them to ask questions and valuing their opinions—a way of treating children that is recently emerging as a preferred educational approach.

Extending Sisimpur's Reach: Rickshaw Viewings

While the Sisimpur television show offers an accessible and popular avenue for early learning opportunities, the fact that nearly half (49%) of Bangladeshis reported watching little or no television at the inception of the project (Bangladesh National Media Survey, 2002) and that few families owned televisions severely limited the series' reach. Therefore, in order to extend the impact of the project beyond those who are privileged enough to have regular access to television, it was essential to establish means for overcoming barriers preventing children from watching the show.

To this end, the project partnered with Save the Children to develop a rickshaw-viewing program, in which drivers equipped vegetable carts with television sets, a DVD player, and a generator to facilitate interactive community viewings of the show in rural areas (see Plate 2.2). The program has continued to expand throughout the seasons, reaching more children in a wider geographical area. Additionally, Sisimpur's outreach team developed a program to train rickshaw drivers to mediate the viewing by encouraging children to actively respond to the program. They would pause the tape and ask for predictions of what happens next; sing along with the show and ask children to join in; and ask children open-ended questions about what happened during the show in the last viewing. Because families usually attend these events, the interactive activities not only enhanced the educational value of children's viewing experiences, they also provided parents with a model for activities they can incorporate into their daily routines with their children. The rickshaw-viewing program has been successful in reaching children and families in rural areas throughout the country.

The Way Forward

Sisimpur has made a substantive contribution to early childhood education in Bangladesh. This is borne out by research (described later in this chapter) as well as anecdotes in the popular press (Karim and Ara, 2012). Sisimpur continues to gain ground in the country, with partnerships with other stakeholders in early childhood education, including the Ministry of Primary and Mass Education (MOPME), the Ministry of Women and Children's Affairs (MOWCA), and the Bangladesh Shishu Academy (BSA). BSA has been an implementing partner for Sisimpur programs for three years through its 64 district offices and six sub-district offices. Under this partnership, Sisimpur developed teaching and learning materials focusing on early literacy, math, and healthy habits, which were distributed to teachers, caregivers, and children in over 3,000 BSA centers and MOPME schools. In addition, Sisimpur print materials on literacy (such as big books, storybooks, puzzles, and letter charts) were successfully piloted in 18 MOPME schools. These partnerships will continue to bring Sisimpur content to preschool and early primary classrooms in the country. The project has experienced success on many fronts and aspires to be an enduring presence in Bangladesh.

Indonesia

Within a relatively short period of time, Indonesia has made great progress toward universal primary education. Compulsory primary education was mandated in 1984 (Djojonegoro, 1997), and primary school participation was almost universal (98%) by 2013 (BPS-Statistics Indonesia, 2014). The same magnitude of progress has not been made in the area of early childhood education and development (ECED), however. The ECED sector in Indonesia has been challenged with low government investment, low enrollment among the poor, a lack of teacher training, and low participation among children younger than age three (World Bank, 2012). Disparities in ECED by wealth are marked. In the mid-2000s, the government promoted non-formal ECED (Pendidikan Anak Usia Dini, or PAUD) with an emphasis on providing early education to low-income families, but enrollment in ECED services remains low (at 46%, UNICEF, 2014), particularly among low-income and rural families (UNICEF Indonesia, 2012). At the same time, television penetration in Indonesia is almost ubiquitous (Ministry of Communication and Information Technology, 2012; Synovate, 2008), and anecdotal evidence showed that children spent a great deal of time watching TV in a media landscape that was bereft of high-quality educational and entertaining content. Sesame Workshop identified television as an effective way of delivering informal ECED to a large audience. It is against this backdrop of opportunity and need that the Indonesian co-production Jalan Sesama was created.

As with other Sesame Street co-productions, Jalan Sesama's curriculum addressed multiple domains of development: physical, cognitive, emotional, social, aesthetic, and moral. The importance of teaching early literacy skills, however, surfaced very early, in the project's first educational content meeting in November 2006. Indonesian educational experts expressed the need for Indonesian students to be more prepared for school, develop a love for reading, and be exposed to early literacy before entering into primary school. Consequently, the series often included messages on the love of reading and learning to read, and the program's physical set incorporated a reading corner to bring the audience closer to the world of books. The reading corner was consistently used as a location where the many fun and exciting stories played out.

The Jalan Sesama team also developed special formats to address academic skills such as literacy and problem solving. A recurring animation format called *Gatot Kata* is one such example. *Gatot Kata* teaches early literacy skills using a familiar character, Gatot Kacha from the Mahabharata. (There is also a play on words in the format's title: "kata" means "word" in Indonesian.) In each segment, Gatot Kata introduces three different words that begin with the same letter. The audience sees visuals and is asked to guess which picture represents a word that starts with the letter. Gatot Kata then highlights the correct answer with the letter and word, so that the child sees the letter, its sound, and its use in a word.

In another format that features both live action and Muppets, *Agen Rahasia 123* (*Secret Agent 123*), a bumbling secret agent Muppet character solves problems—with the help of children—in the real world created by his nemesis, a rogue goat. For instance, in one segment, the goat knocks over a set of angklung (bamboo musical instruments) in a music room, and Agen Rahasia must re-arrange them from smallest to largest before the students return. A child inevitably ends up helping him to solve the problem.

These Jalan Sesama formats exemplify the integration of education, creativity, and localization that has worked effectively across co-productions around the world. Interestingly, *Gatot Kata* and *Agen Rahasia 123* draw from very different points of cultural reference: *Gatot Kata* is derived through an iconic character in popular wayang kulit (traditional shadow puppetry), whereas *Agen Rahasia* is an endearing but blundering version of James Bond, a modern Western character. That the production team draws from both local and international influences is testament to the creativity, humor, and relevance that are inherent to our co-productions.

Delivering educational content in a non-didactic way is at the heart of Jalan Sesama's approach. Its importance was also underscored in discussions (Zuhdi, 2008) with the Ministry of Education and Culture (MoEC, formerly the Ministry of National Education). As a project that aims to further early childhood education in Indonesia, it was critical for the team to understand the Ministry's philosophy about pedagogical issues such as teaching early literacy, and to ensure that Jalan Sesama's approach was aligned accordingly. MoEC emphasized that foundational literacy skills should be forwarded in fun and interesting ways in the early years, and that the project should also help teachers facilitate children's literacy skills through engaging and child-centered activities. The team continued to foster close communication and collaboration with MoEC through the production process, and MoEC's endorsement of the series was an important validation of its value. In 2010, MoEC awarded Jalan Sesama with a certificate of appreciation for its contribution to early childhood education (JakartaGlobe, 2012).

Community Engagement: Providing Early Childhood (PAUD) Centers with Educational Materials and Training

The partnership with MoEC would prove to be a central aspect of the Jalan Sesama project. In addition to the television series (and with support from USAID), the two worked together to provide PAUD centers with high-quality, child-centered teaching and learning materials on literacy and math. Such materials were sorely lacking in many centers that serve young children. The project's educational goals were designed in accordance with the Ministry of Education's regulation no. 58/2009 on early childhood education (Minister of Education, 2009), as well as Jalan Sesama's *Statement of Educational Objectives*. The regulation addresses standards of early childhood education, namely standards for children's development; teachers and administration staff; content; process and assessment; and facility, management, and budgeting. Jalan Sesama's educational objectives were created in accordance with the standards for child development.

Jalan Sesama engaged MoEC and other experts in the ECED sector (Association of Early Childhood Educators; Association of the Organizers of Indonesian Kindergarten; and ECED academics from Universitas Indonesia and Universitas Negeri Jakarta) in an intensive review and collaboration process. The Curriculum and Learning Sub-directorate at MoEC also reviewed the materials. MoEC recommended two provinces for the project: West Java (relatively well-resourced) and West Nusa Tenggara (less well-resourced). Before a full-scale roll-out, the team tested the materials with PAUD educators and children to ensure the materials' relevance, comprehensibility, and usability. They then conducted a small-scale pilot and teacher training in two PAUD centers in each province. Teachers in the pilot centers used the materials for four weeks and provided feedback to the team on the training and materials. The Jalan Sesama team improved upon the materials and training based on this input before a full-scale roll-out to over 800 centers in 2012.

Teacher training came to be a unique component of this project. In addition to training workshops, the team also produced a series of teacher training videos that introduced the materials and modeled their use in the classroom. In the training workshops, teachers practiced using the materials and learned how to create their own lesson plans with them. The training videos offered many alternate ways of using the materials. Different celebrities hosted each video so that they were appealing for the teachers. The Jalan Sesama team brought their creative talents to bear on producing content for a different audience: educators rather than children. The videos were innovative and engaging and could be shared among educators at the same center so that the teachers who did not have the opportunity to attend the training could still benefit from the suggestions and modeling in the videos.

This mode of engagement was so successful that the team received funding from the JP Morgan Foundation to adapt the materials for Papua—the most remote and under-resourced province in Indonesia. In interviews with ECED stakeholders, they expressed the desire for educational materials that reflected Papuan people and environments. Most of the materials they received were created in Java or Western countries and did not represent their lives. What the team thought could be relatively simple adaptations turned out to be substantial re-versioning of the materials to ensure that they suited the Papuan context. Food, housing, transportation, cultural festivals, animals, clothing, and musical instruments were all different in Papua compared to the rest of the country. The Bahasa Indonesia in the Papuan materials was also modified (and in some instances simplified) to suit Papua. Plate 4.1a–b shows pages from a math big book that illustrate the difference between the Java (Plate 4.1a) and Papua (Plate 4.1b) versions of the materials. Our Papuan advisors emphasized the importance of representing images that Papuans are familiar with. The book depicts Papuan human characters, local settings (such as homes, animals, and transportation), and variations in text (see Plate 4.1b). Testimonials suggest that the materials resonate with local educators. As a Papuan teacher (Susan Xie, personal communication, February 16, 2012) said, "The other thing that made the program special was that the Papuans normally recieved story books about Indonesian children depicting children from other Islands except Papua. Here, with Jalan Sesama, the books are in Bahasa Indonesia, yet the pictures illustrate Papuan children. This make us feel strongly that we are part of Indonesia."

The school engagement projects in West Java, West Nusa Tenggara, and Papua solidified MOEC's recognition of the value of Jalan Sesama to the ECED sector in Indonesia. It is remarkable that a children's media project has achieved such broad reach (Synovate, 2008) and engaged in such deep collaboration with the Ministry, ECED experts, and PAUD educators. An evaluation of the project's impact (described later in this chapter) further affirms its value to ECED stakeholders.

China

From the early introduction of formal schooling to modern-day compulsory education, reading, writing, and arithmetic skills have been regarded as essential building blocks for school readiness in China. These basic academic skills have been the areas of increasing emphasis for preschoolers' learning as they approach school age in both urban and rural regions. The Chinese cultural practice of child rearing also places a strong emphasis on socializing children to become a person who values books that symbolize learning and a love of learning (Li and Li, 2002). More recently, several of our projects have focused on the *processes* that underlie life-long adaptive learning skills instead of traditional academic skills. Along with the growing awareness of the need to develop science and technology in contemporary society, critical thinking, problem solving, communication, and other commonly called 21st century skills (Partnership for 21st Century Skills, 2011) have gained attention among early childhood educators. Such awareness has also been embedded in the Workshop's co-productions in China for nearly two decades. Sesame Workshop's entrée into China began as early as 1983 with a television special, *Big Bird in China*. In this Emmy Award-winning program, Big Bird and his friends went to China to seek answers to a series of Chinese puzzles they learned about in New York City's Chinatown. Their search took them to China's mountains, rivers, cities, and villages where they made new friends, met legends, and eventually found all the answers to the puzzles. This was followed by a major television series, Zhima Jie, in the late 1990s with the hope of reaching children of both rural and urban areas.

The first season of Zhima Jie included many segments from Sesame Workshop's extensive library of content that focused on science topics and observation skills. Later, in complementing the content on Zhima Jie, a series of sixty-one 30-second spots (*Let's Discover Together*) was created to enhance the science content. They featured a variety of science and technology phenomena that young children may encounter in their everyday lives to connect children's daily experiences with basic notions of science, technology, and engineering. For example, one spot helped children raise the question about how their shadows on the ground change during the day. Another spot introduced the notion of dissolving by putting salt in a glass of water to let children taste it. In another segment, the host's invention of a chain allowed children to take a look at the workings of a bicycle chain. In another, the host asked children to estimate how many ping-pong balls were in a jar.

Several years later in 2008, a unique show, *One World, One Sky*, co-produced by Sesame Workshop, Beijing Planetarium, and Chicago Alder Planetarium, made its debut in both the United States and China. The show was meant to stimulate children's wonderment about the sun, stars, constellations, and the sky. It took on a contemporary conceptualization of science and science education to place young children's learning of science in the context of humanity. The show encouraged children to use their imaginations to travel to the moon and to take a different perspective on the earth. In addition to introducing young children to astronomy, the show was also an innovative binational collaboration that was infused with important cross-cultural messages. Two different versions of the show were produced, one for China and one for the US. In the Chinese version, Elmo visits Hu Hu Zhu and Da Niao in China; in the US version, Hu Hu Zhu visits Elmo and Big Bird in America. They learn that children in China and the United States see the same sun and moon, and the Big Dipper, underscoring their shared experiences.

In 2010, our co-production *Big Bird Looks at the World* brought our early efforts to promote the 21st-century skills to a larger scale both in content scope and in its reach. With 52 episodes that involved three main knowledge domains: science and discovery, nature and the environment, and health and the human body, the series was dedicated to young children's science learning. Each episode invited young children to start from their daily experiences and to follow Elmo and Big Bird to ask an experience-based science question such as where the sun goes at night, how a tree eats and drinks, why our heart beats, and how a child can avoid passing a cold on to another child. A wide range of science topics exposing children to phenomena from the immense universe like the solar system to the tiny micro world like activities of germs and viruses were presented through a number of episodes. Young children viewing the show can easily share the experience-based questions Elmo and Big Bird ask about the sun's whereabouts at night and a better way to prevent invisible germs passing from one child to another. These important science questions are couched in preschool-friendly ways but actually lay the foundations for understanding about the universe and the micro world. Indeed, the topics on health and the human body bring home the basic science of health for children, so their knowing "what" is to help their knowing "how."

Through various new broadcast arrangements, the show in its first season reached children and their families in 20 provinces and cities, followed by a summer replay in 2012 on the national broadcaster, China Central Television (CCTV) for children all over China. China's television ownership rate is high (95%; Cable and Satellite Broadcasters Association of Asia, 2010), which in principle allows children in rural areas similar access as urban children to the series *Big Bird Looks at the World*.

In China's *Big Bird Looks at the World*, science is the perfect vehicle for engaging children in these processes and engendering their interest in the world around them. The series emphasizes the experiential, hands-on aspects of learning and provides scenarios for children that put them in an active role of determining the questions, investigating, collecting evidence, and drawing conclusions based on evidence. Such a process enables children to draw deeper meaning from their learning experiences and become more active, successful learners (Sesame Workshop Global Education Department, 2012). Through the lens of scientific investigation, children learn to ask questions, make observations, and form conclusions. Everyday experiences become the basis for inquiry, from noticing that the moon looks different on different nights, to wondering what fills a balloon, to finding out what sinks and what floats. Children build their working knowledge of the world as they create connections and make meaning of new discoveries. Through Muppets and live-action films, the series models children engaged in hands-on activities to find answers to their questions as they describe, compare, investigate, and work with others. Because science education also taps into multiple domains of child development, the series also supports children in developing language and reasoning skills, problem-solving abilities, and socio-emotional skills like social understandings of an observed event, sympathy, and collaborative efforts.

Unlike most television programs for young children in China, the series exposed preschool-aged children to science and technology words that were not in their vernacular. Learning words like "experiment," "alive," "chrysalis," and "dissolve," helps build children's scientific vocabulary and provides a means for young children to express themselves as scientists do. In this way, children are introduced to the basics of scientific inquiry. The series underscores the use of the five senses in observation, asking "how," "what," and "which;" and designing and building tools and technology to solve problems. Every effort was made to use objects that are familiar to the child in locations that fit with the child's environment in order to develop their familiarity with science concepts and their relevance to daily life. Following its launch in 2010, *Big Bird Looks at the World* began occupying a noticeable place in children's media in China. Its presence on the Sesame Workshop China website (Zhima Jie, 2014) and Central China Television Channel 14 (CCTV Shaoer, 2014) allows the series to continue to reach a broad audience.

Afghanistan

In Afghanistan, formal schooling starts at age seven, in first grade. The Afghan constitution (Article 43) has granted free education up to baccalaureate to all Afghans, male and female (Ministry of Justice, n.d.). Therefore, the Afghan government considers access to and quality of formal schooling a priority. The government, however, faces many challenges in the provision of education, including a lack of trained teachers (especially female teachers), adequate school infrastructure, a lack of teaching and learning materials, and cultural barriers to girls' education. The Ministry of Education (MoE) estimates that as many as half of school-age children may be out of school (Ministry of Education, 2010). With the current challenges and some 15 million students enrolled (Froutan, 2011), the Ministry of Education is focusing its efforts to realize the Afghan government's commitment to free schooling for all Afghans.

There is a patchwork of services for young children in Afghanistan, with some early childhood education and daycare centers run by the Ministry of Labour, Social Affairs and Martyred and Disabled and other private pre-school and early child development (ECD) programs offered by local and international NGOs (Ministry of Education, 2010). The Ministry of Education has not focused on early childhood education in the same way it has formal schooling, which has resulted in a lack of cohesive early childhood education infrastructure and services. Only 1% of children under five years of age attend an early childhood education program (UNICEF, 2013). Recently, the Ministry of Education has realized the need to develop an early childhood education program, which will be an integral part of the existing formal schooling. The MoE is currently drafting an ECE strategy that envisions "quality pre-school services for young children 4–6 years old that enable them to grow and thrive physically, mentally, socially, emotionally and morally" (Ministry of Education, 2010). Due to the lack of early childhood education (ECE) teachers and age-appropriate school infrastructures, the MoE has recognized the role of private schools and centers in providing ECE and has partnered with international NGOs such as Agha Khan Development Network and BRAC Bangladesh to pilot ECE programs in select schools in Kabul.

Despite increasing attention to ECD, children are currently entering primary school without adequate knowledge and skills or preparation for the transition to the school environment. Low literacy rates (45% among males and 17% among females (the primary caregivers); UNESCO, 2012) also mean that many children cannot receive help with schoolwork from their parents. Many would argue that one of the reasons behind the current high primary drop-out rate (only 39% of girls and 60% of boys complete primary school; UNESCO, 2012) is the fact that Afghan children lack the strong foundation for academic success that can be established in early childhood.

Baghch-e-Simsim

In the face of all the existing challenges such as security, capacity, resources, infra-structure, and the absence of an established ECE system, Baghch-e-Simsim (BSS) is an alternative edutainment model that prepares young children for formal schooling and teaches them basic life skills. With the vision of responding to Afghanistan's critical need for high-quality early education resources, the BSS project focuses on literacy and numeracy and aims to build the core life skills of a new generation of Afghans in a context that values and promotes education for all, respect for humankind, gender equity, and cultural diversity.

Based on Sesame Workshop's educational model, BSS is one of only a few ECE media programs that addresses the developmental needs and educational priorities of Afghan children. The program focuses on cognitive, emotional, physical, and social development needs and includes cross-cutting themes such as girls' empow-erment, mutual respect, cultural diversity, and national identity. The program is produced for television and radio in Dari and Pashto, the two official national lan-guages of Afghanistan; the television content targets children ages three to seven years, while the radio format also includes segments on positive parenting. Radio programming is especially important in reaching rural areas where households cannot necessarily afford a television set. Both TV and radio complement each other to help *BSS* achieve greater reach and impact.

Girls' Empowerment

Afghan girls face cultural and structural challenges to education and full social, economic, and political participation in society. In response to these challenges, Baghch-e-Simsim has made girls' empowerment one of the core tenets of the program. One strategy of addressing girls' empowerment is through the positive representation of girls and women as role models in many of the locally produced live-action films (LAFs). In Season 1, the live-action film "First Day of School" depicts six-year-old Zynab's first day at primary school. Through her narration, we sense her excitement and apprehension that morning, and see how much she loves school. The film also contains many implicit messages. Zynab's family shares in the excitement of the morning. Her father helps her to pack her schoolbag and her mother makes sure she has a healthy breakfast; her brother is part of the morning's preparations. The engagement, encouragement, and reactions of others including boys and men—implicitly model support for girls' education.

Thus, in addition to promoting the achievements of young Afghan girls, we also model parental and community support and equitable treatment of both genders. Many live-action films explore themes of community while modeling gender equity and division of labor between boys and girls and adult men and women. For example, modeling mothers and fathers sharing household chores and parents encouraging play and exploration among both sons and daughters. In the live-action film "Friday Prayer", the local Baghch-e-Simsim team wanted to encourage girls' participation in the social and religious community. The film portrays a girl accompanying her father and little brother to the masjid and greeting everyone after the prayer. The inclusion of the young girl in this important ritual and community experience suggests that religious values can co-exist with and embrace girls' empowerment in Afghanistan, with the support of community members.

Further, BSS instills hope and inspires girls with a sense of confidence and optimism about the future. While exploring professions and members of the community, the program introduces the audience to women in unique and non-traditional professions. For example, one film features a female civil engineer. In reality, engineering is still considered a male profession in Afghanistan and there are currently only a few female engineers in the whole country. To challenge this perception and inspire girls to pursue a non-traditional profession, the local team was able to find a woman engineer to feature as the lead for this film. This LAF brought widespread attention to the fact that women, too, can be engineers and showed the young girls watching BSS that they can aspire to professions beyond what they may see in their daily lives.

Given that Afghan girls do not have the same access to education as boys (40% of students enrolled in primary school are female; UNESCO, 2012), Baghch-e-Simsim also has great potential to benefit young girls by providing them with basic academic knowledge and school-readiness skills. The series' Muppet characters offer literacy and numeracy lessons in fun and age-appropriate ways. Every episode introduces a letter and a number and reinforces these through visual aids and audio examples, depending on whether it is a TV or radio program. Likewise, the series builds children's vocabulary through introducing three words that start with the letter featured in the episode.

Although it is sometimes challenging for the BSS program to adhere to traditional social norms because doing so may reinforce gender and ethnic stereotypes, the local team tries to challenge perceptions in a nuanced way and offer alternatives that represent the principles and goals they want to promote while still reflecting the Afghan context.

Our Impact

Sesame Street is the most extensively researched television program in history (Truglio and Fisch, 2001, xvii). In its early years, research focused on its educational impact in the United States, with an array of evidence documenting the series' positive effects on children's school-readiness skills (Wright et al., 2001; Zill, 2001) and vocabulary acquisition (Rice et al., 1990). Long-term impact was also evident in a longitudinal study (Anderson et al., 2001), which revealed that adolescents who watched Sesame Street as preschoolers had better grades in high school, read more books for pleasure, and placed higher value on academic achievement than non-viewers.

More recently, we have accumulated a substantial body of studies that affirm the value of Sesame Street internationally. In fact, enough studies have been conducted on the impact of Sesame Street co-productions that researchers were able to conduct a meta-analysis—a "study of studies"—that examined its effects across different countries.[2] This research is described earlier in Chapter 1. The next section examines the effects of exposure to Sesame Street are children's acquisition of literacy, math, and science knowledge. The studies described focus on projects that are highlighted in this chapter, but research has found parallel trends in other countries, including India (GyanVriksh Technologies, 2009), Palestine (Fluent Research, 2011), South Africa (Khulisa Management Services, 2005), and Tanzania (Borzekowski and Macha, 2010).

Effects on Literacy, Math, and Science

Many international studies have documented Sesame Street's positive impact on children's literacy, math, and science knowledge, both in the short term and longitudinally.[3] These studies range in scope and methodology. Some employ what is considered the "gold standard" in summative evaluations—the randomized controlled trial (RCT)—and others use a naturalistic approach where researchers measure the amount of viewing that is occurring "in real life" and link it to learning outcomes, while statistically controlling for important factors that may confound the relationship between the two. The former is particularly valued for its scientific rigor and allows researchers to more confidently attribute causality in their findings. The latter, on the other hand, is not subject to the artifact of experimental manipulation that the RCT is. Both approaches have inherent strengths and drawbacks; they also complement each other and when evidence from both designs is available, allow us to draw firm conclusions regarding Sesame Street's impact based on a convergence of findings. What is particularly encouraging is the finding that the benefits from exposure to Sesame Street are sometimes strongest among children who need it the most—those who are economically disadvantaged or who live in rural areas.

Evidence from Longitudinal Naturalistic Research (Bangladesh)

A nationally representative longitudinal study in Bangladesh (ACPR, 2008) is an example of a naturalistic study. Conducted by a Dhaka-based research agency, this study was unusually large in its scale—over 6,000 children throughout the country participated. Over a three-year period, researchers measured the frequency with which children watched Sisimpur and assessed their performance on a range of measures on literacy, math, and social and cultural knowledge. Through multivariate analyses, researchers examined the link between watching Sisimpur and these learning outcomes, while carefully controlling for socio-demographic variables and children's prior performance to ensure that any relationships detected are over and above the influence of these factors. The first measurement began shortly before Sisimpur was on air in order to establish a baseline measure of children's skills before any exposure to the series. Follow-up "waves" of assessments then took place one and two years thereafter. Such a design allows researchers to examine both concurrent (i.e., relations between viewing and outcomes within each wave) and longitudinal (i.e., relations aggregated across all three waves) effects.

The results within each wave were remarkably consistent: children who watched Sisimpur had higher scores in measures of literacy (letter identification, vocabulary, and reciting letters) than those who did not watch. These results remained robust even when crucial factors like the child's age, gender, mother's education, household income, and (perhaps the most important) the child's prior performance were taken into account. Additionally, the amount of exposure differentiated children's scores: children with the highest exposure (i.e., viewed Sisimpur at least twice a week) demonstrated the highest literacy skills, followed by those who had some exposure (i.e., viewed at least once a month but less than twice a week); children with no exposure had the lowest scores. Another noteworthy finding is that watching Sisimpur may confer developmental gains in academic skills. Children who had no exposure demonstrated literacy skills at levels equivalent to those of a child who is one year older but had no exposure (see Figure 4.1 for a graphical representation using overall literacy skills at Wave 2). Similar patterns also emerged for math outcomes (counting and number identification). It is worth noting that exposure to Sisimpur was often as strongly related to learning outcomes as mother's education and household income. This suggests that Sisimpur has the potential to compensate for some educational disadvantages that children may experience due to their socio-economic background.

When researchers examined the effects of Sisimpur over time, they uncovered further evidence of its educational value. Consistent with findings within waves, viewing Sisimpur was associated with higher scores over time in literacy and math outcomes. Interestingly, the analyses showed that the effects of Sisimpur depend in part on socio-economic factors. Viewing seems to confer benefits to children from rural households and those in lower-income urban households. Watching Sisimpur does not seem to differentiate children from higher-income urban families. The latter group of children may have a greater abundance of educational opportunities and materials, and viewing Sisimpur may not contribute

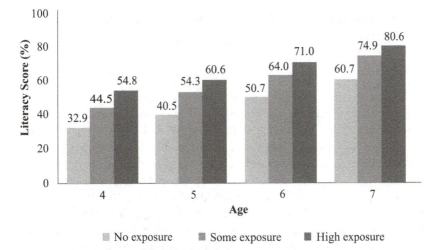

Note: Means are adjusted for child's gender, residence, mother's education, family income, and performance at Wave 1. The sample includes children tested at Waves 1 and 2 ($N = 4{,}688$).

FIGURE 4.1 Overall literacy skills by exposure and age (Bangladesh)

any additional benefits. It thus appears that the positive impact of the program may be the most potent among children who need it the most and have few opportunities to be exposed to educational content.

Evidence from Experimental Studies (Indonesia, Afghanistan, and China)

The Bangladesh evaluation just described was large and long term in scope. While extremely worthwhile, such a study requires considerable time, capacity, and financial resources that are usually limited. Other studies investigating Sesame Street's impact often involve smaller samples and are shorter in duration. We describe several interesting examples below from Indonesia (Borzekowski and Henry, 2011; Myriad Research, 2012), Afghanistan (Glevum International, 2012), and China (Hsueh et al., 2012). Each examined different learning outcomes based on the project's educational focus. The research from Indonesia and Afghanistan investigated the co-production's impact on children's cognitive, literacy, math, health, social development, and cultural knowledge; the outcomes examined reflect a whole-child approach that the co-production took in its educational direction. The study from China centered in a much more targeted way on science outcomes, as was the focus of the series *Big Bird Looks at the World*.

All were experimental studies (a few were randomized controlled trials) that took place in schools.

Indonesia

The evaluation of Jalan Sesama's impact took place in a community that was relatively remote and low-resourced (Borzekowski and Henry, 2011). A total of 160 children ages three to six years took part in this study. Children were randomly assigned to a "high-exposure" group (watched three to four episodes of Jalan Sesama a week), a "low-exposure" group (viewed one episode a week), or a "control" group (watched an alternate children's program). Researchers assessed them on a range of skills before and after a 14-week exposure period. (Because the focus of this chapter is on academic skills, we will focus on cognitive, literacy, and math outcomes accordingly.) Analyses indicated that children who had high exposure performed better on tests of early cognitive skills, letter recognition, number recognition, and counting compared with those who had no exposure. These effects were over and above those of the child's gender, age, baseline score, and parent education. Interestingly, low exposure (i.e., watching once a week) was not linked to better performance in these areas, suggesting that a threshold "dosage" of more than one episode a week may be needed to create impact. The intervention did not have significant effects on skills that are not emphasized in the series, such as early reading and writing, and arithmetic.

Impact of MoEC partnership

Researchers also evaluated the impact of the MoEC partnership in PAUD centers described earlier in this chapter. PAUD centers (N = 823 children; 408 in the intervention group, 415 in the control group) in two provinces participated in a four-month intervention (Myriad Research, 2012). Children who participated in the Jalan Sesama project showed greater gains than the control group in several literacy and math skills tested, including letter identification, knowing the initial letters of words, number identification, and relational concepts. The intervention had greater impact in West Nusa Tenggara—an area of greater need and fewer resources—than West Java. Interviews with MoEC personnel revealed that they valued the project, especially the collaboration and coordination with MoEC, teacher training, and the creativity and innovation of the materials. They expressed the need for a longer training workshop and materials that will encourage greater creativity in teachers. Teachers themselves appraised the materials very positively and felt that the materials were varied in the skills they addressed and were more appealing than existing materials. Teachers also thought that the training was useful and relevant for their needs, and helped to promote confidence in their teaching. They appreciated the chance for professional development and would have liked the training to be longer (Myriad Research, 2012).

The research affirms the contribution that Jalan Sesama has made to ECED in Indonesia, both in mass media and in early childhood classrooms. The team's capacity extended beyond media production, to adding value in professional development among teachers and developing content for formal educational settings.

Afghanistan

A small-scale pilot study in Afghanistan suggests that children learn basic skills from watching the series. In an eight-week intervention with 101 children in two schools in Kabul, children watched Baghch-e-Simsim three times a week and were assessed on literacy, math, and socio-emotional skills. Compared to children in the control group, those who watched Baghch-e-Simsim made greater gains in phonemic awareness, counting, gender equity attitudes, and knowledge about emotions, over and above the effects of age (Glevum Associates and Sesame Workshop, 2013). The study comprised a small sample and larger-scale evaluations are necessary to verify its impact, but the research indicates that the co-production holds promise for children in Afghanistan.

China

In addition to literacy and math, research has also uncovered Sesame Street's educational impact in the domain of science. Researchers examined children's learning of science content from *Big Bird Looks at the World (BBLW)*, the Chinese co-production of Sesame Street (Hsueh et al., 2012). A large sample of over 1,900 children in two provinces participated in the RCT. Children in schools were randomly assigned to an intervention group that watched BBLW five times a week, or to a control group that carried on with their usual classroom activities. The outcomes examined mapped onto the series' curriculum and comprised three main domains: science and discovery, nature and the environment, and health and the human body.

The researchers found that children who watched *BBLW* scored higher on all three domains tested than children who did not watch (see Figure 4.2). Interestingly, the effect sizes found in this study (ranging from .27–.36; see Figure 4.2) mirror that from the effect size of .29 in the meta-analysis (Mares and Pan, 2013). Importantly, the series had particular benefit for children in rural areas in some areas of knowledge. Rural children were especially likely to show gains in their knowledge of hygiene, health, and animals' body coverings compared to urban children. These findings were especially encouraging given that there is a greater need for educational resources in rural areas, and rural–urban disparities in education has been an important topic of focus in China (Peng and Yan, 2011; Yan and Wei, 2013).

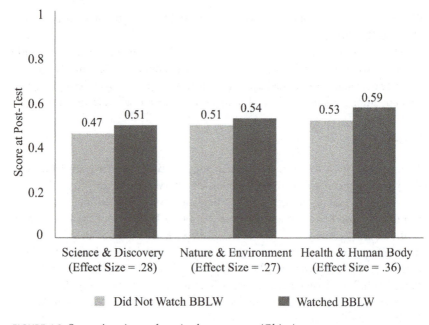

FIGURE 4.2 Scores in science domains by exposure (China)

Broader Cultural Impact

Our international projects often have ripple effects that extend beyond children's learning. Assessing our projects' broader cultural impact on early childhood is challenging, but qualitative studies suggest that we are making a difference there too. An anthropological study of Sisimpur's cultural impact (Kibria and Jain, 2009) examined how caregivers in rural areas of Bangladesh viewed the project. The findings indicate that the project is elevating the importance of ECE among parents and educators. Parents felt that Sisimpur has provided useful information for the family (on good hygiene practices, for example), that it is a source of shared enjoyment, and its depiction of rural culture was especially valued. They appreciated the series for its pro-social content and saw it as being aligned with their own values. Many parents also reported that Sisimpur helped them become more aware of the importance of paying attention to and building a close relationship with their children; they became more thoughtful about how they interacted with children as a result. Teachers also affirmed the project's value in helping children be prepared for school, noting that the use of play and songs helped to motivate children in their learning. Some teachers drew inspiration from the series' child-centered approach and its appealing characters and used them effectively in their classrooms.

In Afghanistan, a study commissioned by the US State Department described Baghch-e-Simsim's positive impact on young children and families (Glevum International, 2012). In a series of focus groups conducted in Kabul, Herat, and Kandahar, mothers affirmed BSS's value. They credited the series for sparking enthusiasm about learning and attending school among their children. Many mothers described their children imitating characters from BSS and asking questions about what they saw in the show. They also noted that the show promoted good behavior and valuable social lessons such as friendship and unity. Similar to Sisimpur in Bangladesh, BSS also helped mothers understand how to treat their children, and to encourage their learning and self-expression. They also saw BSS as being consistent with Afghan culture and values. Perhaps most remarkably, a few mothers mentioned that adult males in the family (i.e., children's fathers and grandfathers) had decided to permit girls to attend school.

Conclusions

Building on the vision of its founder Joan Ganz Cooney, Sesame Street is extending its mission of using media to provide learning opportunities for children who may need it most. That vision has taken on a life of its own and Sesame Workshop has an important stake in using media to fulfill international development and early childhood education goals. Sesame Street co-productions have at their bases well-defined educational goals, teams of creative and passionate educators and producers, informed by research as to what works best for children in a given country or region. The impact that we hope to create in ECD is ambitious, but there is evidence to suggest that such an approach can bear fruit. Media can be an effective educator. In contexts where ECE provision is limited, mass media such as television can reach large numbers of children for a relatively low cost. It is an intervention that is scalable and can have great reach to include those from lower socio-economic families. Formal ECE provided by trained educators will always remain vitally important and although a media project cannot take its place, it can potentially fill gaps left by current ECE systems. Educational media also have the flexibility to serve supplementary or after-school functions.

It is important to note that with one exception, the research reviewed in this chapter (including the meta-analysis) examined unmediated exposure to Sesame Street. That is, children watched the program without any adult facilitation or explanation. While we always emphasize the importance and added value of adult-child co-viewing, that Sesame Street has an educational effect without adult facilitation is testament to its effectiveness as an educational tool.

In many countries, the research indicates that we often have a greater impact on children who may need it the most, whether it is rural and low-income urban children in Bangladesh, rural children in China, or less-resourced provinces in Indonesia. For most children, media is a backdrop to their lives, but media content can produce "drip" effects that can create small changes. Over time, we hope that small changes accumulate, narrow the gaps in educational opportunities, and set children on a positive path toward learning.

Notes

1. School readiness also encompasses a range of other academic and non-academic skills such as socio-emotional competencies and executive functioning. The focus of this chapter, however, is largely on academic skills.
2. A meta-analysis aggregates results from different studies across sample sizes and methodologies. It aims to detect patterns across a diverse body of research in order to understand the magnitude of impact (in this case, the impact of watching Sesame Street on children's learning outcomes).
3. Many of these studies are included in the meta-analysis (Mares and Pan, 2013) just described.

References

Aboud, F. (2006). Evaluation of an early childhood preschool program in rural Bangladesh. *Early Childhood Research Quarterly*, 21, 46–60.

ACPR (2008). *Summary: Sisimpur's reach and educational impact: Evidence from a national longitudinal survey*. Dhaka: Associates for Community and Population Research.

Anderson, D.R., Huston, A.C., Schmitt, K.L., Linebarger, D.L., and Wright, J.C. (2001). Early childhood television viewing and adolescent behavior: The recontact study. *Monographs of the Society for Research in Child Development*, 66(1, 264).

Borzekowski, D.L.G. and Henry, H.K.M. (2011). The impact of *Jalan Sesama* on the educational and healthy development of Indonesian preschool children: An experimental study. *International Journal of Behavioral Development*, 35, 169–79.

Borzekowski, D.L.G. and Macha, J.E. (2010). The role of *Kimilani Sesame* in the healthy development of Tanzanian preschool children. *Journal of Applied Developmental Psychology*, 31, 298–305.

BPS-Statistics Indonesia (2014) *Indikator Pendidikan 1994–2013*, http://www.bps.go.id/tab_sub/view.php?kat=1&tabel=1&daftar=1&id_subyek=28&notab=1, accessed April 19, 2014.

Britto, P.R., Engle, P.L., and Super, C.M. (eds) (2013). *Handbook of early childhood development research and its impact on global policy*. New York: Oxford University Press.

Cable and Satellite Broadcasters Association of Asia (2010). *China*, http://www.casbaa.com/advertising/countries/china.

CCTV Shaoer (2014). *Zhima Jie: Daniao kan shijie*, http://shaoer.cntv.cn/children/C28472/classpage/video/20110808/101261.shtml.

Cole, C., Biel, L., and Pai, S. (2007). Projecting youth voices: *Sisimpur* Rural Filmmakers' project in Bangladesh. *Journal of Children and Media*, 1, 88–92.

Currie, J. and Thomas, D. (1995). Does head start make a difference? *American Economic Review*, 85, 341–64.

Djojonegoro, W. (1997) *Fifty years of Indonesian education development*. Jakarta: Depdikbud.

Engle, P.L., Black, M.M., Behrman, J., Cabral de Mello, M., Gertler, P., Kapirro, L. et al. (2007). Child development in developing countries 3: Strategies to avoid the loss of developmental potential in more than 200 million children in the developing world. *Lancet*, 369, 229–42.

Engle, P.L., Fernald, L.C.H., Alderman, H., Behrman, J., O'Gara, C., Yousafzai, A., et al. (2011). Child development 2: Strategies for reducing inequalities and improving developmental outcomes for young children in low-income and middle-income countries. *Lancet*, 378, 1339–53.

Engle, P.L., Rao, N., and Petrovic, O. (2013). Situational analysis of young children in a changing world. In P.R. Britto, P.L. Engle, and C.M. Super (eds), *Handbook of early childhood development research and its impact on global policy* (pp. 35–64). New York: Oxford University Press.

Fluent Research (2011). Shara'a Simsim *impact assessment study: Report of research findings*. New York: Fluent Research.

Fong, M.W. (2009). Technology leapfrogging for developing countries. *Electronic Journal of Information Systems in Developing Countries*, 36, 3707–12.

Froutan, A.A. (2011). Building a solid foundation for a brighter future in Afghanistan through education, November 8, http://www.unicef.org/infobycountry/afghanistan_60442.html.

Glevum Associates and Sesame Workshop (2013). An impact assessment of *Baghch-e-Simsim*: A report on findings from a pilot experimental study. Gloucester, MA: Glevum Associates.

Glevum International (2012). *Focus group report: Sesame Street*. Gloucester, MA: Glevum.

Grantham-McGregor, S., Bun Cheung, Y., Cueto, S, Glewwe, P., Richer, L., Trupp, B., and International Child Development Steering Group (2007). Developmental potential in the first 5 years for children in developing countries. *Lancet*, 369(9555), 60–70.

GyanVriksh Technologies (2009). *The reach and impact of the* Galli Galli Sim Sim *television show in India: Endline report of a naturalistic longitudinal study*. Hyderabad: GyanVriksh Technologies.

Heckman, J.J. (2008). The case for investing in disadvantaged young children. In First Focus (ed.), *Big ideas for children: Investing in our nation's future* (pp. 49–58). Washington, DC: First Focus.

Heckman, J., Pinto, R., and Savelyev, P.A. (2012). *Understanding the mechanisms through which an influential early childhood program boosted adult outcomes*, NBER working paper no. 18581. Cambridge, MA: National Bureau of Economic Research.

Hsueh, Y., Zhou, Z., Su, G., Tian, Y., Sun, A., and Fan, C. (2012). Big Bird Looks at the World *Season 1 evaluation report*. Memphis, TN: University of Memphis.

JakartaGlobe (2012). *Moving Sesame Street's Lessons Online*, January 23, http://www.thejakartaglobe.com/archive/moving-sesame-streets-lessons-online/.

Karim, K.M. and Ara, G. (2012, March 22). The cartoon disease gets a cartoon therapy. *Dainik ProthomAlo*, March 22, https://www.prothom-alo.com.

Khulisa Management Services (2005). *Impact assessment of* Takalani Sesame *season II programme*. Johannesburg: Khulisa Management Services.

Kibria, N. and Jain, S. (2009). Cultural impacts of *Sisimpur, Sesame Street*, in Bangladesh: Views of caregivers of children in rural Bangladesh. *Journal of Comparative Family Studies*, 40, 57–75.

Li, J. and Li, J.M. (2002). "The Cow Loves to Learn": The Hao-Xue-Xin learning model as a reflection of the cultural relevance of *Zhima Jie*, China's *Sesame Street*. *Early Education and Development*, 13(4), 379–94.

Ludwig, J. and Miller, D.L. (2007). Does Head Start improve children's life chances? Evidence from a regression discontinuity design. *Quarterly Journal of Economics*, 122, 159–208.

Mares, M.L. and Pan, Z. (2013). Effects of *Sesame Street*: A meta-analysis of children's learning in 15 countries. *Journal of Applied Developmental Psychology*, 34, 140–51, doi: 10.1016/j.appdev.2013.01.001.

Minister of Education (2009). *Peraturan Menteri Pendidikan Nasional No. 58 Tahun 2009 tentang Standar Pendidikan Anak Usia Dini* (Minister of National Education's regulation no. 58 year 2009 on early childhood education standard). Jakarta: Ministry of Education.

Ministry of Communication and Information Technology, Indonesia (2012). The usage of ICT by households and individuals in Indonesia, http://www.itu.int/en/ITU-D/Statistics/Documents/events/wtim2012/011INF-E_doc.pdf.

Ministry of Education, Islamic Republic of Afghanistan (2010). National education strategic plan for Afghanistan, http://www.iiep.unesco.org/fileadmin/user_upload/News_And_Events/pdf/2010/Afghanistan_NESP.pdf.

Myriad Research (2012). Jalan Sesama*'s educational impact: Evidence from an experimental study of a Sesame Street outreach project in Indonesia*. Jakarta: Myriad Research.

Naudeau, S., Martinez, S., Premand, P., and Filmer, D. (2011). Cognitive development among young children in low-income countries. In H. Alderman (ed.), *No small matter: The impact of poverty, shocks and human capital investment in early childhood development* (pp. 9–50). Washington, DC: World Bank.

Partnership for 21st Century Skills (2011). Framework for 21st century learning, http://www.p21.org/storage/documents/1.__p21_framework_2-pager.pdf.

Peng, J.Y. and Yan, C.Y. (2011). 彭俊英、鄢超云 (2011）：关于发展乡镇中心幼儿园的一些思考——基于对四川省30所乡镇中心幼儿园的调查，幼儿教育，2011年第3期[Thoughts on developing preschools in counties and towns: Based on the survey of 30 county-center and town-center preschools in Sichuan province. *Young Children's Education (You'er Jiaoyu)*, 3, 10–12].

Rice, M.L., Huston, A.C., Truglio, R., and Wright, J.C. (1990). Words from "*Sesame Street*": Learning vocabulary while viewing. *Developmental Psychology*, 26, 421–8.

Sesame Workshop Global Education Department (2012). *Introducing STEM to Sesame Workshop's international coproductions*. Unpublished manuscript.

Synovate (2008). *Reach and perception of* Jalan Sesama *(Wave 1)*. Jakarta: Synovate.

Truglio, R.T. and Fisch, S.M. (2001). Introduction. In S. Fisch and R.T. Truglio (eds), *'G' is for growing* (p. xvii). Mahwah, NJ: Erlbaum.

UNESCO (2000). The Dakar framework for action, http://unesdoc.unesco.org/images/0012/001211/121147e.pdf.

UNESCO (2012). World atlas of gender equality in education, http://unesdoc.unesco.org/images/0021/002155/215522E.pdf.

UNICEF (2013). Afghanistan: Statistics, http://www.unicef.org/infobycountry/afghanistan_statistics.html.

UNICEF (2014). State of the world's children 2014 in numbers: Every child counts, http://www.unicef.org/sowc2014/numbers/documents/english/SOWC2014_In%20Numbers_28%20Jan.pdf.

UNICEF Indonesia (2012). Issue briefs: Education and early childhood development (ECD), http://www.unicef.org/indonesia/A3-_E_Issue_Brief_Education_REV.pdf.

United Nations (2013). The millennium development goals report, http://www.un.org/millenniumgoals/pdf/report-2013/mdg-report-2013-english.pdf.

World Bank (2012). The Indonesia early childhood education and development (ECED) project: Findings and policy recommendations, http://documents.worldbank.org/

curated/en/2012/10/16960151/ndonesia-early-childhood-education-development-eced-project-findings-policy-recommendations.

Wright, J.C., Huston, A.C., Scantlin, R., and Kotler, J. (2001). The Early Window Project: *Sesame Street* prepares children for school. In S.M. Fisch and R.T. Truglio (eds), *"G" is for growing: Thirty years of research on children and Sesame Street* (pp. 97–114). Mahwah, NJ: Lawrence Erlbaum Associates.

Yan, C.Y. and Wei, T. (2013). 关于发展农村学前教育的几点思考，社会与公益，2013年第6 [Thoughts on developing rural preschools. *Society and Public Service*, 6, 67.]

Yoshikawa et al. (2013). *Investing in our future: The evidence base on preschool education*, http://www.srcd.org/sites/default/files/documents/washington/mb_2013_10_16_investing_in_children.pdf.

Zhima Jie (2014) *daniao kan shijie*, http://www.sesamestreetchina.com.cn/.

Zill, N. (2001). Does *Sesame Street* enhance school readiness? Evidence from a national survey of children. In S.M. Fisch and R.T. Truglio (eds), *"G" is for growing: Thirty years of research on children and Sesame Street* (pp. 115–30). Mahwah, NJ: Lawrence Erlbaum Associates.

Zuhdi, M. (2008). Meeting of *Jalan Sesama* team and Director of Early Childhood Education, Ministry of National Education of the Republic of Indonesia, July 25 (meeting minutes).

PLATE 1.1 *TIME* magazine cover

PLATE 1.2 Sketch of Alam Simsim's Egypt set, with library tent, vegetable cart, store, playground, and other curricular affordances

PLATE 1.3 Grover's thumbs-up gesture

PLATE 1.4A Formative research alteration: prototype (shirt at waist level)

PLATE 1.4B Formative research alteration: revision (shirt converted to tunic)

PLATE 2.1 Dutch postage stamp

PLATE 2.2 Rickshaw viewing, Sisimpur Bangladesh

"Di jalan, ada **3** burung terbang dan **4** kambing."

1   **2**   **3**   **4**   **5**   **6**   **7**   **8**   **9**   **10**

PLATE 4.1A

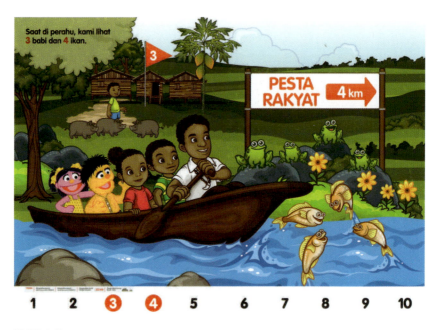

Saat di perahu, kami lihat
3 babi dan **4** ikan.

1   **2**   **3**   **4**   **5**   **6**   **7**   **8**   **9**   **10**

PLATE 4.1B

PLATE 4.1 Big Book pages. Both pages teach the numbers 3 and 4, but the Papuan version is adapted to depict Papuan human characters, local settings, and a localized version of Bahasa Indonesia.(4.1a) shows a page from a math big book from Java, while (4.1b) shows a page for a math big book from Papua

PLATE 5.1 Early draft of the Chandarua Salama poster

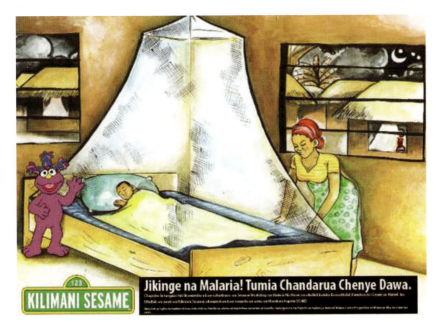

PLATE 5.2 Final version of the Chandarua Salama poster

PLATE 6.1A Tuktuki/Sisimpur (Bangladesh)

PLATE 6.1B Khokha/Alam Simsim (Egypt)

PLATE 6.1C Chamki/Galli Galli Sim Sim (India)

PLATE 6.1D Putri/Jalan Sesama (Indonesia)

PLATE 6.1E Sivan/Rechov Sumsum (Israel)

PLATE 6.1F Lola/Plaza Sésamo (Latin America)

PLATE 6.1G Kami/Takalani Sesame (South Africa)

PLATE 6.1H Raya/Global Health Initiative

PLATE 8.1 Story Pond floor mat for preschool centers

5

FEATHERED AND FURRY HEALTH COMMUNICATORS

The Sesame Street Approach to Child Health and Wellbeing in Egypt, Sub-Saharan Africa, and Beyond

Abigail Bucuvalas, Zainab Kabba, Jean Baxen, Janice Fuld, and Ayobisi Osuntusa

Around the world, young children face serious and often deadly health challenges. Infectious diseases such as diarrhea, pneumonia, malaria, and HIV and AIDS lead to inexcusable annual mortality rates among children under the age of five years, particularly in low resource settings. Consider that 6.6 million children under the age of five years died in 2012, the vast majority from preventable causes (WHO, 2013b). Challenges that result from infectious diseases have been well documented. For example, 3.4 million children were living with HIV at the end of 2011 (WHO, n.d.), and approximately 760,000 children under five years die from diarrheal disease every year (WHO, 2013c). Thousands upon thousands of children remain at risk for polio, measles, diphtheria, tetanus, pertussis, and other vaccine-preventable illnesses, despite widespread knowledge about and capacity for effective inoculation (WHO, 2013b). At the same time, non-infectious diseases steer millions of children towards unhealthy adolescence and adulthood. In 2012, over 40 million children under the age of five years were overweight or obese, with a surprising 30 million of these children living in developing countries (WHO, 2014b). Type 2 diabetes, which frequently results from being overweight and physically inactive, is becoming more and more common in children (WHO, 2013d). An individual who is overweight and/or has Type 2 diabetes is at an elevated risk for cardiovascular disease, which is the most common cause of death worldwide. It is noteworthy that over 80% of deaths from cardiovascular disease occur in low- and middle-income countries (WHO, 2013a).

Access to high-quality medical services varies by region, country, and proximity to an urban center, as well as by income level and other demographics. Regardless of the accessibility of medical services, clear and relevant health education has the capacity to reduce child morbidity and mortality from many life-threatening diseases. Proven health solutions, such as insecticide-treated bed nets and balanced diets rich in fruits and vegetables, are frequently available and affordable even in marginalized communities. Unfortunately, a large amount of health information is conveyed in dense and scientific language, and still more gives insufficient consideration to local cultures and contexts. As a result, potentially life-saving information is rendered unfamiliar, unappealing, and effectively useless to the families and children it aims to reach and empower. In order to maximize the positive impact of recognized health solutions, health educators and practitioners must commit to providing persuasive information in a way that propels both children and adults to adopt new health behaviors.

It is at the interface of public health and medical fields where Sesame Street's Muppets enter and have relevance. These furry, family-friendly communicators have access to children and caregivers, along with decades of experience in capturing their attention. As a result, they are uniquely positioned to support children's physical, emotional, and psychological development and wellbeing. Around the globe, the Sesame Street Muppets have encouraged vitamin-rich diets by calling on children to eat a rainbow of colors, addressed the fears of a doctor's visit by braving routine vaccinations, and reminded millions of young viewers and listeners to wash their hands and brush their teeth with catchy songs and positive modeling.

Granted, some health topics are more sensitive than others, and some of the world's deadliest diseases are challenging to explain to Sesame Street's youngest learners. In addition, there is some appeal in sheltering children from learning about frightening diseases and their impact in the hope that they won't need to understand certain issues until they are older. Even so, in the spirit of supporting children with the tailored information they may need in order to thrive in their current realities, Sesame Workshop has a history of embracing opportunities to educate children in developmentally appropriate ways about healthy habits as well as more controversial health topics. We do so by leveraging the natural kindness, curiosity, and charm of the Sesame Street Muppets.

In the US, research has demonstrated that children's parasocial relationships with media characters have the capacity to enhance their learning (Lauricella et al., 2011). It therefore seems likely that locally developed Muppet characters, designed to mirror children's own natural curiosity and to be charismatic, funny, and deeply relevant, are qualified envoys for delivering health education around the world. How is a Muppet selected for a critical health task? Many times, existing local Muppets address health-related objectives such as encouraging daily healthy habits or explaining ways to prevent specific infectious diseases. Less commonly, a new Muppet is painstakingly created to communicate essential health information about a particularly challenging or uncomfortable topic, such as HIV and AIDS or safe sanitation. This chapter describes how the lovable Muppets, via Sesame Street programming ranging from broadcast television and radio to community- and school-engagement initiatives, have generated learning, shifts in attitudes, and action around diverse health topics—controversial and not—all around the world. While this chapter includes reference to Sesame Workshop's health programming in various parts of the world, it focuses on some of our most salient health-education efforts in Egypt and several countries in sub-Saharan Africa.

Healthy Habits

Around the globe, Sesame Street Muppets have encouraged children and care-givers to engage in healthy habits related to nutrition, exercise, basic hygiene practices, and preventive health-care behaviors such as visiting the doctor and receiving routine vaccinations (Cole et al., 2010). The Alam Simsim project in Egypt, initially funded by the United States Agency for International Develop-ment (USAID), is one example where a special initiative presented messaging about health knowledge and behaviors across various categories, including medi-cal check-up visits, the DPT1 (Diphtheria, Pertussis, and Tetanus) vaccine, hand and face washing, using a personal rather than a shared towel, brushing teeth, proper sneezing techniques, and good nutritional practices such as eating fruits and vegetables and drinking milk (SPAAC, 2004).

The broadcast of Alam Simsim launched in 2000 with a whole-child cur-riculum, aiming to address topics important to young Egyptian children's early learning, physical health, and socio-emotional wellbeing. By the end of 2001, 92% of caregivers in the television broadcast audience in Egypt with at least one child who was between the ages of two and eight years old were familiar with Alam Simsim, with nearly equal awareness levels in urban and rural households. These caregivers reported that 80.2% of their children watched Alam Simsim about two times per week, with an additional 18.8% of children watching from time to time (Synovate, 2007). This high degree of familiarity with Alam Simsim and its Mup-pet characters, from the curious and inventive four-year-old girl named Khokha to the enthusiastic and ageless male named Filfil, meant that the series had the potential to be a good vehicle for promoting educational messaging.

Prior to the launch of the first season of Alam Simsim, project staff and stake-holders conducted a special seminar on health, and a well-known doctor wrote a topical paper on health that framed some of the key issues confronting Egyptian children (Younis, 1998). The Alam Simsim team considered these health issues alongside decades of experience of maximizing the strengths of children's televi-sion. For example, while schistosomiasis was identified as a critical issue, experts felt it would be extremely difficult to use Sesame Street content to convey the primary preventive measure for the disease—not swimming in fresh water—without risking imagery or language that inadvertently promoted the swim-ming practices that put children at risk. The team therefore decided that while schistosomiasis constituted an important concern, it was best to use Alam Simsim to convey other equally important health education messages.

Khokha, Filfil, and their young and gentle friend Nimnim were natural mes-sengers for challenging and sometimes unappealing recommendations about nutrition, personal hygiene, and visiting the doctor. These characters conveyed health tips in a child-friendly, non-threatening way, a contrast to the intimidation—however unintentional—that is frequently associated with health clinics and medical professionals. And their recognizability, thanks to the success of the television program, allowed for their use on health-focused outreach kits containing a variety of print materials, including books, posters, a healthy habits calendar, and flash cards, as well as audiotaped songs (SPAAC, 2004). During a nine-month pilot project in 2003–4, 20 NGO partners distributed these materials to over 10,000 families. From these families, 300 caregivers and 200 children ages four to seven years old participated in a research study aiming to measure the educational impact of the Alam Simsim outreach program.

Researchers collected pre- and post-intervention data in Cairo and Beni Suef. They used a semi-structured survey tool, which was supported with occasional ethnographic observations, to compare experimental and control communities. The study revealed that caregivers and children who were exposed to the Alam Simsim outreach program reported statistically significant positive changes in children's personal care and hygiene practices, including handwashing with soap and water before eating, using a personal towel to dry hands after handwashing, brushing teeth on a daily basis, brushing teeth before bed, turning away from others when sneezing, and covering the nose with a handkerchief when sneezing (SPAAC, 2004). Caregivers and children who participated in the program also reported a significant increase in their consumption of vegetables, fruit, and milk. Finally, caregivers exposed to the program demonstrated a significant increase in awareness of 16 different vaccinations (SPAAC, 2004).

Alam Simsim's positive impact on the healthy habits of Egyptian caregivers and children underscored the capacity for Sesame Street programming to reach its audience with appealing messages about a wide variety of healthy habits, with the Muppets playing a vital role in conveying those messages. Indeed, there was some precedent for the research findings in Egypt; the practice of Muppet promotion for healthy behaviors originated well before the launch of the Alam Simsim program.

For decades, Plaza Sésamo in Latin America has used Muppet characters both to promote health learning through the television program and also to support a campaign for building public awareness of critical health concerns. (See Chapter 9 for more detail about the Plaza Sésamo program.) In the 1990s, the Plaza Sésamo project received a grant from UNICEF to create content with a special focus on general health, nutrition, and safety. Later, beginning in 2007, the Plaza Sésamo team provided its support, and its characters, to Vaccination Week in the Americas, a Pan American Health Organization (PAHO) event. Since 2003, this event has resulted in the vaccination of more than 465 million children and adults throughout Latin America (PAHO, 2014). Also starting in 2007, in partnership with Tetra Pak (a company that produces food carton packaging), Sesame Workshop developed an extensive campaign that presented Plaza Sésamo Muppets with messages about nutrition, exercise, and personal hygiene on milk boxes that were served in school lunch programs throughout Mexico. An assessment found positive effects: children chose healthy foods associated with the show's characters, and families reported positive changes in the children's eating and hygiene habits (CINCO, 2009). More recently, the Plaza Sésamo Muppets have been used for widely broadcast public service announcements (PSAs) on flu prevention and emergency preparedness as well as community outreach activities on healthy habits and knowledge about the body.

Efforts of other programs have been more modest but also demonstrate the usefulness of enlisting Muppet characters in the service of healthy habits aims. In the late 1990s, the Ulitsa Sezam project in Russia, for example, included a special outreach component funded by Nestlé that used a well-received booklet featuring the program's characters to present general health and nutrition information (Nestlé, 1998). In the decade following the successes of the Alam Simsim, Plaza Sésamo, and Ulitsa Sezam initiatives, Muppets have been employed to communicate to children and their families about nutrition, exercise, personal hygiene, and more in countries all around the world, including Bangladesh, Brazil, Colombia, India, Indonesia, Nigeria, South Africa, Tanzania, and the United States. And there is evidence that these programs are succeeding in their health education aims. An increasing body of research has emerged that points to the positive impact of this programming, underscoring the continued value of using Sesame Street's international Muppets to promote general health and wellbeing aims (Borzekowski and Macha, 2010; Borzekowski and Henry, 2011; Cespedes et al., 2013).

HIV and AIDS

The impact of the HIV and AIDS pandemic on the sub-Saharan region is well documented (UNAIDS, 2011; 2012a; 2012b). It manifested differently on this continent than in other parts of the world, both in terms of who presented with the disease as well as with respect to its scope and impact. In South Africa and throughout the region, the disease was contracted primarily through heterosexual intimate relationships and mother-to-child transmission. It affected the working-class populace, who were poor and perceived to have less education. By the mid-2000s, over 10% of the population over the age of two years was living with HIV, and prevalence was significantly higher among females (13.3%) than males (8.2%) (Shisana et al., 2005). Responses to mitigating the pandemic included a call for more information to be made available for people to educate themselves about HIV contraction and its consequences. The assumption was—and still is—that possessing "enough" information would lead to behavior change and a subsequent reduction in infection rates.

But, many communities around the world don't commonly discuss deeply private and intimate aspects of human life in public, and discussions about sex are no exception. In South Africa in the early 2000s, this made conversations about HIV and AIDS difficult because they are so integrally tied to sex, sexuality, values about who has the right to have sex, the stage of life when one should have sex, and so forth. Discussions about HIV and AIDS thus appeal to aspects of lives that are tied up with morality, beliefs, and values, making messages about contraction and what to do once infected difficult to openly mediate. These realities shape how people think about, talk about (or remain silent about), and respond to issues perceived to be private, taboo, and/or sacred. They also regulate behavior and actions, signaling what is and is not allowed, and what an individual can say and do. In a sub-Saharan African context in general and a South African context in particular, discussions about HIV and AIDS carry particular meanings, often with negative consequences for those who dare bring up such topics in public. Particularly as the epidemic was emerging, stigmatization, ostracization, and being labeled as deviant were often the consequence; the individual who discussed HIV and AIDS was seen as deviating from the norm (Parker and Aggleton, 2003). Messaging about aspects of daily life perceived to be secret in contexts with high behavior regulation calls for sensitivity and has implications not only for how one constructs the message, but also for who communicates the message, and how the message is delivered.

The South African social and cultural context is complex. The country's economic landscape is characterized by a strong economy with a burgeoning middle class on the one hand and by large-scale unemployment that disproportionately impacts the nation's poor on the other hand. The latter are deeply affected by HIV infection, and women and young people are particularly vulnerable. Children are impacted both by mother-to-child transmission and by the AIDS-related deaths of their primary caregivers. In 2005, 3.3% of children between the ages of two to 14 years were estimated to be living with HIV or AIDS, and over 2.5 million children ages two to 18 years were classified as single or double orphans (Shisana et al., 2005). The complex intersection between gender, poverty, and social and cultural practices in South Africa create challenges for educational messages about HIV and AIDS, the mediators of these messages, and the contexts in which the messages are delivered. How could a relatively new, child-facing brand such as Takalani Sesame contribute to breaking the proverbial silence about aspects of human life in contexts where the kind of information to be discussed would be perceived as extremely private? How could this brand introduce a mediator without invoking questions about the mediator's right to weigh in on the disease? How could the Takalani Sesame platform be leveraged to reach and appeal to all who needed to hear critical messaging about HIV and AIDS? Such questions gave rise to creativity that found expression through a multi-pronged approach to addressing the issue with age-appropriate television, radio, and outreach content. At the heart of the initiative was a new Sesame Muppet called Kami, who was carefully "conceived" at a time in South Africa when issues of judgment, morality, and misinformation about HIV and AIDS made it difficult to discuss the disease in private conversation, let alone through a social medium such as television and especially through a children's program.

In 2002, supported by funding from USAID, Sanlam (the project's corporate sponsor), and others, the Takalani Sesame team created an HIV/AIDS education program whose central vehicle was five-year-old Kami. This special Muppet character was thoughtfully designed to help dispel several commonly held misbeliefs about people living with HIV and AIDS (Segal et al., 2002). She was female (to represent the disproportionate number of HIV-positive women) and asymptomatic (to counter the belief that people who are HIV positive are sickly). She was a monster Muppet with human features, an important decision given the need to convey the human experience of the disease through a character who would not be affiliated with a particular cultural group. Kami speaks clearly and openly about the experiences of living with HIV, with a particular focus on experiences about stigma and her mother's AIDS-related death, and she importantly does so through the eyes of a young child. Kami, living on Takalani Sesame and covered in bright yellow-orange fur, has brought conversations about HIV and AIDS into the public space in a way that a human could not. She acts as a communicator and advocate for HIV and AIDS, sharing health information as well as the difficult and painful social realities of living with HIV, addressing such issues as the pain of stigma and the consequences of labeling and ostracizing, as well as the value of living with hope, sharing emotions, and talking with friends about living with HIV and about losing someone to AIDS. Despite being a Muppet—or probably because she's a Muppet—Kami has been able to humanize the pandemic. Kami's friends on Takalani Sesame support her efforts by conveying accurate information about the disease and by modeling natural, positive interactions with someone who is living with HIV. They learn about the disease from Kami, and as they learn, the children and families viewing the show learn along with them.

When Kami was introduced to the Takalani Sesame cast, she arrived armed with a supplement to the pre-existing, broad-scope (literacy, numeracy, and life skills) curriculum. The new HIV/AIDS curriculum was developed by the South African team and included educational objectives determined through meetings with health education and child development experts, as well as formative research with children and adults who were impacted by the disease (Segal et al., 2002). The objectives were divided into knowledge, attitudes, and skills related to HIV and AIDS. The knowledge objectives addressed the acquisition of age-appropriate information related to the disease, transmission, standard precautions, symbols of HIV and AIDS (i.e., the red ribbon), death and dying, and body awareness. The objectives focused on the humanization and destigmatization of individuals living with HIV and AIDS, and on the importance of open discussion about the disease. The skills objectives aimed to prepare young children to cope with HIV and AIDS, to cope with how illness may impact daily life, and to cope with the death of loved ones (Segal et al., 2002). The in-country Sesame team employed these educational objectives to shape new messaging for Takalani Sesame television, radio, and print materials, and Kami and her friends brought this messaging to life through open, honest, and age-appropriate discussion.

One of the most compelling components of the HIV and AIDS work that was executed by the Takalani Sesame team was a multimedia program called *Talk to Me*. The *Talk to Me* program provided tools for caregivers to use when discussing HIV and AIDS with their children, aiming to promote open conversation about the disease. These tools included a one-hour, George Foster Peabody award-winning television special consisting of four short documentaries about South African families coping with—and communicating about—different aspects of HIV and AIDS as well as a storybook intended for classroom use. The storybook featured the Takalani Sesame Muppets and human children navigating challenges associated with the loss of adult family members and friends. The program was broadcast in partnership with LoveLife, who provided a phone hotline that viewers could call for more information.

In 2004, a research team assessed the impact of the *Talk to Me* program materials through a cluster randomized trial intervention with children and their caregivers in the Kwa-Zulu Natal province. The majority of caregiver participants felt the materials were relevant to their lives and reported feeling more prepared to discuss HIV and AIDS with their children (Schierhout, 2005). Research results also demonstrated a positive association between exposure to the *Talk to Me* program and increased communication about HIV between children and caregivers. Caregivers who were exposed to the program were more than twice as likely to talk to a child in their household about HIV compared to those unexposed (Schierhout, 2005). Many of these children were older than the traditional Sesame Street audience, demonstrating the high relevance of the Takalani Sesame-branded content for viewers of all ages during this particular time and context in South African history.

The Takalani Sesame team also commissioned a study to evaluate the educational impact of the project's television and radio programs, including impact on children's learning about HIV and AIDS (Khulisa Management Services, 2005). This research included children and caregivers from Kwa-Zulu Natal and Limpopo provinces. Children who were exposed to Takalani Sesame content demonstrated gains in basic knowledge about HIV and AIDS, knowledge about blood safety, attitudes related to destigmatization, and skills related to coping with illness. Moreover, these learning gains were significantly greater than those that occurred in matched control groups. The research also assessed parent and educator willingness to discuss HIV and AIDS with children, and educators exposed to Takalani Sesame programming were far more likely to include HIV and AIDS content in their lesson plans than educators in the control groups (Khulisa Management Services, 2005). The impact of the program was further illuminated in a national study of HIV/AIDS incidence, prevalence, and communication practices commissioned by the Nelson Mandela Foundation. The data indicated high awareness of the Takalani Sesame program even in rural areas without good access to electricity, despite the fact that the youngest people sampled in the study were youth aged 12 to 14 years, far older than the typical Sesame target audience. And while the results do not speak to knowledge gained through exposure to the program, they provide evidence of its wide reach and underscore Takalani Sesame's value as a communication device for HIV/AIDS education (Shisana et al., 2005).

What lessons should be drawn from these research studies? In short, Muppets like Kami and her friends can deliver carefully developed messages that support communication about and destigmatization of sensitive, difficult, and frightening health topics like HIV and AIDS in South Africa during the early and mid-2000s. More broadly, these studies point to the Muppets' ability to model positive ways for children and families to learn about and cope with challenges in their own lives.

A few years after the Takalani Sesame impact assessments were completed, USAID leveraged their investment in South Africa by providing funding for a Sesame Street pilot project that brought age-appropriate HIV and AIDS messaging to children living in diverse regions of Nigeria. In animated and print form, Kami debuted in Nigeria alongside Big Bird in 2008, reaching over 30,000 children—the majority of whom were orphans and vulnerable children—and 600 caregivers during the first year of project activities, which focused on reaching children in need at the community level. After the pilot, the Sesame Square television co-production was launched with additional support from USAID, and for the last five years, Kami has continued to deliver HIV and AIDS-focused messages in Nigeria, in the context of a whole-child curriculum, via television, print, and mobile phone. She has also led Sesame's HIV and AIDS education efforts in Tanzania through Kilimani Sesame programming, where familiarity with the show's characters was linked to greater HIV and AIDS learning gains (Borzekowski and Macha, 2010). The project in Tanzania, however, has focused more on another, equally pressing health challenge.

Malaria

Malaria is a potentially deadly disease that is caused by four parasite species transmitted through mosquito bites. In sub-Saharan Africa, where the majority of malarial deaths occur, a child dies from malaria every minute (WHO, 2014a). Malaria is the most prominent cause of child mortality in Tanzania (REPOA, 2008). Because young children lack protective immunity against malaria, preventive behaviors are critical (WHO, 2014a). Insecticide-treated bed nets are the pre-eminent means of malaria control, but they can be prohibitively expensive for some of the world's most vulnerable families. To promote bed net use and to curb the cost of the nets, the Tanzania National Voucher Scheme was launched in 2004 as the Ministry of Health and Social Welfare's system to mitigate the spread of malaria in the country (Center for Health Market Innovations, n.d.). Implemented at a national level since 2006, the program targets pregnant women and infants by distributing vouchers to pregnant women during their first antenatal visit. The voucher has an approximate value of $2.50 and can be put towards the purchase of a bed net, which is sold for between $3 and $10, depending upon the net's quality and size (Center for Health Market Innovations, n.d.).

While national policies such as the Tanzanian voucher system can address financial barriers to proven malaria prevention behaviors, they may be inadequate at reducing social barriers. To support the efforts of the Tanzanian government in the mid- and late-2000s, the Muppets stepped in to normalize the routines associated with malaria prevention, including sleeping under treated bed nets, so children would regard such practices as a regular part of their everyday lives.

In 2008, Sesame Workshop launched the pilot program Kilimani Sesame, a multimedia early childhood education initiative in Tanzania. The project was a culmination of two years of multiple partnerships between government and non-governmental organizations (NGOs) and local media producers. The Kilimani Sesame Muppets, Kami, Lulu, Zikwe, and Neno, speak Kiswahili and deliver educational messaging in an engaging, child-friendly way. Broadcast by the Tanzania Broadcasting Corporation and on Television Zanzibar, thirteen 30-minute television episodes featured locally produced live-action films that depicted lives of Tanzanian children. A particularly compelling film addressed malaria prevention through a story about the proper use of an insecticide-treated bed net, told from the perspective of a young girl. In addition, thirteen seven-to-ten-minute original radio episodes and songs were developed. Produced in Kiswahili, these episodes feature Kilimani Sesame characters as well as Tanzanian children. Although the Workshop did not commission viewership and listenership research, it is estimated that as many as 5 million children and caregivers benefited from the pilot radio and television episodes (Sesame Workshop, 2008).

Reaching beyond television and radio, the Tanzanian education team led the design of three bilingual storybooks for children and one caregiver guide for classroom educators in government schools. The print materials were developed in Kiswahili and English (the two official languages of Tanzania), and promote general health, hygiene, good nutrition, and awareness about HIV and AIDS, in addition to malaria education messages. One storybook, *Chandarua Salama* (The Safe Net) focuses on the importance of sleeping under a treated bed net. In this book, the Muppet Neno—whose appearance and personality closely match Elmo's—questions why he needs to sleep under a bed net. Lulu and Kami present accurate, age-appropriate health information as they encourage Neno to use the net to stay safe from malaria, but they add that it can also be fun, inserting an element of play to their advice, appealing to the nature of children in early childhood. And true to the child's perspective, Neno concurs by saying, "Kami and Lulu, you were right. It's nice and cozy in here. It feels like my own tent and I am safe" (Muganzi, 2010, 16). By appealing to the perspective of a child, the Muppets offered a sound argument to children for sleeping under a treated bed net. Thanks to extensive and enthusiastic NGO partnerships, these malaria education print materials were distributed throughout Tanzania, with an estimated reach of over 400,000 children (Sesame Workshop, 2008).

Encouraged by the positive response to the pilot program and the effectiveness of the project's educational programming, Sesame Workshop forged a
partnership with Malaria No More in 2009, supported by Mattel and Freedom
to Create, to employ existing and new Kilimani Sesame materials. Collaboration across multiple Tanzanian government sectors supported the creation of
these materials, which aimed to further promote malaria awareness and prevention to children and caregivers. The process of developing a new poster to
promote bed-net use in the home provides insight into the detailed attention
that in-country education teams place on underscoring key messages to support
the educational goals of every Sesame Street project. In this case, using the idea
of promoting widespread use of bed nets within the country as a conceptual
framework, the first renderings of the poster (Plate 5.1), while beautifully illustrated, did not sufficiently focus attention on the intended behavior—sleeping
under a bed net. Moreover, Lulu's image served only to brand the poster and
was not incorporated into the scene in a way that would emphasize the educational health objective. After review and deliberation, the image that was
ultimately used (Plate 5.2) zooms in on one home, where the bed net is promi-
nently featured in the foreground of the scene. Lulu appears inside the home,
where she plays a supporting role similar to her role in the storybook. In this
way, the poster highlights the importance of bed-net use on a nightly basis, a
familiar message for children who have already read the storybook. This process of refinement is a key element in developing materials that are impactful
and that support holistic educational engagement with children.

The 2009 partnership brought together the Malaria No More goodwill
ambassadors and Tanzanian music stars Marlaw, Banana Zoro, Mwasiti, and
Natasha along with the Muppet Lulu to leverage mass media to reach parents
(along with children) with key information about malaria prevention at home.
Each of the music stars recorded a Kiswahili television PSA with Lulu, encouraging parents and children to avoid going outside at night when malarial mos-
quitoes are most active, to wear long sleeves and long pants when outside for
long periods of time, and to sleep under a treated bed net. These PSAs successfully conveyed critical health information in a memorable but non-threatening
way by coupling the lovability of the Muppets with the star power of the aforementioned celebrities.

Sesame Workshop commissioned the Bloomberg School of Public Health at
Johns Hopkins University, who worked in association with a ten-person Tanzanian research team, to evaluate the impact of Kilimani Sesame's health education
content, as well as its effects on literacy, mathematics, and socio-emotional skills.
The subsequently published research examined children's pre- and post-exposure
performance on a series of tests designed to measure outcomes related to educational messages presented in the program (Borzekowski and Macha, 2010). Participants included 223 preschool-aged children and caregivers in the rural and urban
locales of Kisarawe and Dar-es-Salaam, respectively. The six-week intervention

included radio, television, and print materials, as well as mediation and activities by adult teachers. Researchers conducted one-on-one interviews with both children and parents in Kiswahili. Children were randomly assigned to groups that received either high or low exposure to the intervention. High exposure included 18 hours of educational activities, supported by 20 radio episodes and 16 television episodes. Children in the low-exposure group were shown half of the materials compared to the high-exposure group, totaling six hours of exposure for the duration of the intervention period (Borzekowski and Macha, 2010).

Analyses found that children performed significantly better on tests related to information about malaria and general health knowledge (i.e., recognition of a medical provider, awareness of healthy foods and behaviors, and knowledge of what to do when ill or in an emergency situation) after exposure to the Kilimani Sesame intervention compared to their performance before exposure to the show. Children who had greater exposure to Kilimani Sesame gained more knowledge about malaria, even after accounting for factors such as location, gender, age, and baseline performance. Furthermore, researchers found that high engagement with the program series was associated with increased educational benefit. An analysis examining children's receptivity to and engagement with the program (as measured by the ability to identify Kilimani Sesame characters) found that children who had the greatest engagement with the Sesame content performed significantly better on a range of health measures than those who were less engaged, again after controlling for factors including location, gender, age, baseline Kilimani Sesame character recognition, and baseline performance on each outcome. Children who were the most engaged showed the greatest improvement in malaria knowledge, general health knowledge, and positive health behaviors (Borzekowski and Macha, 2010).

Lulu's ability to lead Sesame's communication about malaria and other health topics in Tanzania clearly demonstrated a Muppet's ability to address the risks of the mosquito-borne illness. Kami and Zobi, the Muppet stars of Sesame Square in Nigeria, followed Lulu's example and have recently reached millions of young Nigerian children and their caregivers with messages about the importance of sleeping under an insecticide-treated bed net to protect against malaria. As is generally the case with Sesame Workshop's international co-productions, they did so not only via national broadcast (in this case, on the Nigerian Television Authority) but also through engaging print materials and even a pilot feature phone initiative.

Global Health

Until recently, nearly all of Sesame Workshop's health programming was developed around specific disease or wellness topics on a country-by-country basis (Cole et al., 2010), addressing issues such as those described above. But children reside in a world where threats to their health and wellbeing are not confined by national borders, or by the broadcast ranges of Sesame Street co-productions, and there is a common set of health issues that are relevant across regions and cultures. Diarrhea caused by inadequate and/or unsafe water, sanitation, and hygiene (WASH) facilities leads to over 700,000 annual deaths in children under five years (CDC, 2013). Moreover, WASH-related illnesses have been linked to other serious health problems, including malnutrition (Griffiths, 2014) and a variety of neglected tropical diseases (CDC, 2013). Around the world, discussions about sanitation and related behaviors have the potential to be awkward and embarrassing, and in many places, communication about toileting is essentially unthinkable. Even so, it is critical to overcome such barriers because the health information conveyed during these discussions has the potential to be life-saving.

Although the Millennium Development Goal to halve the number of people without improved sanitation was not met, more than 2 billion people have gained access to improved sanitation since 1990 (World Bank, 2015). The new Sustainable Development Goal for sanitation aims to provide adequate and equitable sanitation and to end open defecation by 2030, impacting well over 1 billion people. More than half of the affected countries are in sub-Saharan Africa, and 82% of those who practice open defecation live in only ten countries (UNICEF, 2014). Thanks to a generous grant from the Bill & Melinda Gates Foundation (BMGF) in 2012, Sesame Workshop began to confront the challenge of how best to improve sanitation and related hygiene practices in three vastly different settings: remote tea estates in Bangladesh, crowded Kolkata slum communities in India, and rural and semi-rural areas in Nigeria's Federal Capital Territory. Each country already had an existing co-production with its own popular Muppets, but none of these Muppets were particularly well suited for use among all three countries. Moreover, given the discomfort that surrounds toileting discussions, what kind of Muppet would be an ideal bearer of detailed information about sanitation and hygiene behaviors?

Through a collaborative and painstaking process involving educators and producers in Bangladesh, India, Nigeria, and the US, a new Sesame Street Muppet was carefully developed. In a fashion similar to the process for creating Kami in South Africa, the development of the aqua-green Muppet called Raya involved cooperation between creative teams and educators—in this case from multiple countries—who worked together to create an appealing character who would also be able to carry the depth of the health messaging the curriculum required across different countries, communities, and cultures. With human-like features, Raya is an extremely neat and clean, occasionally absent-minded six-year-old girl who remembers and eagerly shares all sorts of facts about health and every other topic imaginable. For the BMGF-funded "Cleaner, Healthier, Happier" project, Raya sings about toilets, reminds Elmo how to properly wash his hands, and misplaces her potable water and super powerful foot protectors (i.e., sandals) in plain sight. She aims to be the slightly quirky, no-nonsense friend who will remind your daughter that dangerous germs are everywhere, and who then will offer her a long list of practical ways to stay safe.

The "Cleaner, Healthier, Happier" project included PSAs for national broadcast in the three participating countries, as well as school- and community-based interventions with video and print components in the aforementioned target communities. One of the most exciting—and unique—aspects of the project is the extent to which it was driven by research. Early in the project, in-country research teams conducted needs assessments in order to prioritize key sanitation and hygiene issues, which were selected from a broader range of topics identified by in-country advisories. Video and print materials were tested through formative research with children and adults before they were put into use in classrooms and communities, ensuring their appeal and clarity for target audiences. During a pilot phase for the interventions, a third-party researcher from the University of Maryland partnered with three research agencies, one in each participating country, to conduct evaluations of the project's educational impact. The pilot phase studies aimed to assess how different approaches to educational messaging impacted children's gains in knowledge, attitudes, and behaviors, and findings helped to guide decision making about the roll-out of the outreach interventions.

At the time of writing, findings from Bangladesh, India, and Nigeria indicate that participation in the "Cleaner, Healthier, Happier" pilot interventions had better outcomes in WASH-related knowledge, attitudes, and/or behaviors than those who did not participate, with specific results varying by country (Borzekowski et al., 2015a; Borzekowski et al., 2015b; Borzekowski et al., 2015c). It is extremely encouraging that the pilot phase activities achieved signs of educational impact among young children in such dissimilar low-resource communities. These findings informed in-country scale up of the programs that ultimately reached well over 100,000 children between the ages of three and seven years old across the three participating countries. Replication and research in multiple communities are needed to further validate these promising results. In addition, also in all three countries, Raya enjoyed very high levels of appeal. Among children who took part in the pilot phase of the interventions, Raya ranked highest (among six characters tested) in positive attributes: as someone whom children liked best, who tells children important things to do, is never sick, and loves her shoes (Borzekowski et al., 2015). Over a relatively short period of time (three months or less), children understood who Raya was and the positive behaviors and attributes associated with her.

Raya's first journey with Sesame Street health programming has charged her with discussing sanitation and hygiene in Bangladesh, India, and Nigeria, and this work will likely continue. She was designed, however, with the hope that she will be equally welcomed by children all around the world as a reliable source of broad health and wellness information. Indeed, going forward, Sesame Workshop aims to build a library of health content that is optimized for adaptation across diverse languages, cultures, and contexts. By employing a global curricular framework with straightforward, overarching health messages for children and families, and by strategically selecting production formats and technologies that allow for localization during post-production, the Workshop aims to maximize the effectiveness, utility, and economic value of any new health content that it produces.

Conclusion

In sub-Saharan Africa and around the world, Sesame Street Muppets have proven themselves to be effective and influential health communicators for young children. Through Sesame Street international content, they have conveyed critical health-education messages related to healthy habits, sanitation and hygiene, vaccination, road and household safety, and specific diseases, and they have supported significant changes in health knowledge, attitudes, and behaviors in children and adults. Experiences within and beyond the sub-Saharan African region have informed—and continue to inform—the creation of new health content that can be leveraged in global ways. As technology becomes increasingly affordable and accessible, we can expect Sesame's target audiences to engage with their favorite healthy Muppets through media platforms ranging from television and radio to print and e-book to mobile phone and tablet. And no matter the platform, research will continue to guide the process of developing, refining, and implementing health content and interventions, supporting Sesame Workshop international teams in sharing both successes and lessons learned, honing best practices for Muppet-led multimedia health education for children and families.

References

Borzekowski, D.L.G. and Henry, H.K.M. (2011). The impact of Jalan Sesama on the educational and healthy development of Indonesian preschool children: An experimental study. *International Journal of Behavioral Development*, 35, 169–79.

Borzekowski, D.L.G. and Macha, J.E. (2010). The role of Kilimani Sesame in the healthy development of Tanzanian preschool children. *Journal of Applied Developmental Psychology*, 31, 298–305.

Borzekowski, D.L.G., Bickford, A., & Khan, Y. (2015a). "Me" and "we": The impact of the Sisimpur "Cleaner, Healthier, Happier" intervention among children from Bangladesh's tea estates. College Park, MD: University of Maryland.

Borzekowski, D.L.G., Bickford, A., & Mehrota, D. (2015b). "Me" and "we": The impact of the "Cleaner, Healthier, Happier" intervention among children from the Kolkata slums. College Park, MD: University of Maryland.

CDC (2013). Global WASH fast facts: Information on water, sanitation, and hygiene, http://www.cdc.gov/healthywater/global/wash_statistics.html.

Center for Health Market Innovations (n.d.). Tanzania National Voucher Scheme, http://healthmarketinnovations.org/program/tanzania-national-voucher-scheme.

Cespedes, J., Briceno, G., Farkouh, M.E., et al. (2013). Targeting preschool children to promote cardiovascular health: Cluster randomized trial. *American Journal of Medicine*, 126, 27–35.

CINCO (2009). Impact assessment of the community program "Hábitos saludables para toda la vida", unpublished report.

Cole, C.F., Kotler, J., and Pai, S. (2010). "Happy healthy Muppets": A look at Sesame Workshop's health initiatives around the world. In P.A. Gaist (ed.), *Igniting the power of community: The role of CBOs and NGOs in global public health* (pp. 277–94). New York: Springer.

Griffiths, J.K. (2014). Food is necessary . . . but not sufficient: Biological insights into malnutrition, http://agrilinks.org/sites/default/files/resource/files/1)Griffiths%20Nepal%20Meeting%2 0Talk%20Nutrition%20Innovation%20Lab%20Africa%2010%20AM%203.11.2014.pdf.

Khulisa Management Services (2005). *Impact assessment of Takalani Sesame: Season II programme*, unpublished report.

Lauricella, A.R., Gola, A.H., and Calvert, S.L. (2011). Toddlers' learning from socially meaningful video characters. *Media Psychology*, 14, 216–32, DOI:10.1080/15213269.2011.573465.

Muganzi, A.A. (2010). *Chandarua salama/The safe net.* Sesame Workshop outreach material.

Nestlé (1998). *Ulitsa Sezam good nutrition activity booklet* (English translation). Moscow: Nestlé.

PAHO (2014). Vaccination week in the Americas, http://www.paho.org/vwa/.

Parker, R. and Aggleton, P. (2003). HIV and AIDS-related stigma and discrimination: A conceptual framework and implications for action. *Social Science and Medicine*, 57(1), 13–24.

REPOA (2008). Children and vulnerability in Tanzania: A brief overview, http://www.repoa.or.tz/documents/REPOA_Brief_9_Mar_2008.pdf.

Schierhout, G. (2005). *Impact assessment of a new programming component on HIV and AIDS*, unpublished report.

Segal, L., Cole, C.F., and Fuld, J. (2002). Developing an HIV/AIDS curriculum for Takalani Sesame, South Africa's Sesame Street. *Early Education and Development*, 13, 363–78.

Sesame Workshop (2008). *Sesame Workshop final report to USAID*, unpublished report.

Shisana, O., Rehle, T., Simbayi, L.C., Parker, W., Zuma, K., Bhana, A., Connolly, C., Jootse, S., Pillay, V., et al. (2005). *South African national HIV prevalence, HIV incidence, behavior and communication survey, 2005.* Cape Town: HSRC Press.

SPAAC (2004). Alam Simsim outreach program impact report. Study commissioned by Sesame Workshop. New York: Social Planning, Analysis and Administration Consultants.

Synovate (Cairo). (2007). *Alam Simsim* marketing survey in Egypt. Report commissioned by Sesame Workshop. New York: Synovate.

UNAIDS (2011). AIDS at 30: Nations at the crossroads, http://www.unaids.org/sites/default/files/media_asset/aids-at-30_1.pdf.

UNAIDS (2012a). Global AIDS response progress report 2012: Republic of South Africa, http://www.unaids.org/sites/default/files/country/documents//ce_ZA_Narrative_Report.pdf.

UNAIDS (2012b). Regional fact sheet 2012, http://www.unaids.org/sites/default/files/en/media/unaids/contentassets/documents/epide miology/2012/gr2012/2012_FS_regional_ssa_en.pdf.

UNICEF (2014). Progress on drinking water and sanitation, http://www.unicef.org/publications/files/JMP_report_2014_webEng.pdf.

WHO (2013a). Cardiovascular diseases, http://www.who.int/mediacentre/factsheets/fs317/en/.

WHO (2013b). Children: Reducing mortality, http://www.who.int/mediacentre/fact sheets/fs178/en/.

WHO (2013c). Diarrhoeal disease, http://www.who.int/mediacentre/factsheets/fs330/en/.

WHO (2013d). What are the risks of diabetes in children? http://www.who.int/features/qa/65/en/.

WHO (2014a). Malaria, http://www.who.int/mediacentre/factsheets/fs094/en/.

WHO (2014b). Obesity and overweight, http://www.who.int/mediacentre/factsheets/fs311/en/.

WHO (n.d.). Treatment of children living with HIV, http://www.who.int/hiv/topics/paediatric/en/.

World Bank (2015). Goal 7: Ensure environmental sustainability by 2015, http://www.worldbank.org/mdgs/environment.html.

Younis, A.S. (1998). Egyptian child health and nutrition. Topical paper commissioned by Children's Television Workshop, New York.

6

EMPOWERING GIRLS AND BOYS TO BE LIFE-LONG LEARNERS

Gender Equity Lessons from Sesame Street Programs in Egypt and Palestine

Charlotte F. Cole, Alyaa Montasser, June H. Lee, Cairo Arafat, and Nada W. Elattar

> *Maybe I'll be a police officer . . . maybe a journalist . . . maybe an astronaut!*
> Alam Simsim's Khokha, Egypt

Gender equity is a foundational element of Sesame Workshop's international work.[1] Over the years, and across the various Sesame Street international co-productions, messages of inclusion and respect have been implicitly woven into the fabric of program content. While much of Sesame Workshop's gender equity efforts have specifically focused on empowering girls who are growing up in environments where they suffer gender-based discriminatory practices, our approach from the beginning has regarded boys as a critical part of the gender inclusion equation. We work to provide positive role models that help break down gender stereotypes, counter negative attitudes, and close the significant gaps that have resulted from inequitable practices. We believe that for changes to take hold, children of both sexes need exposure to culturally relevant content that introduces proactive, empowering messages to oppose the negative attitudes that have resulted from girls' historically limited educational experiences and the prejudicial attitudes and practices that are part of the lives of many.

Additionally, while the needs of girls have been a consideration, our programming has also directed specific attention to the changing dynamic for boys and the need, in some locales, to provide content that targets their unique concerns. Through a summary of our overall approach and descriptions of the impact of two different co-production projects, this chapter provides a window into Sesame Workshop's gender equity content. The examples provide insights from separate angles: Egypt's Alam Simsim's focus on girls' education and the boys' empowerment messaging that has been a strong part of our work on Shara'a

Simsim in Palestine. Together, the two projects illustrate Sesame Workshop's process for developing and testing the impact of content for girls and boys that is age-appropriate, culturally-relevant and compelling.

The Gender Equity Focus on International Co-Productions

The focus on gender equity in Sesame Workshop's international work has its origins in the elevated attention that the international development community began giving to the value of investing in girls. This thinking culminated at the turn of the century with the articulation of the United Nation's Millennium Development Goals and, in particular, Goal 3: "to promote gender equality and empower women" (United Nations, 2006). The drive was pushed forward further with empirical evidence illustrating that educating girls has a magnifier effect that results in dramatic social improvements, including fewer teenage pregnancies, improved health and disease prevention, lessened incidence of child marriage, and a greater skilled workforce, all aspects that contribute to overall poverty reduction (World Bank, 2014).

These sensibilities have directly influenced the development of Sesame Street's international co-productions in several important ways. Production teams have actively worked to present balanced representations of both genders, with an eye toward neither glorifying nor belittling either. Teams have developed strong female Muppet and human characters that have an equal play as protagonists in storylines to their male peers. Traditional gender roles are challenged in culturally relevant contexts with men, for example, taking active roles in their children's education, and with women portrayed as professionals and community leaders. Additionally, Sesame Workshop invested in research to examine the impact of these efforts to both evaluate their effect and to apply lessons learned to future production.

The need for a special focus on the development of girl characters is punctuated by recent multi-country research (Smith et al., 2014) on gender representation in popular films. A study—commissioned by the Geena Davis Institute on Gender and the Media—shows under-representation of females on the screen (less than 30% rather than 50%) and a dearth of women in roles of authority such as CEOs, scientists, and other professions. Yet, while the data demonstrate a worldwide absence of positive female role models in the entertainment media, the research also points to the potential of media to transform our unconscious biases when content carries more gender-balanced depictions.

For the past few decades, international producers of Sesame Street have made a concerted effort to develop strong female protagonist characters. Table 6.1 provides a list of some key female Muppet characters from different co-productions, shown also in Plate 6.1. In addition to developing females with strong, vibrant personalities and aspirations, fundamental to Sesame Workshop's approach is the concept that girl and boy characters interact with one another in a respectful and supportive manner. This, along with well-planned human/Muppet dialogue and action, is one of the best ways to underscore the program's gender equity aims. Sesame Workshop seeks to engrain in both boys and girls positive values of care, kindness, and appreciation so that all children grow up to become productive citizens.

TABLE 6.1 Descriptions of selected female Muppet characters

Co-production	Character	Description
Sisimpur (Bangladesh)	Tuktuki	Tuktuki, a Muppet on Sisimpur in Bangladesh, has an insatiable curiosity about the world. (She also appears on Baghch-e-Simsim in Afghanistan as Gulguly.)
Zhima Jie (China)	Lily	Lily is a rambunctious four-year-old female tiger. She is very proud of her growl which punctuates her expressions when she is excited. She's powerful, energetic, and imaginative. Lily can also be self-centered and short-tempered, but she always comes round to see the other's point of view.
Alam Simsim (Egypt)	Khokha	Khokha is a proactive, inquisitive girl Muppet who has high hopes for the future. She dreams of being an engineer, a doctor, and a lawyer all at the same time.
Galli Galli Sim Sim (India)	Chamki	A vibrant five-year-old girl Muppet who has a flair for language and learning. Chamki is also a bright and energetic problem solver.
Jalan Sesama (Indonesia)	Putri	Putri is a friendly and active four-year-old girl who asks many questions, is independent, expressive, fun, and playful. Putri's hobbies are dancing and singing with her friends and playing soccer. Putri also has a wild sense of imagination.
Rechov Sumsum (Israel)	Sivan	Sivan is a seven-year-old computer whiz and video gamer with a passion for technology. She has a physical disability which is why she sits in a wheelchair. She has a great sense of humor, speaks with confidence, and is a born leader.
Plaza Sésamo (Latin America)	Lola	Lola is a four-year-old Muppet who is sure of herself and wants to do everything on her own. Curious and inquisitive by nature, Lola is most motivated by learning new things and growing. Although she cannot read very well yet, she wants to learn and can recognize a few letters and words.

(Continued)

TABLE 6.1 Continued

Co-production	Character	Description
Shara'a Simsim (Palestine)	Haneen	A five-year-old girl monster who loves learning new things, especially reading. She is lively, energetic, has a wild imagination, and loves to sing. She is best friends with Kareem (a Muppet rooster) and wants to learn lots of things that Kareem already knows because he is older than she is. Her favorite phrase is "I can do that!"
Takalani Sesame (South Africa)	Kami	Kami is an affectionate, articulate, literate, and inquisitive girl monster and is great fun to be with! She is HIV positive, non-symptomatic, and has a wealth of accurate information about living with the illness.
Global Health Initiative	Raya	Raya is a six-year-old girl who is very neat and clean because she pays special attention to her hygiene. She just loves to gather facts! Raya's planning on being a doctor when she's big, so she sometimes spends time practicing on whomever agrees to subject themselves to her ministrations.

Case Studies: Egypt and Palestine

While the topic has been a core value of all Sesame Street international co-productions, a few have made special efforts to incorporate a gender equity focus in their curricular development processes. Several projects, for example, have sought advice from experts in the form of topical reports, including one written for the project in India (Capoor and Gade, 2004) that was used to shape the approach to gender on Galli Galli Sim Sim. Other efforts have included seasonal emphases such as a focus on gender in the eighth season of Plaza Sésamo in Mexico. It began with a seminar that was designed to help the production team engage thoughtfully around gender concerns when devising program content (Platón and Lembert, 1999). The need for gender-neutral terminology was one key element discussed in that meeting: *firefighter* (instead of *fireman*), *police officer* (instead of *policeman*), *flight attendant* (instead of *stewardess*). In Spanish, however, because it is a language that uses male and female forms of words, employing generic forms is complex. The word for *children*, for example, like most plural words in Spanish, uses the male ending (os)—*niños*. Applying neutral language requires what some people consider to be convoluted and forced communication: *niños y niñas*, rather than *niños*. Instead of the two-word pairing, the team recommended the use of more inclusive singular words like, la *niñez* or *infancia*, which at the time were beginning to be used more and more frequently in Spain and Latin America (Plaza Sésamo Education and Research Team, 1999).

The execution of seminars and the authorship of papers, guidelines, and other supports that were developed over the years for Sesame Street co-production projects underscore the complexity of the issue as well as the seriousness to which Sesame Workshop has addressed the topic. The approaches taken in Egypt and in Palestine, which are detailed below, highlight two different examples of how co-production teams have applied a gender equity focus on international co-productions of Sesame Street.

Girls' Education and Alam Simsim

Alam Simsim was conceived of as a tool to promote early childhood education across a range of curricular domains. The project was built on the belief that educating children while keeping them entertained (*edutainment*) was an effective mode for reaching and teaching. Almost from the beginning, the series gained great popularity in Egypt (MEMRB, 2002), reaching a majority of the television viewing audience, punctuating its potential as a high-impact educational endeavor.

From the beginning, the project enlisted the power of Egypt's history and traditions in the service of encouraging girls' aspirations. Specifically, the series aimed to empower girls and help bridge the education gap between girls and boys. Building on the success of Sesame Street in the United States and elsewhere, Alam Simsim was created to provide a uniquely Egyptian experience that was inclusive of the country's ancient and rich customs, while providing contemporary images, messages, and stories.

The foundation for including a special focus on gender equity and girls was laid by Rouchdy (1998) in a report on gender that the Alam Simsim team commissioned at the initiation of the project. Designed to provide background information on the status of women and girls, the paper presented the historical underpinnings of gender issues as they related to education in contemporary Egypt. It argued for the need for the Sesame Street project to direct explicit attention to girls'/women's concerns. Rouchdy noted that girls and women were marginalized as a result of what she called "structural constraining factors" in Egypt that included the difficulties the educational system had in retaining children in school and the economic cost of education to poor families. She also pointed to urban–rural differences and the particular constraints for rural families. Her conclusion asserts that the Sesame Street project could potentially play a critical role in presenting the "voice" of girls and women (p. 91) by calling upon examples from contemporary times and the past.

Rouchdy's points were further honed during a meeting, convened in keeping with Sesame Workshop's production model (see Chapter 1), that brought together Egyptian educators, psychologists, teachers, and other child-development experts to, in collaboration with the production team, shape an educational plan for the program. The results of the meeting were summarized in an educational framework, or "curriculum document" as it was called, which included four key domains and prioritized gender equity as an implicit education thrust for the program (Alam Simsim Education Team, 1999; see Table 6.2). In particular, the document advocated that program content underscore five points related to gender equity: equal rights, self-esteem, emotional expression, professional attainment, and civic and community responsibility. Each point was further sharpened as follows:

1. **Equal rights**: Promote the belief that girls and boys have equal rights and responsibilities.
2. **Self-esteem**: Encourage boys and girls to experience and express feelings of self-worth, pride, and confidence in their abilities.
3. **Emotional expression**: Promote the belief that boys and girls have feelings and that there are not gender-specific ways to express them (e.g., it is okay for boys and girls to cry when feeling pain).
4. **Professional attainment**: Promote the belief that professions are not gender-specific and that boys and girls can grow up to be what they would like to be.
5. **Civic and community responsibilities**: Promote the belief that household, community, and civic responsibilities are not gender-specific (e.g., boys and girls can help around the house, women can hold government offices; all have an obligation to make a contribution).

To carry out these aims, the team developed Muppets and human characters to support the broader gender equity goals. Khokha, a four-year-old girl Muppet, became a central vehicle for Alam Simsim's gender messages. Smart, inquisitive,

TABLE 6.2 Summary of educational framework: Alam Simsim, Egypt

Child's world	Social relations	Symbolic representation	Cognitive organization
• Self • Health and wellbeing • Child's capacities • Natural environment • Human-made environment	• Social groups and institutions • Social interactions	• Reading fundamentals • Writing fundamentals • Other forms of expression • Numeracy and geometry • Pre-science	• Perceptual discrimination • Relational concepts • Classification

active, and positive, she never stops wanting to know and learn more. She asks many questions, constantly seeking solutions to problems, and is often seen in her pretend workshop making or creating something new and fun. Of equal importance is the support she gains from other (and in particular, male) characters. Her male Muppet colleagues, Filfil, a purple-hued, ageless sack puppet character and Nimnim, a gentle, nature-loving full-body puppet (the size of the US's Big Bird), learn, sing, and play with her as she embarks on a new adventure every day. Together, the characters challenge the more established but outdated norms on what "girls should be like" and how people should interact with them. Khokha not only embodies a new "image" of the Egyptian girl, but presents a "voice" that is both audible and convincing. Through Khokha and the interactions with the other characters, Alam Simsim "remakes" Egyptian girls by encapsulating the modern and progressive girl while ensuring she is fully aware of her heritage, history, and culture. Alam Simsim strikes a balance between the old and the new, linking the past—through basic knowledge of Egypt's long and rich cultural history—with the future—through developing the basic skills and learning to cope with a technologically advanced world. Khokha's personality and relationship with her Muppet friends and the other human characters on the show is especially designed to encourage girls to seek out learning, to be interested in education, and to model gender equity in a child-friendly manner.

Khokha and the other female characters boldly show proactive, positive life strategies in the face of problems and in their everyday lifestyle. Human characters, such as Khala Khaireya, a motherly figure, is an educated housewife, combining the old, traditional wisdom with the modern attitude of today's women; Abla Nabila is the educated and helpful librarian; Mona is Khaireya's teenage daughter who studies in Alexandria and combines playfulness and eagerness to learn.

The characters engage with one another on Alam Simsim's set, which is an identifiable modern street in Egypt. It includes a traditional grocery store that also sells food and other goods, as well as a library from which everyone can borrow books. There is a carpenter's workshop, some homes, but also an outdoors area and a garden for playing. The human characters are made up of girls and boys, women and men, Christians and Muslims who all live in this neighborhood and interact with mutual respect with each other.

Like Sesame Street in the United States, Alam Simsim follows a "magazine format." Curricular messages are presented using a combination of studio, live-action documentaries and animations strung together into half-hour episodes. For example, Khokha is seen in one segment contemplating and imagining all the different career options that she may have: an astronaut, a doctor, a police officer, etc.; in this case simultaneously addressing the direct goal of describing "professions" and the indirect message that girls can choose to have the career that they like and that the choice is vast. The magazine format makes it possible to further underscore the gender equity messaging with live documentaries of, for example, female professionals at work, or furthering the girl-empowerment goals featuring real-life girls (not actors) engaged in activities that demonstrate their activities, achievements, and contributions to their communities.

In addition to such explicit illustrations, the program also indirectly extends the gender equity messaging through the everyday antics of the program characters and their stories. In showing positive communication between the characters and in providing an environment that supports curiosity, discovery, and the capabilities of all, Alam Simsim works to transform the images young children hold in their minds about the accomplishments, achievements, and aspirations of young girls. By presenting both boys and girls, women and men, engaged in daily life activities that show equitable participation of both genders in community and home life, the program works to shift the mindset of its viewers.

Formative Research

To ensure the success of these efforts, Alam Simsim used formative research at the early stage of its production process to assist in the development of culturally relevant content. While time, funding, and other factors constrained the team's ability to introduce a formative research process that is as extensive as that used on the domestic (US) program (see Fisch and Bernstein, 2001), the team did benefit from various formative research efforts over the course of the program's history.

Some of the formative research was related to general concerns, such as children's viewing habits and their reactions to initial prototypes of the characters and early content (live-action films) produced for the program. This was the primary focus of the program's first formative study, which tested 60 four- to six-year-old girls and boys from mid- to low-income households in Cairo Governorate (Boulaq El Dakrour) and Dakahliya Governorate (Mit El Faramawy) (Alam Simsim Research Team, 1999a). Other research delved more specifically into children's learning from content (Alam Simsim Research Team, 1999b). In some instances the production team used the results of formative research to fine-tune segments, but more typically results provided "lessons learned" for producing new material.

Perhaps the most valuable aspect of this research was that, as with most formative research conducted for Sesame Street co-production projects, it employed samples with balanced representation of girls and boys. While balanced gender sampling is something that modern social scientists take as a given (and something that has always been a part of Sesame Street's approach), it was not always the tradition (see, for example, Gilligan, 1982). This is a critical component of our study design in that it enables assessment of gender differences in comprehension, appeal, and other elements and has allowed us to test differences in girls' and boys' comprehension of and engagement with program content.

For the most part, the research team detected few differences between the reactions to content for boys and girls. Findings from the previously mentioned, second formative study, which included 48 children (sixteen four- to six-year-olds) from a low-income, rural area in Upper Egypt (Talah-El Menya) were typical.

It found, at baseline, low levels of basic literacy and what the researchers framed as "moderate" math skills of both boys and girls and no gender differences in skill attainment, with slight improvement in some skills, such as recognition of geometric shapes, noted on average for all groups after exposure (Alam Simsim Education Team, 1999). This suggests that the content was equally appealing and comprehensible for both girls and boys.

In addition to the insights gained from comparing the data obtained from girls and boys on various tests related to these elements, formative research on Alam Simsim included studies that specifically related to the program's gender content. For example, the team gained insights on children's understanding of gender identity depicted on the screen. One study showed that children thought a girl protagonist in a segment was a boy (Montasser et al., 2002). In the segment, entitled *Ramadan Cannon*, a girl, her brother, and other members of her family arrive by taxi to break the Ramadan fast with their grandfather, who works as the person who fires the cannon singling the end of the fast each day during Ramadan. The team believed that the children's gender confusion could potentially undermine the segment's focus on the importance of the girl's point of view and her role in this important family tradition. It underscored the need for program content to more potentially highlight girls in active roles to counter stereotypic visions of females.

Another formative study portended findings from a later more comprehensive study (see the discussion of Rimal et al. (2013) in the ensuing section on impact) of changes in gender role perception. After viewing two short, live-action documentary films portraying boys and girls in non-traditional gender roles (a boy baking and a girl aspiring to her pilot father's profession), some of the children sampled showed changes in the perceptions of gender roles (tested both before and after exposure), acknowledging that boys could bake and girls could pilot airplanes (Alam Simsim Research Team, 1999a).

Impact of the Gender Equity Approach

Two more comprehensive studies of Alam Simsim provide data specifically related to the impact of the program's gender equity orientation. The first, a study of cultural impact (SPAAC, 2005), was designed to assess the degree to which Alam Simsim catalyzed changes in attitude and knowledge on a range of curricular priorities. The researchers used a qualitative methodology that included separate focus groups with children, mothers, and teachers as well as in-depth interviews with other stakeholders, namely Al Karma Edutainment production team members, Ministry of Education officials, and Egyptian television officials involved with children's programs.

Regarding gender equity, researchers concluded that the program had contributed to shifting perceptions of girls' capabilities and achievements and an increased sense that girls should be educated and can grow up to be "something important"

(p. 32). The comment of one 35-year-old, illiterate mother hones the point: "Particularly my daughter, I was going to [take] her out of school . . . enough education. After we watched a few episodes, I told my daughter you shouldn't leave school" (p. 32). Additionally the interviews with mothers provided evidence that the precocious girl Muppet, Khokha, was admired, a fact that was further punctuated by data that show she was elected as the favorite character for girls.

Rimal et al. (2013) used a different approach to examine the impact of Alam Simsim's gender equity influence. One of the earliest attempts to systematically look at the impact of gender equity messaging in an international Sesame Street co-production, they created an index to measure children's attitudes that was based on data from a 13-point questionnaire. Their measure included queries related to responsibilities, personality characteristics, and career possibilities; they asked children whether boys, girls, or both could have a given characteristic or role and reflect aspects of gender equity messaging highlighted in the series. The questions included points such as "who knows a lot" and "who is good at reading." While further research is necessary to validate the measure and examine what the notion of gender equity means for a preschool-aged child, the pattern of findings that emerged was illuminating. Many results were gender specific: in general, girls regarded girls in a positive light and boys regarded boys in a positive light. Girls, for example, tended to view girls as making most of the rules, whereas boys tended to view boys as making most of the rules. Similarly, a majority of the girls reported that girls like to take care of others, while boys were likely to respond that boys like to take care of others. The questions about career choice were a place where the responses of both boys and girls followed a similar pattern. Both genders tended to view careers such as police officers and pilots as boys' professions, with nurse and doctor being possible for either gender.

While the analysis of the relationship between exposure to Alam Simsim and the measure of gender-equitable attitudes illustrated that exposure to the program was associated with more gender-equitable attitudes—which is positive and noteworthy for the series—the findings have been received with a note of caution. It's clear that more work needs to be done to refine the measure so that it reflects an agreed-upon convention of gender equity and its various dimensions. Nevertheless, such research is an important rudimentary step toward unpacking the complexities of evaluating this kind of impact and is something that can be used as a point of departure for the future study of gender equity on Sesame Street and within other children's media endeavors.

Into the Future

Through its popularity, appeal, and recognized educational impact, Alam Simsim holds a notable place in the cultural fabric of Egyptian society. In its comprehensive commitment to the child's development (cognitive, socio-affective, and physical wellbeing), the program has upgraded learners' abilities to move from simple memorization (the more traditional pedagogical approach in Egypt) to genuine analysis and creative thought that has been cast in a culturally appropriate context of social inclusion and respect. This orientation not only benefits the individual child but contributes to a better-educated and more thoughtfully engaged citizenry. In modeling positive messages about the capabilities and achievements of women and girls in Egypt, Alam Simsim took a bold positive step that has contributed to an evolution in education that will help solidify a wide-spread recognition of the importance of the principles of inclusion and cohesion. This, in turn, holds promise to elevate opportunity and instill desire for life-long learning.

Yet, the sustainability of the program is currently in question. Continued broadcast of the series has been interrupted due to the current political climate; while re-runs of the series air periodically, the Egyptian producers continue to seek funding for new production so that a new generation of boys and girls may reap the benefit of Alam Simsim and the principles of its social-inclusion modeling.

Boys' Empowerment: Shara'a Simsim in Palestine

Since its premiere in 1998, Shara'a Simsim, the Palestinian adaptation of Sesame Street, has become a respected source of literacy and other learning fundamentals for Palestinian boys and girls living in the West Bank and Gaza, a region of the world where the majority of young children (roughly two thirds) don't have access to preschool education (UNICEF, 2010a; 2010b; ANERA, 2014). The project reflects the context in which it was developed. It offers preschoolers living in a conflict-ridden environment a means for shifting thinking away from confrontation and negativity to more positive and constructive attitudes. In so doing, it provides a foundation for formal education and responsible citizenship in the nascent Palestinian state by exposing children to positive role models and strengthening their self and mutual respect.

Like Alam Simsim, from the beginning the program has presented a broad curriculum designed to address a full array of children's cognitive, socio-emotional, and physical wellbeing needs. Table 6.3 provides a summary of the curricular framework of its most current season. It includes eight broad areas: math, literacy, emotions, socio-emotions, health and safety, nutrition and healthy eating, human diversity, and resilience. The categorization is similar in nature to the "whole child" framework of Sesame Street's domestic (US) program (see Chapter 3).

Beginning with the fourth season of the program, Palestinian educators working on the project, responding to the contemporary status of young boys in Palestine, instituted a special focus on the emotional wellbeing of Palestinian boys. Educators were reacting to alarming regional trends with respect to boys with measures such as results of standardized tests of academic achievement showing girls out-performing their male peers (World Bank, 2006, 21).

Placed in context, the statistics pointed to a need for action. Palestinian boys were living (and continue to live) within a societal context and economic reality

TABLE 6.3 Summary of educational focus for Shara'a Simsim, Palestine, Season 4

Content area	Focus
Math	Counting
	Number recognition
Literacy	Vocabulary development
	Letter recognition
Socio-emotions	Sharing
	Helping others
	Respecting others' opinions
Health and safety	Cleanliness
	Dental hygiene
	Nutrition
	Healthy eating
Human diversity	Appreciation of similarities and differences
	Respecting ethnic and cultural diversity
Resilience	Task persistence
	Problem solving
	Self-esteem

that provided little hope for the future. With large portions of the Palestinian population living in poverty and high levels of unemployment (World Bank, 2006), children have been growing up in a highly stressed environment that has promoted little opportunity. Within this milieu, boys were confronted with specific social pressures that pushed them to defend family and honor (Palestinian National Authority, n.d). Furthermore, societal expectations of boys and girls differ. Ingrained biases have resulted in societal norms that permit boys, for example, to expect immediate gratification, whereas girls are taught early on to be compliant and disciplined (Joseph, 1994). These patterns begin early with child-rearing practices that set boys and girls on different paths. The effects of the variation in the way children are treated ends up inadvertently building girls' achievement. Anecdotal theorizing about toilet-training methods is one example. It's common practice to allow toddler boys to run about naked, while such exposure for girls is viewed by some as shameful. One speculation is that this results in girls, who wear underwear to cover their bodies, learning control by necessity. Seemingly, they then become toilet trained at an earlier point than their male peers, at least in part due to their differential treatment (C. Arafat, December 16, 2014, personal communication to C. Cole). In sum, the essential idea is that in many instances girls are required to learn discipline and control at an early age. Skills such as potty training, good hygiene, self-regulation, and helping others are practices that generalize to societal interactions in a positive way.

Shara'a Simsim's "boys' empowerment" messaging strives to serve as a catalyst for change by promoting children's positive sense of their own Palestinian identity. The series emphasizes the importance of the broader community in the lives of children (the neighborhood, school, community groups, etc.) and presents social values such as helping others, volunteering, cooperation, and shared responsibilities. At the core of its orientation is a key message: "I can . . ." And embedded in this are strategies for helping children cope with the hardships they confront and giving them concrete ways to improve their lives (Arafat, 2007, 2008).

Sometimes the stories presented are metaphoric: a young bird falls out of a tree and needs kindness and attention. Other times, the lessons are more direct: the characters Haneen and Kareem collect books that are discarded by others and give them to a civic group who helps to set up a children's library (Arafat, 2007). In all elements, though, through the games, stories, and antics of the characters, viewers are exposed to a model of communication that requires teamwork, cooperation, and respect for all. In each of the episodes, children and adults are seen as caring, kind, warm, and sensitive and are presented in a human context that also shows that they have flaws: they are forgetful, fearful, mistaken, and confused sometimes. Bad things do happen on Shara'a Simsim, but the overarching message is that when people work together, they can change things for the better.

A critical element of the boys' empowerment messaging is its focus on improving self-regulation skills. The character Kareem, for example, is seen persisting at tasks in order to succeed, taking responsibility for his actions, controlling his anger, and using his head to think through solutions rather than acting viscerally. For instance, in one segment Kareem is at school and is busy building a tower of blocks. Along comes another puppet who knocks Kareem's tower down. Kareem gets very angry and wants to act out by hitting, but decides to talk with his teacher first. He does so and they are able to solve the problem by letting the other puppet know that this behavior is not accepted and that Kareem is very angry. But then both Muppets work together to build a better tower. Another story included Kareem and Haneen playing outdoors and Kareem had made a kite. A big storm comes along and destroys his kite and makes a big mess of the neighborhood. Haneen becomes very distraught. But Kareem stops and thinks of ways that they can fix up the neighborhood. He calls his friends, gathers cleaning tools, and then they start to clean up together. At the end, they work to rebuild his kite. In both cases, a focus was on persistence, addressing anger in a proactive manner (yet never denying the presence of anger), and coming up with solutions that are reasonable and effective.

Additionally, boys and girls, men and women are seen supporting each other's success. Rather than taking a bifurcated stance of what boys or girls can do, the program emphasizes the aspirations, achievements, and responsibilities of all. So, while the program maintains a special focus on boys' empowerment, it does so within an inclusive context that models gender equity and cooperation.

Formative Studies

Formative research was conducted throughout the course of each season of the program (Shara'a Simsim Research Team, 2006, 2007). For instance, the team used formative testing to help shape the newly designed Muppets Haneen and Kareem and to gain insights to help develop other characters. Researchers showed boys and girls between the ages of three to eight years various images and voices of the characters. There was a strong tendency for the girls to prefer Haneen (the girl monster Muppet) over Kareem (the boy rooster Muppet) in terms of both image and voice. Young boys reported that they liked Kareem because he was big and strong. The girls noted that Haneen was pretty and funny. During the testing of human characters, both boys and girls identified the female storekeeper as a favorite person they would go to for information and help. However, neither boys or girls favored a male "fix-it" repair person who was very gentle and friendly. The boys reported that they preferred a different male "fix-it" repair person who had a more rugged voice and appearance. The input helped the team to revise basic elements of the characters' voices and personalities (C. Arafat, personal communication to C Cole, February 2015).

Additional formative research was conducted throughout the season that tested children's comprehension of basic elements of the curriculum such as the learning of numbers, letters, shapes, skills like cooperation, sharing, taking turns, and other social skills. No significant differences were noted between boys and girls during the testing on comprehension. However, during the testing of visual attention, boys tended to show higher levels of activity (poking others, calling out, squirming) compared to girls, although they had similar rates of visual attention (C. Arafat, personal communication to C Cole, February 2015). Such findings did not lead to specific changes in the materials produced as the main take away from comparing gender data was that both boys and girls enjoyed and benefited from the content.

Impact Studies

While there are no studies to date specifically examining the impact of the boys' empowerment curriculum, a limited amount of research on the effect of the program as a whole shows that it is having a positive effect with respect to its broader educational goals. Children who watch Shara'a Simsim score higher on a range of educational outcomes than those who don't watch it, especially with respect to socio-emotional themes like task persistence, cooperation, sharing, and helping others (Fluent Research, 2011). Researchers found no gender differences in children's learning from the program, which suggests that both boys and girls benefited. While the Fluent Research (2011) study was relatively small scale, involving 344 boys and girls, it is worth noting that the research was a randomized controlled trial, where households were randomly assigned to either watch Shara'a Simsim on TV and DVD, or an alternate educational children's Arabic-language program, *Dragon Tales*.[2] Participants were asked to view the programs over a course of ten weeks. Interestingly, Dragon Tales (an animated series produced by Sesame Workshop) also contained pro-social content, but where there were differences between the two groups, they favored viewers of Shara'a Simsim. While it is impossible to draw conclusions from one study, one speculation is that Shara'a Simsim's cultural relevance was one reason that it yielded greater educational impact compared to a program that was simply dubbed.

The Future of Shara'a Simsim

Shara'a Simsim continues to reach out to young children in Palestine. Recently the production team has completed a new activity book that is being used in Gaza to help children traumatized by conflict and war to cope with stress. The activity book was specifically designed to be used in the classroom or at home and to encourage children to express his/her feelings and share them with an adult. Adults also receive a brochure that explains how children perceive conflict and ways that they can also support children in dealing with stress and help them to re-adjust to returning to school. The team has produced new songs to support children's psycho-social development and allow them to sing and dance and use movement to relieve tension and stress in their lives. The songs were specifically designed as sing-along stories that help children to act out their thoughts and feelings in a positive and proactive manner.

In addition, Shara'a Simsim and Penmedia, the organization that produces Shara'a Simsim, has partnered with another non-profit organization, called Partners for Sustainable Development (PSD). PSD has been working closely with the Ministry of Education to develop supplemental digital-based educational material to support the national educational curriculum. They have focused on learning materials for grades 1 to 12. Penmedia/Shara'a Simsim is collaborating with them in adapting existing materials (educational segments, activity books, etc.) to be used as part of the available library of educational materials that children in preschools through grade 3 can access to support early literacy and social and cognitive development. This is being done through upgrading the existing Shara'a Simsim website and linking with the PSD educational portal.

Shara'a Simsim is currently seeking funding to produce Season 6 of the show. There is high local demand for the program that was and continues to be aired on national and local television stations; however, there is a lack of national resources available to fund a new season and international aid is required. The program has been instrumental in raising parent and educators' awareness on the importance of early childhood education and support and its impact on school preparedness. Organizations such as UNICEF and UNESCO have advocated for continued investment in early childhood initiatives (UNESCO, 2014) to promote quality and inclusive education for all children and support programs that can reach out to vulnerable and marginalized children—like Shara'a Simsim.

Conclusion

Over the last decade and a half the international development community has made great progress toward the United Nation's Millennium Development Goals in general and specifically with respect to those related to gender issues. Statistics point to key achievements such as equal primary education enrollment of girls and boys and increases in the political participation of women (United Nations, 2014). But while there is much to celebrate, a closer look at these statistics highlights the need for continued attention to gender issues. According to the grossest indicator—gender parity in enrollment—progress has been made in the early grades, but few countries have achieved equality at all levels of education. Additionally, there remain "hotspots" in 23 countries where obstacles to school enrollment are particularly acute for girls, as well as a number of countries where boys are at a disadvantage (Winthrop and McGivney, 2014).

Underlying these statistics are differing needs for boys and girls. Factors such as early marriage, inadequate sanitation, safety, and differences in parents' perceived value of education for boy and girl children are often cited as barriers for girls; the presence of violence and gangs (something that affects male youth more forcefully than female), education quality, and inadequate linkages between education and future economic opportunity have been recognized barriers for boys (see Winthrop and McGivney, 2014). Furthermore, some theorize that the same social biases that allow boys a privileged status in some parts of the world, permitting them to behave without self-regulation, responsibility, and attentiveness, inadvertently places them at a disadvantage, as their societal context does not push them to build the non-academic skills valued as necessary to be successful in the education environment (Cornwell et al., 2013; Sommers, 2013). Additionally, disparity favoring girls is seen as related to teaching methods that value (and in some cases inculcate) passive learning and behavioral compliance. It is theorized that expected classroom behavior is, at least in part, more consistent with the way many girls are socialized and results in them achieving at a higher level (UNICEF 2005; Winthrop and McGivney, 2014).

Yet whatever the reasons, all children have the right to educational opportunity that prepares them for the future. Underlying all the statistics are prevailing inequitable attitudes (many of which are unconsciously engrained in societal ethos) around the potential of girls and boys to achieve and become productive members of society. Media are perhaps one of the most promising tools for changing those perceptions. While there are separate needs for each gender, and the differing thrusts of the Alam Simsim and Shara'a Simsim programs provide examples of how Sesame Workshop has developed programming to address those differing needs in a directed way, it is clear that progress will not be made until we can move from a binary orientation to a stance that values gender equity. There is a need for boys and men to be invested in the equity of girls and women and vice versa. At the heart of Sesame Street's co-production efforts regarding gender, this is the ultimate aim.

While the current research on Sesame Street's impact regarding gender equity has limits with respect to its comprehensiveness and the robustness of its design, the results are encouraging as a preliminary indicator. The studies of the Egyptian and Palestinian programs have been linked to changes in perceptions such as parents being more willing to send their girl children to schools, and fathers noting changes in their attitudes about child care and a desire to be more directly involved in it. These data parallel that gleaned from other countries including a qualitative study of Baghch-e-Simsim, the Sesame Street program in Afghanistan (Glevum International, 2012), described in Chapter 4. Indeed, Alam Simsim and Shara'a Simsim laid the groundwork for the creation of girls' empowerment content for other co-production projects, especially those in Afghanistan, India, and Bangladesh.

Notably, all of Sesame Workshop's co-production projects strive to ensure gender equity, fair and equal treatment of boys and girls, and pro-social messaging. Programs like Alam Simsim and Shara'a Simsim have further transformed the thinking through their special curricular emphasis on gender. Boys and girls everywhere have the right to high-quality education that empowers them to reach their highest potential. Sesame Street's international co-productions endeavor to provide an engaging learning experience that uplifts all.

Notes

1. This chapter is dedicated in loving memory to our dear friend and colleague, Dina Amin, for her commitment to educating and entertaining children in Egypt and beyond. We miss you, always.
2. Dragon Tales is an animated production of Sesame Workshop originally produced in English for a domestic, US audience. It has a pro-social curricular focus. Image Production House dubbed 78 30-minute episodes (all three seasons of Dragon Tales) into modern standard Arabic for satellite broadcast in various parts of the Middle East and North Africa on Soread 2M, ART, Orbit, Oman, and Tunisian networks.

References

Alam Simsim Education Team (1999). *Statement of educational objectives for Alam Simsim (English translation of Arabic)*, Unpublished document. New York: Children's Television Workshop.

Alam Simsim Research Team (1999a). *Alam Simsim formative research summary of findings*, June, unpublished document. Cairo: Al Karma Productions.

Alam Simsim Research Team (1999b) *Alam Simsim second research study, Talah-El Menya*, September, unpublished document. Cairo: Al Karma Productions.

ANERA (2014). Early childhood development in the West Bank and Gaza, Volume 5, http://www.anera.org/wp-content/uploads/2014/02/ECD_Report_West_Bank_and_Gaza_WEBVIEW.pdf.

Arafat, C. (2007). Shara'a Simsim-Palestine: A safe, fun and educational street for Palestinian children. *TelevIZIon*, 54–5.

Arafat, C. (2008). *Statement of educational objectives: Shara'a Simsim*, unpublished document. New York: Sesame Workshop.

Capoor, I. and Gade, J. (2004). *Gender in equalities matters! A situational analysis of gender discrimination in India*, unpublished report for Sesame Workshop.

Cornwell, C., Mustard, D.B., and Van Parys, J. (2013). Noncognitive skills and the gender disparities in test scores and teacher assessments: Evidence from primary school. *Journal of Human Resources*, 48(1), 236–64.

Fisch, S. and Bernstein, L. (2001). *Formative research revealed: Methodological and process issues in formative research*. In S. Fisch and R. Truglio (eds), *"G" is for growing: Thirty years of research on children and Sesame Street* (pp. 39–60). Mahway, NJ: Erlbaum.

Fluent Research (2011). *Shara'a Simsim impact assessment: Report of research findings*. New York: Fluent Research.

Glevum International (2012). *Focus group report: Sesame Street*. Gloucester, MA: Glevum.

Gilligan, C. (1982). *In a different voice*. Cambridge, MA: Harvard University Press.

Joseph, S. (1994). Women in the Middle East: Images and reality: Family and gender in the Arab world, *MERIP/Middle East Report*, 199–200.

MEMRB (2002) *Results of omnibus survey of reach of Alam Simsim*. Middle East Market Research Bureau.

Montasser, A., Cole, C.F., and Fuld, J. (2002). "The tower in red and yellow": Using children's drawings in formative research for Alam Simsim, an educational television series for Egyptian Children. *Early Education and Development*, 13(4), 395–407.

Palestinian National Authority (n.d.) *Palestinian National Authority strategy to combat violence against women 2011–2019*, http://www.unwomen.org/~/media/headquarters/media/stories/en/palestinianauthoritynationalstrategytocombatpdf.pdf.

Platón, Y. and Lembert, M. (1999). *Encuernio de Género [Gender Seminar Report]*, unpublished Document. New York: Sesame Workshop.

Plaza Sésamo Education and Research Team (1999). *Guidelines for presenting segments about gender equity* on *Sesame Street coproductions*, unpublished document, Children's Television Workshop.

Rimal, R., Figueroa, M.E., and Storey, J.D. (2013). Character recognition as an alternate measure of television exposure among children: Findings from the Alam Simsim program in Egypt. *Journal of Health Communication: International Perspectives*, 18(5), 594–609, DOI: 10.1080/10810730.2012.743625.

Rouchdy, M. (1998). *Girls' Education in Egypt*, paper commissioned by Children's Television Workshop, New York.

Shara'a Simsim Research Team (2006). *Formative research report*, unpublished document for Sesame Workshop, New York.

Shara'a Simsim Research Team (2007). *Formative research report*, unpublished document for Sesame Workshop, New York.

Smith, S.L., Choueiti, M., and Pieper, K. (2014). *Gender bias without borders: An investigation of female characters in popular films across 11 countries*. Report commissioned by Geena Davis Institute, http://seejane.org/symposiums-on-gender-in-media/gender-bias-without-borders/.

Sommers, C.H. (2013). *The great divide: The boys at the back*. New York Times Opinionator blog, February 2, http://opinionator.blogs.nytimes.com/2013/02/02/the-boys-at-the-back/?_r=0.

SPAAC (2005). *The cultural impact of Alam Simsim: An Egyptian adaptation of Sesame Street*. Cairo: Social Planning, Analysis and Administration Consultants.

UNESCO (2014). *The EFA package for Palestine: A partnership between the Ministry of Education and Higher Education and the United Nations to promote quality and inclusive education for all children*, http://www.unesco.org/new/en/ramallah/about-this-office/single-view/news/the_efa_package_for_palestine_a_partnership_between_the_ministry_of_education_and_higher_education_and_the_united_nations_to_promote_quality_and_inclusive_education_for_all_children/#.VNfIRPnF-So.

UNICEF (2005). *Gender achievements and prospects in education: The gap report* (pp. 44–9). New York: UNICEF.

UNICEF (2010a). *My right to safe access to school and to a child-friendly learning environment*, UNICEF, http://www.lacs.ps/documentsShow.aspx?ATT_ID=6284.

UNICEF (2010b). *The situation of Palestinian children in the Occupied Palestinian Territory, Jordan, Syria and Lebanon: An assessment based on the Convention on the Rights of the Child.* New York: UNICEF, http://www.unicef.org/oPt/PALESTINIAN_SITAN-final.pdf.

United Nations (2006). *Millennium project, http://www.unmillenniumproject.org/goals/.*

United Nations (2014). *Millennium Development Goals report.* New York: United Nations, http://www.un.org/millenniumgoals/2014%20MDG%20report/MDG%202014%20English%20web.pdf.

Winthrop, R. and McGivney, E. (2014). *Raising the global ambition for girls' education.* Washington, DC: Brookings Institution.

World Bank (2006). *West Bank and Gaza: Education sector analysis: Impressive achievements under harsh conditions and the way forward to consolidate a quality education system.* Washington, DC: World Bank, http://www-wds.worldbank.org/external/default/WDSContentServer/WDSP/IB/2007/10/05/000310607_20071005161816/Rendered/PDF/410430GZ0Educa1or0Analysis01PUBLIC1.pdf.

World Bank (2014). *Brief: Girls' education*, December 8, http://www.worldbank.org/en/topic/education/brief/girls-education.

7

RIPPLE EFFECTS

Using Sesame Street to Bridge Group Divides in the Middle East, Kosovo, Northern Ireland, and Elsewhere

Charlotte F. Cole and Lewis Bernstein

> *Educational media provide a wonderful tool for translating the open-mindedness and optimism of children into a vision of peace in the world. They offer a perfect channel for them to imagine a world very different from the one we know.*
> Kofi A. Annan, former secretary general of the United Nations, May 22, 2002

At the heart of Sesame Workshop's work in regions of conflict and post-conflict is the aim of helping children from oppositional groups understand their common humanity. On Sesame Street, this is done through carefully designed program content that presents positive images of a child's own group and that of the "other" within a context that is engaging, child-relevant and fun. Developing this content is far from a simple process. It takes careful planning, training, and participation in an active dynamic (see the description of the Sesame Workshop Model in Chapter 1) that involves a collaboration between Sesame Workshop and local partners who work together to shape a given project, from its early conception and design to its implementation and distribution. Research examining the educational impact of various co-production projects has shown that the production process results in programming that positively impacts children's cognitive, physical, and socio-emotional wellbeing (Mares and Pan, 2013).

Less tangible, although arguably equally important, is the impact these programs have beyond their immediate child-level educational influence. In regions of conflict, their "ripple effects" are responsible for bringing groups of people from oppositional groups together, resulting in more than just the specific educational aims of the Sesame Street programming. They contribute to what Ambassador Dennis Ross (President Clinton's special envoy to the Middle East beginning in 1993) called the diplomatic benefit of "people-to-people" projects that bring peace processes from the level of government-to-government negotiation to the practical reality of daily life (Ross, 2002). This horizon is where, as Ross explains, "you break down the barriers . . . make it hard to stereotype, and . . . make it very difficult to demonize" (pp 70–1).

This chapter illustrates the way in which engagement in Sesame Workshop's co-production process works at two distinct levels: that of the child and that of the broader community.[1] In leveraging what Kofi Annan (in the opening quote) refers to as "the open-mindedness and optimism of children," these projects contribute to a larger milieu that is helping to build a collective consciousness for peace. Offering examples from the Middle East, Kosovo, Northern Ireland, and elsewhere this chapter describes how the process itself has contributed to Sesame Workshop's broader goal of promoting respect and understanding across group divides. With its various collaborative components and broadcast-driven timelines, the course of production places teams of people in a creative discourse whose prescribed schedules and deadlines necessitate dialogue, resolution, and decision making around difficult and often contentious issues. Not only have these co-production projects resulted in providing highly effective learning experiences for children, they bring together stakeholders from oppositional groups who become part of a rigorous exchange that promotes cooperation, collaboration, and respect across group divides. And the willingness of all parties to engage in the process comes from a shared desire to build a better world for children. Thus, in effect, through the Sesame Workshop process, children become the galvanizers of peace.

Rechov Sumsum/Shara'a Simsim

As mentioned in her foreword to this book, Sesame Workshop's founder Joan Ganz Cooney once noted that one of her greatest hopes was that someday Israelis and Palestinians would be sitting around a table laughing about a shared Bert and Ernie segment from Sesame Street and maybe peace would then break out in the Middle East. Cooney, of course, said that facetiously, but with an underlying deep hope. The Oslo Accords signed by Israelis and the Palestinians in 1993 brought Sesame Workshop an opportunity to explore and implement Cooney's dream and the possibility of suggesting to Israelis and Palestinians that they start to build a vision of the Middle East that included teaching their youngest children about each other to build a sense of shared humanity. It was something Sesame Workshop believed in and hoped to try, but the question lingered as to whether individuals and organizations in the region would be willing to partner with Sesame Street in this way.

In many ways the project was an analogue to the early history of Sesame Street. Propelled by the optimism the Oslo Accords presented, Sesame Workshop sought to see first-hand if the Israelis and Palestinians shared our outlook about educating their youngest children through Sesame Street. With funding from the Charles H. Revson Foundation, in 1994 Sesame Workshop sent a small team of executives to meet with Israeli and Palestinian psychologists, writers, animators, and politicians from all sides of the political spectrum. The group went to the Middle East to ask three basic questions:

1. Is it important to teach children at a very young age to humanize the other?
2. Is it an important idea?
3. And finally, is it a feasible idea and, were there Israelis and Palestinians who would be willing to be involved in a Sesame Street project?

We discovered very quickly that there was unanimity about the import and significance of the idea. At the same time we learned that most felt it was not feasible. The Israelis were willing but expressed skepticism about any Palestinian group's willingness to work with them. The Palestinians noted two large concerns: there was too much of a gap between the harsh reality of their lives and an imaginary Sesame (fantasy?) street where one could humanize the other; and there was an imbalance between the groups that would be too hard to overcome in that Israelis had been producing educational television for their children for years, but they had never done so.

Over the course of many discussions and discourse, we told both sides that we would work to serve as an intermediary to bridge their differences. We told the Israelis that we would bring Palestinians to the party. And we told the Palestinians that Sesame would help narrow the experience gap by training their talent to be able to produce quality educational television that was authentically theirs. And to our amazement both sides agreed and Rechov Sumsum/Shara'a Simsim (as the project came to be known in Hebrew and Arabic) was born.

The success of the project can best be seen within its historic perspective. During its evolutionally course (which is detailed later in this chapter), in line with the socio-political barometer of the region, it moved from the aspirational idealism of a single, joint Palestinian–Israeli program to—in its current form, more in-keeping with the contemporary situation in the region—separate, independently produced programs. Accordingly, the developmental course of the joint Sesame project advanced through fits and turns that paralleled those of the turbulent situation on the ground in Israel and Palestine.

Though the project, which began in the mid-1990s, had started at a point of optimism, it was implemented against a harsh reality, with major events, such as bus bombings, the assassination of the Israeli Prime Minister, the destruction of the Palestinian production facilities, any one of which could have led to the dissolution of the project. On the most practical level, these realities made it difficult, and in some instances impossible for members of the production team to engage in a cooperative, face-to-face discourse. Basics such as the ability of the group to meet were complicated by restrictions and, at times, prohibitions from traveling across borders and check points. There was, as well, at the emotional level, the psychological complexities with which members of the team—on both the Palestinian and Israeli sides—had to contend. The personal histories of many of the people on the project had been directly impacted by the political turmoil in grave and traumatic ways. There were, for some, huge personal risks of engagement with the "other."

Yet, it is these very challenges, and the way they were overcome, that, when seen through the project's evolutionary lens, are testament to the triumph of Sesame Workshop's approach. In implementing a method of engagement that allows for and promotes partnership dynamics that launch from and respect local context, needs, and sensibilities, the project team navigated a shifting course that resulted in the creation of high-quality educational content that advanced children's learning and much more.

As with all international co-productions of Sesame Street, Sesame Workshop engaged in a carefully planned, yet highly flexible, development process to hone the project's educational goals and establish the necessary working relationships on the ground. (The project's key milestones are presented in Table 7.1.) In this case, that process began with fact-finding trips during which members of Sesame Street's New York office travelled to the region to talk with government and non-government stakeholders in the education, broadcast, production, and other sectors in Israel and Palestine. Based on the results of these visits, which took place in 1994–5, the approach evolved in many ways.

TABLE 7.1 Rechov Sumsum/Shara'a Simsim's project milestones

Date	Activity	Description
September 1993	**Signing of Oslo Accords**	
February 1994	**L. Bernstein authors funding proposal to Charles H. Revson Foundation**	Title: *And a Child Shall Lead Them: Humanizing the Other in the Middle East with Sesame Street*
March 1994	**Letter of endorsement**	Israeli Educational Television (IETV)
July 1994	**CTW: Fact-finding trip to Israel**	CTW participants: L. Bernstein and B. Urist
August 1994	**CTW: Fact-finding trip to Israel, West Bank, and Gaza**	CTW Participants: L. Bernstein, C. Cole, G. Gettas, D. Jacobs, and G. Knell
May 1995	**Palestinian–Israeli/ Palestinian mini seminar, East Jerusalem**	To discuss Palestinian-specific content ideas
May 1995	**Israeli/Palestinian–Israeli mini seminar, Haifa**	To discuss Israel-specific content ideas
June 1995	**Letter of endorsement**	Palestinian Broadcasting Company (PBC) and the Jerusalem Film Institute (JFI) as Palestinian production partners

(Continued)

TABLE 7.1 (Continued)

Date	Activity	Description
July/August 1995	**Interim meetings**	To further discuss how Palestinians should be portrayed on and participate in the series. Suggested further research on Israeli/Palestinian attitudes and stereotypes
May 1995	**Position paper**	M. Mar'i: Teaching Tolerance and Understanding through Sesame Street for Israeli and Palestinain-Israeli Children
July 1995	**Position paper**	I. Levin: Preliminary Thoughts on Planning a TV Program for Preschoolers: Enhancing Tolerance between Israeli Jews, Palestinain-Israelis, and Palestinians
September 1995	**Position paper**	C. Arafat: Sesame Street Position Paper: West Bank and Gaza Strip
November 1995	**Position paper**	N. Yirmiya: Sesame Street Position Paper
November 5, 1995	**Assassination of Yitzhak Rabin**	
November 7–8, 1995	**Curriculum seminar: Tiberias**	To frame project curriculum parameters
February 1996	**Curriculum document draft (finalized in February 1997)**	
April 1996	**New York workshop**	Production-training workshop
July 1996	**Israeli-Palestinian writer's workshop, Neve Shalom, Israel**	CTW participants: L. Santeiro, M. Loman, plus 12 Israeli writers; six Palestinian writers; production representatives from IETV and JFI (character descriptions created)
September 1996–March 1997	**Sesame assigns resident writer/producer to work with Palestinian team**	
January 1997	**IETV production begins**	Israelis create ten hours of studio material, 60 minutes of live-action material, and 20 minutes of animation
April 1997	**Palestinian team at IETV studio**	Film one week of "cross-over" segments, where the Israeli Muppets and characters visit the Palestinian street

TABLE 7.1 (Continued)

Date	Activity	Description
April 1997	**LAF training**	For Palestine production team by CTW
June 1997	**Palestinian team at IETV studio**	Cross-over segments filmed where the Palestinian Muppets and characters visit the Israeli street
October 1997	**Summative evaluation research meeting in New York**	To discuss planning of research with University of Maryland (N. Fox and M. Killen)
October 1997	**Gaza Community Health Conference**	CTW presentation: C. Cole, viewing of Shara'a Simsim segments and discussion of show's educational goals
March 1998	**Summative evaluation: training of researchers, Tel Aviv, Ramallah, and Acre**	CTW Participant: B. Richman
April 1, 1998	**Press conference, Dan Pearl Hotel, Jerusalem**	To announce launch of Rechov Sumsum, Shara'a Simsim
April 1, 1998	**Rechov Sumsum/Shara'a Simsim lau`nch**	Rechov Sumsum: April 1–14, 13 30-minute programs broadcast on IETV, remaining 45 programs broadcast during summer
		Shara'a Simsim: 20, 15-minute programs air on Al-Quds educational television, broadcast three times a week over a 20-week period
April–September 1998	**Summative evaluation research conducted in Tel Aviv, Ramallah, and Acre**	Wave 1: April 1998 Wave 2: May/June 1998 Wave 3: June/July 1998 Wave 4: September 1998
July 1998	**Market research (parents)**	Telephone interviews
July 7, 1998	**Summative evaluation meeting (New York)**	Non-CTW Participants: N. Fox, L. Leavitt, M. Killen, and G. Lesser
		Purpose: To discuss coding system for summative evaluation qualitative data and project information dissemination
November 1998	**Japan Prize Foundation's President's Prize**	Rechov Sumsum/Shara'a Simsim "In Harmony" episode
November 2–3, 1999	**Rechov Sumsum/Shara'a Simsim Research Symposium, American Colony Hotel, Jerusalem**	Results of summative evaluation presented to CTW, IETV, Al-Quds, and invited international conflict-resolution experts

One of the most significant changes was the consideration of the needs of three separate groups, rather than two. While the program had initially envisioned a joint Palestinian–Israeli project, discussions with people on the ground led the team to incorporate the distinct needs of a third group—Palestinian citizens of Israel—who shared a perspective different from both Israeli Jews and from Palestinians living in the West Bank and Gaza. A comment from one of our advisors from the Palestinian Israeli community to one the authors of this paper hones this point: "Who is more 'Jewish'? Your cousins who may be living in California as assimilated Jews or me? I am living in Israel; I speak Hebrew; my life follows the Jewish calendar. And yet I am a proud Palestinian living in Israel" (Bernstein, personal communication, 1994). After that discussion, we made sure that in planning the series we included representatives of the Palestinian Israeli community. Further, we were also advised to conduct parallel discussions among the different groups before convening a joint Palestinian–Israeli meeting (as had been our initial intention).

To accommodate these needs, we altered our plan and added two "mini seminars," one for Israelis and one for Palestinians. These day-long meetings took place prior to a larger meeting that brought both groups together. While we had also contemplated holding a third meeting just for Palestinian citizens of Israel, our advisors from this group suggested instead that they join both of these introductory meetings.

During these meetings, one held in East Jerusalem and the other in Haifa in May of 1995, as well as in a joint Palestinian/Israeli meeting held months later in Tiberias in November 1995, Israeli and Palestinian stakeholders joined together representing both government and non-government entities from the fields of education, broadcasting, and production. The sessions led to the creation of an educational framework for the project (described below) and also underscored a larger aim: the value of convening groups of people from oppositional groups to discuss a resource designed to benefit "their" children and prepare them for a brighter future.

The session in Tiberias was the first time some of the attendees had been in a room with people from the "other" group and for many this was not an easy context to navigate. Yet, despite grave differences in outlook, perception, and opinion, the attendees participated in a productive way with even a sense of shared comradery. Their commitment was underscored by the project's various challenges, including the assassination of the Israeli prime minister that happened the same week as the scheduled meeting in Tiberias. Remarkably, while Sesame Workshop entertained the idea of cancelling this meeting altogether—feeling it might be too difficult and insensitive to convene a group of Israelis and Palestinians in the aftermath of such an event—our Israeli and Palestinian partners on the ground opted for the meeting to take place, acknowledging that Rabin stood for peace in their collective future, and regarding it as even more important to move forward with peace-related activities, given the troubling circumstances.

The meeting resulted in a productive discussion about what children should learn from the series that provided the foundation for developing the project's curriculum and program content. The concept of presenting positive, authentic images of Palestinian and Israeli culture was a primary focus which highlighted the benefit of filming stories using cameras held by individuals from the cultures presented. From these discussions there also emerged the sense of the importance of creating two streets—one Israeli and one Palestinian—to present the program's core Muppet stories. The team agreed that it was simply too far from reality to create a Sesame neighborhood—analogous to America's multi-cultural neighborhood—in which Israelis and Palestinians would be together. But they did decide that it would be possible to include some segments in which characters from the two different streets "crossed over" to the other.

There was much dialogue both at that session and throughout the course of the project about disequilibrium. Life was not equal. Nor was life fair. Nor would the political and military circumstances change rapidly no matter how optimistic we all could be. Our Israeli partner, Israel Educational Television (IETV), has been producing television for 25 years. Our Palestinian partner at Al Quds Institute for Modern Media was just beginning. Our Israeli partners believed that peace was possible and that we needed to model what that might look like; our Palestinian partners were much more skeptical about the future. After all, they did not yet have a state; the reality was very far from achieving that goal and a real peace. Sesame Workshop aimed to navigate the disequilibrium and help create a meaningful experience for all children viewing.

We further explained that from its inception the Sesame Street program would be seen as a kind of Rorschach test in which everything would be viewed through one's personal political filter. We were committed to keeping our eye on the child and not on the politics. Each side would need to create segments about their own culture, their own symbols, and their own language. And by doing so we hoped that Palestinian and Israeli children would not only gain pride in their own cultures, but, through authentic messages, learn to respect each other.

The Project Curriculum

As with other Sesame Street projects, the curriculum for the program took a "whole-child" perspective and included a full range of curricular domains that, in this case, were categorized into four areas: 1) mutual respect (human diversity, commonality and understanding); 2) the child's world (body parts, child's powers, health, reasoning, problem solving); 3) reading, mathematics, and writing (symbolic representation, numbers, geometric forms); and 4) cognitive organization (perceptual discrimination, relational concepts, classifying). But although mutual respect and inclusion goals have been a part of educational frameworks for Sesame Workshop co-production, Rechov Sumsum/Shara'a Simsim marked the first time that it was a leading focus with anti-sectarianism being a major priority (Cole et al., 2001). This element of the curriculum, inspired by the outcomes of the various advisory sessions, focused on articulating goals that would help children understand each other and to demystify and break down negative stereotypes.

The great hope for the project is expressed in the document's introduction:

> [W]e are committed to portraying authentic illustrations. While on the one hand the streets of Rechov Sumsum/Shara'a Simsim depict a fantasy place where we can go beyond our present reality, the images on the program must be presented in a manner that is true to the customs and beliefs of the cultural groups represented. Segments produced about a given group must be produced with the advice of members of that group. We endeavor to take care that the context of the implicit messages that emerge carries details that are truly reflective of a given culture in a respectful and dignified manner . . . we wish to present believable situations and events in a fashion such that children watching the series will find aspects of what is presented that reflect a part of themselves and their own life experiences . . . We let children see that it is possible to break the barrier of fear that exists, to respect one another and even to develop friendships among each other.
>
> Children's Television Workshop, 1996, 8

Devising content that represented the curriculum offered many challenges to the team. Some of the most difficult content to develop was associated with the "cross-over" segments where characters from one street visited the other. These segments were at the heart of the program's ability to demonstrate each side's willingness to accept the other. And these segments proved to be some of the most poignant and powerful of the series.

Yet they were not without controversy. For example, even to this day, each partner has a Rashomon-like interpretation of one segment that is perhaps emblematic of what Sesame Workshop set out to do. It was called "the bicycle." The plot was as follows:

> A young Israeli boy of about age nine, who is taking a bike ride, finds himself lost on Shara'a Simsim (the Palestinian street) where he discovers he has a flat tire, a scary situation in its own right and all the more a cause for concern in that the Jewish boy in this fictional story is lost in a Palestinian neighborhood (a circumstance that would arouse fear for many Israelis who would have great concern for the boy's safety). He looks at his tire and in Hebrew expresses distress ("*Oh no, what am I to do?*"). Our two Palestinian Muppets hear him, and respond in Arabic, saying, "*What's the matter? Can we help you?*" The Israeli boy replies in Hebrew thanking them and telling them he has a flat tire. The Palestinian Muppets see the flat tire and have an idea. They leave momentarily and then bring back at first a tire that's too big. And then one that's too small. And then one that is just right. The Israeli boy tells them he will bring back the tire and thanks them. He then asks if

they will join him for a bike ride. The Palestinian Muppets at first respond positively, but then they remember that their bicycle is missing a wheel, as they gave it to the Israeli boy to fix his bike! At the end, the Israeli boy thanks them and promises to return the wheel.

As a story, its content is a powerful way to promote respect and understanding. An Israeli boy gets lost on a Palestinian street and is welcomed by two Palestinian Muppets who extend compassionate help. And yet, when the Palestinian team of writers wrote the segment, the Israeli head writer had strong reservations about producing it believing that it would not-so-subtly be metaphorically interpreted as the Palestinians giving up, once again, what they own to an Israeli. The Palestinian head writer responded by asserting that the scenario was reflective of Palestinian culture and fit with the tradition of extending hospitality to a person in need. In the end, the decision was made to produce the segment as it was regarded as important from a child's perspective and an example in which politics needed to take a back seat. And yet to this day, there is controversy within the members of the production team about who even wrote that segment, and who was and wasn't opposed to producing it. It is a perfect example of a Sesame segment as a kind of "Rorschach-test" reflection of individuals' interpretations.

Impact

Sesame Workshop commissioned a series of studies to look at the impact of the program both from the perspective of reach and children's learning. In parallel to some of the challenges of producing the program, studying its impact was far from straightforward. It was, for example, difficult to collect comparative data across the three groups of interest as researchers' access to the communities varied; additionally, infrastructure differences (such as whether, for example, reach data could be collected through phone survey or door to door) resulted in the need for varied research designs when collecting data from the different participant groups. Among other limitations, these challenges made it impossible to make meaningful comparisons across the groups. Researchers were, therefore, only able to capture a preliminary sense of the program's reach and educational impact.

In their survey of parents of young children, Cohen and Francis (1999) found significant access to the program although there were important differences in exposure across the three groups studied (with the Israeli-Jewish children having the greatest exposure, the Palestine children living in West Bank/Gaza the least and the Israeli-Palestinian children somewhere in the middle). Perhaps the most interesting finding from this survey, which included questions to parents about their perceptions of the program, was that the Israeli and Palestinian parents interviewed understood the social mission of the project, generally supported it, and expressed a desire from their children to learn from it.

There is also evidence of impact on Israeli and Palestinian children's perceptions (Cole et al., 2003), although interpreting the data is complex because the content of the programs the children from different groups viewed was not the same. Perhaps one of the most striking findings from this early study was that children demonstrated an innate sense of fairness and justice that was apparent in the judgments they made about different scenarios (see Fox et al., 1999) involving Palestinians and Israelis playing together. In answering questions such as who should use a swing when there is only one swing, fairness trumped ethnicity and politics. Yet, equally potent was the language used by some, albeit a minority of children, when describing people (as prompted by a picture of an adult male) from the "other" culture. While some children used positive or neutral descriptors to articulate their perceptions of the other group, some children provided commentary that was disturbingly negative ("They are stupid;" "They steal our land") demonstrating the degree to which even very young children pick up adult cues reflecting prejudicial thinking and cultural bias and underscoring the need for interventions that start at an early age.

As for the evidence of learning from the program, it is important to view the data in light of how the content was broadcast. IETV aired 63 half-hour episodes of the series; while the Palestinian program, which was only 15 minutes in length, included only 20 episodes that we broadcast on the Ma'an network. Due to the differences in broadcast and the construction of the Hebrew and Arabic episodes the children from the different groups saw different amounts of content about each other. It is perhaps not surprising that there was great variation in impact across the groups studied. On average, the Israeli children demonstrated positive changes in their perceptions of Palestinians, whereas many of the Palestinian groups' perceptions of the "other" became more negative over time. While this finding was not desirable, viewed in light of the reality of the content the children from the different groups saw it was not discouraging: the children with greatest access to the content of the "other" showed positive change. It's not possible, however, to discern from the data, given the limits of the study design, how much the changes in perceptions of either group could be traced to the program itself versus other factors such as the broader influence of the increasingly tumultuous socio-political backdrop. Studies by other researchers, most notably that of Warshel (2007), provide further insights. Warshel examined children's reactions to specific Rechov Sumsum program content and found positive change after exposure that echoed that noted in the Cole et al. study. Additionally, subsequent studies of later variations of the program and related outreach experiences in Israel (Fisch and Oppenheimer, 2012a, 2012b) and Palestine (Fluent Research, 2011) show small but measurable positive effects of the social inclusion messaging.

From a broader perspective, though, perhaps the greatest contribution of the early research is that it pioneered—through the use of the Social Judgment Instrument (Fox et al., 1999; Brenick et al., 2007)—a way of studying cross-group perceptions. (See Chapter 2 for additional discussion.) The instrument which Fox et al. developed for the project offered a way to examine changes in young Palestinian and Israeli children's understanding of and perceptions about each other. Variations of this instrument, which involves having children answer questions about their knowledge and perceptions of their own and the "other" group, have been employed by other researchers who have adapted it and/or used it as an inspiration for measuring children's learning in this curricular domain in other regions (see Cole, 2000; Connolly et al., 2002; Fluent Research, 2008; Najčevska).

In addition to formalized research looking at the linkages between the program's curricular goals and children's learning, there is also some evidence—albeit more anecdotal in nature—that the project had effects beyond its explicit child-level goals. Rechov Sumsum/Shara'a Simsim was, from the beginning, much more than a children's television show. It was a device for bringing together individuals from oppositional sides in a project that allowed not only children to learn about each other, but adults to experience their common humanity. The production process, because it was driven by creative concerns and by deadlines dictated by the need to meet broadcast and other time-sensitive specifics, required a level of cooperation, respect, and collaboration that rose above personal differences and prejudices to be fruitful.

Israeli puppeteer, Gilles Ben-David, who played Moshe Oofnik (an Israeli version of the American Oscar the Grouch Muppet character), summarizes, in a description of his experience working with the Palestinian team, the ways in which engagement in the production process itself activated a higher purpose. As content was filmed, the puppeteers worked in close quarters and, to be successful, needed to assist one another in a cooperative way. He describes the transition from working as actors from separate Israeli and Palestinian production groups to working together as a team.

> There was a small [counter], one and a half or two meters by half a meter, with three puppets, and five operators [behind it], four men, one woman, with cables and microphones, and it's uncomfortable . . . In the beginning it was awkward, everyone keeping to his own space, not to say anything, not to make waves God forbid . . . And slowly we began to laugh, and to help one another, and I said, I'll move my leg this way, maybe you can see the monitor better . . . And slowly, slowly it turned into a real co-production, five actors working hand in hand and trying to help one another.
>
> Quoted in Schoffman, 2000

Beyond the Rechov Sumsum/Shara'a Simsim Project

Since its initial inception, the project shifted from its original vision in ways that aligned with the socio-political reality. Over a multi-decade period the evolution of the project paints a portrait that mirrors Middle East dynamics as the peace process took its various turns. Beginning in 2003, a spin-off version of the program, produced by HOP! called Sippuray Sumsum (Sesame Stories in Hebrew) was developed in conjunction with a Palestinian team (Institute for Modern Media) and a Jordanian team (Jordan Pioneers) who each produced separate Sesame Stories programs (called Hikayat Simsim in Arabic). The base of the program's episodes was animated stories telling the fables/tales of five different cultures: Israeli-Jewish, Palestinian-Israeli, Palestinian, Jordanian, and American. For a total of 13 animations, each production group (including Sesame Workshop) produced three animations with an additional story filmed by Hop! (who provided stories from both Jewish-Israeli and Palestinian-Israeli cultures). These programs were independently managed and each featured their own puppet characters: Noah and Brosh in Israel, Haneen and Kareem (a rooster) in Palestine, and Tonton and Juljul in Jordan. They then shared the animated content across all three programs. While the generalized curriculum goals were similar to the Rechov Sumsum/ Shara'a Simsim project and included a strong pro-social component, the dimension of introducing Palestinian children to Israeli and vice versa, which had been the driving force of Rechov Sumsum/Shara'a Simsim, was not an explicit element of this project.

In 2006, the series went into a final phase where it reverted back to the Rechov Sumsum name, this time with all the content produced by Hop! Both the Jordanian and Palestinian teams continued to sustain their projects, but without any shared content or pretense of collaboration, echoing the contemporary political climate that lessened the groups' ability to work cooperatively. The Israeli series, which is currently still in production, maintains a strong focus on diversity going beyond cultural and ethnic lines to include social inclusion in its broadest forms, as personified in newer characters such as Mahboub, an Palestinian-Israeli Muppet, and Sivan, who has a physical disability (and appears using a wheelchair).

Thus, the transition of the programs parallels the metamorphosis from the more optimistic vision sparred by the peace initiatives of the mid-1990s to the reality of the increased tensions in the region. The program moved from the initial joint Israeli/Palestinian Rechov Sumsum/Shara'a Simsim to the triune of programs that comprised the Sesame Stories project (containing shared animated content but no overt "cross-overs" between the characters), to the completely separate programs broadcast today. Yet, this evolution, while not fulfilling the goals of the initial vision, typifies the success of Sesame Street's approach in flexibly adapting to meet the complex realities on the ground. From the beginning, the project presented an aspirational vision of reality. It sought to move the needle and show how life could be. Yet, throughout its history, it has always been mindful of engaging in messaging that fit the context in which it was placed. If messaging is to be effective it can't sit so far outside the line of acceptability that the material is not broadcastable. While other joint Palestinian/Israeli projects that emerged with similar ideals in the mid-1990s have since been abandoned, in continuing to be aired in Israel, while now far from its initial vision, the Sesame Street project has been, in its persistence, a resource that will, perhaps, sow seeds that impact some recipients in a way that provides a pathway for future work as the socio-political climate changes.

Rruga Sesam/Ulica Sezam: Kosovo

Sesame Workshop's project in Kosovo leveraged the lessons learned engaging in the Middle East and applied them to another region. That the co-production was initially jointly sponsored by the United Nations Development Program (UNDP) and the United Nations Children's Fund (UNICEF) highlights the double purpose the project served. On the one hand it grew from a need for high-quality early childhood education in Kosovo and a recognition from UNICEF and other organizations of the benefit educational television programming could deliver. On the other, the interest from UNDP underscored the potential contribution a program of this nature could make to building capacity in the education and technology sectors in the service of promoting peace efforts in a post-conflict region.

When the program launched in 2004, Kosovo had been mired in a protracted conflict between its ethnic Serbian and Albanian populations. Tensions had resulted in the creation of a dual education system that independently serviced the ethnic Albanian and Serbian communities and led to an inequitable distribution of resources. The situation was further compounded by a dearth of early childhood education opportunities with only a small percentage of children attending pre-school programs. Furthermore, the limited preschool options available were concentrated in urban areas despite the fact that the majority of the population lived in rural areas (MEST/MAFRD, 2004; Statistical Office of Kosovo, 2001; Sesame Workshop, 2002b).

This need, combined with an estimated 85% access to television at the time (Sesame Workshop, 2002b), positioned Sesame Street as an ideal educational tool. From the beginning the program aimed to address two central curricular issues: 1) providing basic literacy, math, and socio-emotional and physical wellbeing skills that might be a part of any early childhood educational framework, and 2) engendering mutual respect and understanding across group divides.

The co-production, which became known as Rruga Sesam/Ulica Sezam ("Sesame Street" in the Albanian and Serbian languages, respectively), was executed on a significantly smaller scale (and budget) than Rechov Sumsum/Shara'a Simsim and some of Sesame Workshop's other co-production projects. It used a unique model that is a good illustration of the creative way Sesame Workshop has leveraged material produced elsewhere to service a variety of needs and to make such projects economically viable (Cole and Lee, 2013). The core curricular areas (literacy, math, and socio-emotional and physical wellbeing) were, for the most part, carried through material produced in the United States: much of the program was developed by re-packaging and dubbing (into the Serbian and Albanian languages) a Sesame Street spin-off series entitled Open Sesame. This show (which was specially designed to broadcast internationally) included segments from Sesame Workshop's content library and featured classic Sesame Muppet characters such as Bert, Ernie, and Grover who presented various curricular goals through their interests and antics.

The Open Sesame content gave Rruga Sesam/Ulica Sezam an identifiably Sesame Street signature with its use of the Muppet characters and the magazine format in an educational context. Importantly, though, the series also incorporated content produced in Kosovo by a locally-based production team. Each episode featured live-action segments, filmed throughout Kosovo, presenting high-interest stories about the daily lives of children. Although most of these segments focused specifically on ethnic Albanian and Serbian children, they also included children from other groups, including ethnic Turkish, Bosniak, Croatian, Roma, and Gorani.

As with the Rechov Sumsum/Shara'a Simsim project, the program's films aimed to provide children with a window into the lives of people from different groups. Stories highlighted family life, traditions, and holidays presenting activities and events from the perspective of a child. The goal was to illustrate the common humanity shared among people of different groups. Importantly, the same films also worked to build children's pride in their own backgrounds and communities by highlighting traditions, achievements, and other elements that elevated children's sense of their own history and cultural contributions through positive images of the variety of lives people lead as well as showing similarities in the human experience.

The program also included a community-engagement component, managed by UNICEF, who distributed throughout Kosovo print materials in the Serbian and Albanian languages to children and their caregivers. Children's books and a facilitator guide extended the messages of respect and understanding presented in the television series as well as honed some of the basic curricular themes. The facilitator's guide, which was designed for use by parents and teachers, provided tips on ways to engage children using materials from the books and television series (Cole et al., 2008; Cole and Lee, 2013).

Impact

A randomized control trial (Fluent Research, 2008) that examined the effects of exposure to the series analyzed the responses of ethnic Albanian and Serbian five- and six-year-olds living in Kosovo. Based on the program's curricular framework, the researchers developed a measure of mutual respect and understanding that was a composite of children's responses to questions that assessed factors such as recognition of similarities and reception to children from other ethnic groups and to those who speak a different language. They found a small but notable positive effect of the Sesame Street programming on children's attitudes, which were most pronounced with the ethnic Serbian children who expressed stronger attitudes of mutual respect than the ethnic Albanian group did (Fluent Research, 2008; Cole and Lee, 2013).

Sesame Tree: Northern Ireland

During the launch event for Sesame Tree's first season, Northern Ireland's deputy first minister, Martin McGuinness, made a powerful speech that followed the screening of an episode from the series. Referring to Reverend Ian Paisley, his counterpart in the new power-sharing government of trouble-torn Northern Ireland, he noted:

> Today we saw a very strong message of sharing that we would all do well to share . . . We have an 82-year-old unionist and a 57-year-old republican agreeing to share power and they have done so since May last year. This is work we can all be involved in, across all the spectrums and age groups, to eradicate sectarianism and racism.
>
> McClements, 2008

McGuinness' message punctuates the power of Sesame Street to not only bring important messages of mutual respect and tolerance to young children, but—through the visibility of such projects—draw attention to critical societal concerns that can be addressed in positive and productive ways.

The content framework for the series was one of the most elegantly conceived of any of Sesame Street's international co-productions. Designed to coordinate with Northern Ireland's statutory curriculum, it was organized around two educational strands: the individual and the community (Table 7.2). Messaging for each episode was themed in such a way that curricular domains from the statutory curriculum were represented through a mix of explicit and implicit representations of core messages.

Table 7.3 illustrates the tightness of the content planning. It lists (for the first season of the series, 20 episodes) the content themes (in the first column) and curricular goals (A–I, shown in Table 7.2) presented in a given episode. Thus, for episode 3, for example, which was the episode shown at the program launch (and the one referenced by McGuinness), the overarching theme was "sharing."

TABLE 7.2 Summary of Sesame Tree's educational goals: linkages to the Northern Ireland curriculum

Strand I: Individual *Personal understanding and health*	*Strand II: The community* *Mutual understanding in the local and wider community*
A. Self-awareness	E. Relationships with family and friends
B. Feelings and emotions	F. Responsibility of self and others
C. Love of learning	G. Responding appropriately to conflict situations
D. Health and safety	H. Similarities and differences between groups of people
	I. Learning to live as a member of the community

TABLE 7.3 Sesame Tree Season 1 content plan

Theme	A	B	C	D	E	F	G	H	I	LAF
1. Two birthdays	O	O							●	Halloween in Derry
2. Nest/home	O	O						●	⊗	Traveller child
3. Sharing					O	●	●		O	Quintuplets
4. Tidying up				O		O	●		●	Beach cleaning
5. Perspective/wee minute	O	●		⊗	O	O				Making scones
6. Special clothes				⊗	O			●	●	Orange march
7. Recycling			⊗						●	Really rubbish orchestra
8. Doing hard things		O	●							Irish dancing
9. Eating crisps/health				●						Rural farmers' market
10. Best colour	●		O							Children painting
11. Turn taking					O	●			●	School skipping
12. Languages	O	O		O			●			Nigerian child at Gaelscoil
13. Can't fly/being special	●			⊗			O			Feeding ducks
14. Looking different	O				●		●			Children saying their name
15. Land and sea/diff needs						●	●	O		Seal sanctuary
16. Patience/birthday cake		●				●		⊗		Hurling
17. Potto's fear/preparation		●	●							Anchor boys
18. Honesty		O							O	Football accident
19. Sing/dance/self-express		●			O					Everybody dancing
20. Empathy		●			O	O			O	A hospital appointment

Key:
● = Explicit educational objective
o = Implicit educational objective
⊗ = Implicit LAF educational objective

As indicated in Table 7.3, program content represented four different curricular areas: (E) relationships with family and friends, (F) responsibility of self and others, (G) responding appropriately to conflict situations, and (I) learning to live as a member of the community. Two key aspects of the episode carry much of the curricular load. The Muppet story with the character Potto and Hilda involves a conflict over sharing grapes; the live-action film features a family which includes quintuplets who, while playing in the garden, need to share the play equipment (a sliding board). In this way, the episode presents objectives F and G explicitly through the storyline and action while indirectly touching upon goals E and I.

In devising program content for Sesame Tree, the team was mindful of one of the most interesting implications of the results from research conducted on our projects in Israel and Palestine: it was apparent that children learned the lessons of respect and understanding at the level these lessons were provided. Allegory, while helpful in forwarding generalizable messages, is seemingly a less potent strategy for dealing with deeply rooted bias and prejudice at group level than is explicit messaging about—in this case—Catholics, Protestants, and other groups living in Northern Ireland. Pro-social messages about sharing, cooperation, fairness, and other social relations are core elements of most early childhood education programs and, accordingly, were important components of Northern Ireland's statutory curriculum. Yet, left at this implicit level they only provide learning at that level. This is because children don't necessarily generalize the lessons to the group-level context. The project's Theory of Change which is operationalized in its curricular framework (Walsh and Kehoe, 2007) and related research (Connolly et al., 2008; Larkin et al., 2009a, 2009b) was centered in the stance that extending learning beyond pro-social relations within a child's own group, to that of members of an oppositional group, requires specific and direct introductions to members of the other group.

To provide for this learning, the production included several live-action films that were designed to both engender pride in a child's own culture (by showing familiar life experiences) and respect across group divides (by introducing children to the daily life experiences of people from other cultural groups). (These are denoted in Table 7.3 by ⊗.) One such piece told the story from a child's perspective of participation in an Orange march (an annual commemorative parade with a controversial history in Northern Ireland). The boy watches his brother, a musician, get dressed and otherwise prepare for the event; the boy then views from the sidelines as his brother marches in uniform with others.

Including this segment in the program was seen by some as a bold move on the part of the producers and the broadcaster BBC-Northern Ireland. The parades have, throughout their history, been contentious and seen by some as sectarian and offensive. Yet, as a curricular aspect of the project was engendering mutual respect, the project team felt it was important to introduce Protestant and Catholic children to real aspects of each other's lives. The segment is presented from the perspective of a Protestant child who is participating in a cultural event; it was balanced by pieces such as one showing a young Catholic girl learning Irish dancing, and another piece depicting a hurling match (a team game of Gaelic and Irish origin). The program also endeavored to depict—to the degree possible—Northern Ireland's rich diversity and included stories of children from marginalized groups such as the Roma community, children with disabilities, and children from immigrant groups.

Extending the Sesame Tree Experience: Website and Community Engagement

A website developed and managed by BBC-Northern Ireland extends the learning opportunities with Sesame Tree games and printable activities.[2] The site also provides guidelines for adults and includes a section for teachers that links program content to Northern Ireland curricular goals.

Additionally, the project's partnership with Early Years, Northern Ireland's largest non-government organization working with young children, has, from the beginning extended learning through a robust Sesame Tree program provided in early childhood community centers and, in the initial days of the project, through a partnership with Northern Ireland's library board in government schools.[3] The program includes a training program for practitioners that offers instruction on how to use the Sesame Tree materials to promote social inclusion and other core curricular aims.

As was the case for Rechov Sumsum/Shara'a Simsim, the project's live-action films provide the foundation for much of the mutual respect learning. The program also includes activity cards that offer practitioners practical ways to engage children. A lesson, for example, on "festivals" shows the Muppet character Hilda (an Irish hare) going to a Halloween celebration. After viewing this segment, practitioners use hand puppets to promote discussions with the children about festivals that, in turn, build their understanding of similarities and differences among a variety of communities within Northern Ireland. As explained on the Early Years website:

> "Tom" the persona puppet that represents a little boy from the Catholic Community may talk to the children about going to a "*St Patrick's Day Parade*" and his experiences there. "Jim" the persona puppet that represents a little boy from the Protestant Community may talk to the children about his experiences of going to an Orange Parade. In addition Kim the persona puppet that represents a girl from the Chinese Community may talk to the children about going to the Chinese New Year Parade. This gives the children some insight into a range of festivals and helps them understand the similarities between festivals.[4]

Impact

The Sesame Tree project included an extensive evaluation component that was managed by Paul Connolly at Queen's University Belfast. The pattern of findings that emerged provided evidence that children exposed to the series were more willing to be inclusive of others in general, and more likely to be inclusive of people from different racial backgrounds. They were also more interested in participating in the cultural events associated with their own and other communities (Connolly et al., 2008; Larkin et al., 2009a, 2009b).

Importantly, the findings related to the television program were strongest with respect to Protestant children's willingness to engage with Catholic communities. This kind of differential cross-group impact, which surfaces in several studies not just of Sesame Street but of other social-inclusion programs, is a critical lesson for projects designed to promote respect and understanding. It highlights the need for matching content to the specifics of the participating groups. This aspect also underscores a limit of television in that its broadness of reach makes it difficult to tailor content to specific needs of particular groups and sub-groups. This is where community-outreach initiatives, such as the previously mentioned Early Years program, may make a particularly potent contribution in that their direct contact with children allows for a deeper, more customized approach.

Research hints at this benefit: a study of outreach materials associated with the Sesame Tree program (Larkin et al., 2009b) showed evidence of positive effects (such as increasing some children's willingness to be more inclusive of others and greater interest in the other group's cultural event) that were detected above and beyond the effects the schools would have achieved using their existing curricular materials. Additionally, the advent of web-based, tablet, and other hand-held technologies hold great potential for offering more individualized experiences whose effects have yet to be fully evaluated.

Other Related Initiatives

Sesame Workshop engaged in a handful of non-Sesame Street initiatives that used children's media to promote respect and understanding across group divides. Two were produced in partnership with Search for Common Ground (an organization that partners with people around the world to engender peace through dialogue, media, and community engagement) and one was a multi-country web-based initiative designed as a resource for educators that was completed in partnership with the Merrill Lynch Foundation.

Partnership with Common Ground Production: Nashe Maalo and Gimme6

The Nashe Maalo ("Our Neighborhood") project in Macedonia was successful both in terms of its educational impact and its reach. Designed to promote intercultural understanding, the drama series (whose five seasons began airing in 1998) included a diverse cast of ethnic Macedonian, Albanian, Turkish, and Roma children. Storylines addressed prejudice and stereotypes.

Findings from an initial small-scale study of program effects (Najčevska and Cole, 2000; Shochat, 2001) were supported by a later evaluation (Brusset and Otto, 2004) that found that the show was well known (94% of the children interviewed had heard of it), and while the effects were small, children who watched the series over time learned more concrete information about other ethnic communities and other languages. There was also evidence of their learning alternative conflict-resolution strategies.

A subsequent project, Gimme6, built on the success of Nashe Maalo. It was a curriculum-based drama series broadcast in Cyprus in 2001–2 that aimed to engender respect and understanding in Cypriot youth. To give ethnic Greek, ethnic Turkish Cypriot, and other children from different ethnic backgrounds a reason to be together, the program was set in the UK (featuring ex-patriates) with content that promoted examinations of pre-conceived notions. High-interest storylines focused on music and sports confronted negative biases about

Turkish Cypriot and Greek Cypriot cultures and challenged gender and other stereotypes.

Research (Faiz, 2002; Hypothesis Group, 2002; Spyrou, 2002) comparing attitudes of children who had seen the show and those who had not linked exposure to the series to increased perception of commonality across groups and more positive attitudes about members of the "other" group. The impact of the program, however, was constrained by the limited reach of the series, which was estimated to have been accessed by fewer than 10% of the Greek Cypriot target audience and only about 5% of the Turkish Cypriot community targeted (Sesame Workshop, 2002a). This limit underscores the importance distribution outlets hold in the overall effectiveness of large-scale media projects, an element that can be particularly tricky when working in a region of conflict or post-conflict.

Panwapa

The vision for Sesame Workshop's Panwapa project emerged from a meeting Sesame Workshop conducted in 2002 to launch a global initiative to use media to build respect and understanding among children from all cultures (Sesame Workshop, 2002c). This summit brought together 35 world leaders in broadcasting, production, child development, academia, government, and the private sector to propose action plans around ways to enlist children's media to promote messages of tolerance. Inspired by the discussions and subsequent thinking about ways of making a global impact, Sesame Workshop partnered with the Merrill Lynch Foundation who sponsored a multimedia project aimed at building global citizenship skills and community activism in young children.

Panwapa, as the initiative was later named (from the word in the Tshiluba language meaning "here on this earth") grew from the belief that, just as literacy and numeracy can be taught step by step beginning with basics such as learning to count and familiarity with the alphabet, there are building blocks of good global citizenship that can be taught incrementally. Children can learn values such as fairness, justice, mutual respect, appreciation for diversity, and personal responsibility (Cole, 2008; Cole and Lee, 2013).

At the center of the program was a website produced in five languages (Arabic, English, Japanese, Mandarin, and Spanish) that enabled children to enter a virtual community hosted by Muppet characters who lived on Panwapa (a floating island that traveled the oceans of the world). The program's key curricular messages were presented in games, videos (with engaging stories featuring the Muppet characters), documentary films, and other activities on the site. Print materials offered parents and teachers ways to extend the messages in the classroom and at home.

The initiative also inspired a partnership between Sesame Workshop and the Museo Memoria y Tolerancia (Museum of Memory and Tolerance[5]) in Mexico City. A Panwapa exhibit designed for museum visitors aged four to 12 years provides a themed hour-and-a-half Panwapa experience that reinforces values such as tolerance, teamwork, respect, and diversity. The exhibit receives an average of 60,000 children each year (E. Hernandez, Museo Memoria y Tolerancia staff, email communication, September 8, 2014).

A study of the impact of the program (Fisch et al., 2009) demonstrated that across samples of children from four countries (China, Egypt, Mexico, and the United States) who had been exposed to Panwapa content for four weeks, there was greater growth in understanding of global citizenship than those with no exposure. Furthermore, parents and teachers in all four countries gave the program high ratings for educational value. Additionally, teachers thought that Panwapa was very appealing to children.

Reach estimates in March 2009, 11 months after the program went live, showed that the site had attracted over a half-million unique users and had visitors from 180 countries including speakers of 51 different languages and dialects with visitors, on average, from over 100 countries each month. Due to a lack of funding, however, the program went offline in 2011.

Discussion

Any diplomatic effort starts with a search for common values and views. The magic of using Sesame Street in these contexts is that its commitment to children and building a better future for them serves as a point of agreement that unifies members of opposition groups in a people-to-people effort that research has shown, at least in a small way, has a positive impact.

Beginning with the Rechov Sumsum/Shara'a Simsim project Sesame Workshop took, what might be called, borrowing from the Hebrew word, a "dayenu" approach; roughly translated, the word means "it would have been sufficient." We had developed a cascading hope that each step of the process would lead to an ensuing positive next step. For that initial project our progression went something like this:

- simply getting our partners from oppositional groups to sit around the advisory table was a small victory;
- facilitating our partners' creation of a joint curriculum was another successful step;
- helping them to produce materials and share together their challenges and successes was another step forward;
- having the Palestinians produce segments initially to be placed in the Israeli broadcast on its own was yet another step forward;
- ultimately creating two programs, one Israeli and one Palestinian, led to a third program: a joint co-production between Israelis, Palestinians, and a new partner, Jordanians, all under the Sesame umbrella;
- and finally, all of this led to a sense that emerged from the results of an international seminar on the program's impact (conducted after the early

research was completed). The session was attended by participants from several countries who expressed a sentiment that, if the Palestinians and Israelis could work as they had on Rechov Sumsum/Shara'a Simsim, maybe other groups could too; it could be done elsewhere and should be tried.

Thus, some of the value of these projects lies in the fact that they were done at all. The process of engagement has led to much more than their initial goals and has also prompted us to realize that there is much more to do. In the decades since the Rechov Sumsum/Shara'a Simsim project began in Israel and Palestine we have built a body of knowledge both about how to develop and distribute effective content to promote respect and understanding across group divides and how to study it. On both accounts, though, the field of using media for peace building is still in its nascent stages.

Regarding developing high-impact content, most of what we have learned has come from the trial and error that Sesame Workshop's experimental approach engenders. We know, for example, that to be effective, messaging needs to be simple (although not simplistic), culturally relevant, and engaging for the target age. It needs to engender both pride in a child's own group and that of the other. Particularly for children from the most disenfranchised or marginalized groups, building a positive sense of one's own culture is an important step in gaining a positive vision of others. Additionally, focusing on commonalities is as critical as respecting differences and it's important to balance opportunities for understanding variations with insights into similarities. At the core of successful projects is the sense of our common humanity: we all eat, sleep, and need love, nurturing, and physical exercise. We all have capabilities and disabilities and we all share a world that is inter-related (Cole, 2002).

In terms of our ability to formally study educational impact, we have made some progress toward the challenge of developing valid and reliable measures. (More about that is presented in Chapter 2.) The early days of our research were greatly assisted by the relevant work of Israeli psychologist Bar Tal (1996, 1997; Raviv et al., 1999; Bar-Tal and Teichman, 2005), whose research focused on studying Israeli youth's perceptions of Palestinians. Building on this work and others, an international team of researchers developed the Social Judgment Interview (Fox et al., 1999; Brenick et al., 2007) that was designed to study the moral reasoning of the children in our target audience. This measure and the data we collected using it proved a powerful tool for understanding Israeli and Palestinian children's perceptions of each other. In the context of the Rechov Sumsum/Shara'a Simsim study, it was less effective, however, at gauging the relationship between exposure to our intervention (Sesame Street) and changes in perception.

Connolly et al. (2002) were inspired by this approach in their studies of perceptions of Northern Ireland's children. Their innovative application advanced the research approach both through their study of the Sesame Tree program (Connolly et al., 2008, Larkin et al., 2009a, 2009b) and through evaluations of other media such as an animated series developed by a team in Northern Ireland for the Peace Initiatives Institute (Boulder, Colorado), which included not only television spots but also an extensive community-engagement program (Connolly et al., 2006). They used various research designs including randomized controlled trials (often seen as the gold standard for such research), which had the advantage of isolating effects specifically attributed to the intervention. Yet challenges still remained regarding establishing the amount of exposure (dosage) needed to detect effects; further, questions remain about the strength of the measures we have in detecting small effects, which, admittedly, are more in tune with what can be reasonably expected from such interventions.

Fluent Research (2008) in Kosovo made additional progress using an index created by combining responses to social-inclusion questions to study children's perceptions. This study, like much of Connolly et al.'s work, employed a randomized design that was more robust than that used for Rechov Sumsum/Shara'a Simsim (Cole et al., 2003). But it was not without its limits, with there again being difficulties in measuring naturalistic exposure to Sesame Street and linking that exposure to learning. (See Chapter 2 of this book for a more extensive discussion.)

In addition to the challenges of measuring changes in children's perception, there are even greater challenges in quantifying the impact of the ripples effects of the program. It's simply not possible to discern what can and can't be attributed to the Sesame Street programming, per se. Factors such as international awards, including, in 1998, the Japan Prize Foundation's President's Prize which Rechov Sumsum won for an episode entitled "In Harmony," is one form of broader international recognition. Another window is the imprint these projects make on the journalistic media with various articles and other stories that are accessed by international audiences. The drawing of world figures to these projects, such as Martin McGuinness (Northern Ireland's deputy first minister) at the launch of Sesame Tree both in Season 1 and in Season 2 (where, in the second launch he was joined by first minister Peter Robinson) (BBC News, 2010), is one indicator of the large-scale effect these programs have. Similarly, a symposium at the close of the Rechov Sumsum/Shara'a Simsim project that took place at the American Colony Hotel in Jerusalem in 1999 included Palestinian, Hanan Ashrawi, and Israeli, Yuli Tamir, both well-known actors in the regional political arena.

While we can't draw conclusions about cause and effect, it is perhaps safe to say that these projects, at least in a small way, contribute to a collective lexicon and give children and adults alike a vocabulary for more peaceful engagement. While the fate of the individual projects is uncertain due to their cost, their complexity, and other concerns, their history has provided, in the words of Kofi Annan, "a channel . . . to imagine a world very different from the one we know."

Notes

1. See Chapter 2, for an explanation of Sesame Workshop's Theory of Change for international co-productions and the various levels of engagement.
2. As of this writing the site is live at: http://www.bbc.co.uk/northernireland/schools/sesame/.
3. As of this writing, project materials are available at: http://www.early-years.org/sesame-tree/s1/background.php.
4. See http://www.early-years.org/sesame-tree/s1/resources.php, accessed September 6, 2014.
5. See http://www.myt.org.mx/museoninios.php.

References

Annan, K. (2002). Messages to Sesame Workshop's summit on the use of educational media to promote respect and understanding. In Sesame Workshop (ed.), *Toward a passport to peace: using media to give children a chance: Proceedings from Sesame Workshop's global summit on promoting respect and understanding among children through media* (p. v). New York: Sesame Workshop.

Bar-Tal, D. (1996). Development of social categories in early childhood: The case of "the Arab" concept formation, stereotype and attitudes by Jewish children in Israel. *International Journal of Intercultural Relations*, 20, 341–70.

Bar-Tal, D. (1997). Formation and change of ethnic and national stereotypes: An integrative model. *International Journal of Intercultural Relations*, 21, 491–523.

Bar-Tal, D. and Teichman, Y. (2005). *Stereotypes and prejudice in conflict: Representation of Arabs in Israeli Jewish society*. New York: Cambridge University Press.

BBC News (2010) Ministers meet the Muppets. *BBC News, Northern Ireland*. November 10, 2010, http://www.bbc.co.uk/news/uk-northern-ireland-11727124.

Brenick, A., Lee-Kim, J., Killen, M., Fox, N., Raviv, A., and Leavitt, L. (2007). Social judgments in Israeli and Arabic children: Findings from media-based intervention projects. In D. Lemish and M. Götz (eds), *Children and media in times of war and conflict*. Cresskill, NJ: Hampton Press.

Brusset, E. and Otto, R. (2004). *Evaluation of Nashe Maalo: Design, implementation, and outcomes: Social transformation through the media on behalf of Search for Common Ground*. Ohain: Channel Research, https://www.sfcg.org/wp-content/uploads/2014/08/nash2004.pdf.

Children's Television Workshop (1996) *Rechov Sumsum/Shara'a Simsim statement of educational objectives*. New York: Children's Television Workshop.

Cohen, M. and Francis, V. (1999). *Rechov Sumsum/Shara'a Simsim quantitative report*. New York: Applied Research and Consulting.

Cole, C. (2002). What we know about how the media promote respect and understanding. In Sesame Workshop (ed.), *Toward a passport to peace: Using media to give children a chance: Proceedings from Sesame Workshop's global summit on promoting respect and understanding among children through media* (pp. 51–63). New York: Sesame Workshop.

Cole, C.F. and Lee, J.H. (2013). Using media to foster mutual respect and understanding among children in a post-conflict region: The Rruga Sesam/Ulica Sezam project in Kosovo. In C. Ramirez-Barat (ed.), *Transitional Justice, Culture, and Society*. New York: International Center for Transitional Justice.

Cole, C.F., Richman, B.A., and McCann Brown, S.A., (2001). The world of Sesame Street research. In S. Fisch and R. Truglio (eds), *"G" is for growing: Thirty years of research on children and Sesame Street*. Mahweh, NJ: Lawrence Erlbaum Publishers.

Cole, F.C., Arafat, C., Tidhar, C., Tafesh, W.Z., Fox, N.A., Killen, M. et al. (2003). The educational impact of Rechov Sumsum/Shara'a Simsim: A Sesame Street television series to promote respect and understanding among children living in Israel, the West Bank and Gaza. *International Journal of Behavioral Development*, 27(5), 409–27.

Cole, C.F., Labin, D.L., and Galarza, M.R. (2008). Begin with the children: What research on Sesame Street's international coproductions reveals about using media to promote a new more peaceful world. *International Journal of Behavioral Development*, 32, 359–65.

Connolly, P., Smith, A., and Kelly, B. (2002). *Too young to notice? The cultural and political awareness of 3–6 year olds in Northern Ireland*. Belfast: Northern Ireland Community Relations Council.

Connolly, P., Fitzpatrick, S., Gallagher, T., and Harris, P. (2006). Addressing diversity and inclusion in the early years in conflict-affected societies: A case study of the Media Initiative for Children—Northern Ireland. *International Journal of Early Years Education*, 14(3, October), 263–78, DOI: 10.1080/09669760600880027.

Connolly, P., Kehoe, S., Larkin, E., and Galanouli, D. (2008) *A cluster randomised controlled trial evaluation of the effects of watching Sesame Tree on young children's attitudes and awareness*. Belfast: Centre for Effective Education, Queen's University Belfast.

Faiz, M. (2002). *The Impact of Gimme6: Report of qualitative interviews with Turkish Cypriot Children*. Lefkosa-Kuzey Kibris: Cyprus Social Research and Educational Consultancy Center.

Fisch, S.M. and Oppenheimer, S. (2012a). *Rechov Sumsum Arabic Special: Comprehension, appeal, and identification with characters among Arab children*. Teaneck, NJ: MediaKidz Research and Consulting.

Fisch, S.M. and Oppenheimer, S. (2012b). *Rechov Sumsum experimental study: Learning among Jewish preschoolers in Israel*. Teaneck, NJ: MediaKidz Research and Consulting.

Fisch, S.M., Yeh, H., Zhou, Z., Xu, C.J., Hamed, M., Khadr, Z., Langsten, R., Noriega, G.M., Céspedes, A.H., Druin, A., and Guha, M.L. (2009). *The impact of Panwapa on children's appreciation of global citizenship. Final report: Impact research in China, Egypt, and the United States*. Teaneck, NJ: MediaKidz Research and Consulting.

Fluent Research (2008). *Assessment of educational impact of Rruga Sesam and Ulica Sezam in Kosovo: Report of findings*. New York: Fluent Research.

Fluent Research (2011). *Shara'a Simsim: Assessment of preschool outreach materials*. New York: Fluent Research.

Fox, N.A., Killen, M., and Leavitt, L.A. (1999). *The Social Judgment Interview coding manual*, unpublished manuscript prepared for Children's Television Workshop, New York.

Hypothesis Group (2002). *The Impact of Gimme6: A quantitative analysis of Turkish Cypriot and Greek Cypriot children's reactions to the series*. New York: Hypothesis Group.

Larkin, E., Connolly, P., and Kehoe, S. (2009a) *A longitudinal study of the effects of young children's natural exposure to Sesame Tree on their attitudes and awareness (report 2)*. Belfast: Centre for Effective Education, Queen's University Belfast.

Larkin, E., Connolly, P., and Kehoe, S. (2009b) *A cluster randomised controlled trial evaluation of the effects of the Sesame Tree schools outreach pack on young children's attitudes and awareness (report 3)*. Belfast: Centre for Effective Education, Queen's University Belfast.

Mares, M.L. and Pan, Z. (2013). Effects of Sesame Street: A meta-analysis of children's learning in 15 countries. *Journal of Applied Developmental Psychology*, 34, 140–51, DOI: 10.1016/j.appdev.2013.01.001.

McClements, F. (2008) From Stormont . . . to Sesame Tree. *BBC News*, March 11, 2008, http://news.bbc.co.uk/2/hi/uk_news/northern_ireland/7289716.stm.

MEST and MAFRD (2004). *A strategy for education for rural people in Kosovo (2004–2009).* Pristina: Ministry of Education, Science, and Technology and Ministry of Agriculture, Forestry, and Rural Development, www.fao.org/sd/erp/ERPkosovoenglihs.pdf.

Najčevska, M. and Cole, C.F. (2000). *Lessons from Nashe Maalo: A research report on what ethnic Albanian, Macedonian, Roma and Turkish youth learned from watching Nashe Maalo.* Washington, DC: Search for Common Ground.

Raviv, A., Oppenheimer, L., and Bar-Tal, D. (eds) (1999). *How children understand war and peace: A call for international peace education.* San Francisco, CA: Jossey Bass.

Ross, D. (2002). Speech by Ambassador Dennis Ross, distinguished fellow and counselor, Washington Institute for Near East Policy (May 28, 2002). In Sesame Workshop (ed.), *Toward a passport to peace: Using media to give children a chance: Proceedings from Sesame Workshop's global summit on promoting respect and understanding among children through media* (pp. 65–71). New York: Sesame Workshop.

Schoffman, S. (2000). *Trenches of peace: Reflections on creative difference.* Report to Children's Television Workshop of qualitative interviews regarding Rechov Sumsum/Shara'a Simsim. New York: Sesame Workshop.

Sesame Workshop (2002a). *Impact of Gimme6: Overview, May 2002*, unpublished report. New York: Sesame Workshop.

Sesame Workshop (2002b). *Report of Sesame Workshop's fact-finding trip to Kosovo*, unpublished report. New York: Sesame Workshop.

Sesame Workshop (2002c). *Toward a passport to peace: Using media to give children a chance.* New York: Sesame Workshop.

Shochat, L. (2001). Nashe Maalo: Kids' TV in Macedonia for violence prevention. *TechKnowLogia*, July/August. Knowledge Enterprise, http://www.techknowlogia.org/TKL_Articles/PDF/296.pdf.

Shochat, L. (2001). Nashe Maalo: Kids' TV in Macedonia for violence prevention. *TechKnowLogia*, July/August. Knowledge Enterprise, http://www.techknowlogia.org/TKL_Articles/PDF/296.pdf.

Spyrou, S. (2002). *The impact of Gimme6: Report of qualitative interviews with Greek Cypriot children: Nicosia, May 2002*, unpublished report. New York: Sesame Workshop.

Statistical Office of Kosovo (2001). *Statistics on education in Kosovo: Version 2.* Pristina: Statistical Office of Kosovo, http://esk.rks-gov.net/ENG/publikimet/doc_details/662-statistics-on-education-in-kosovo-2001.

Walsh, G. and Kehoe, S. (2007). *Sesame Tree Northern Ireland educational objectives and links with the early years curricula in Northern Ireland.* New York: Sesame Workshop.

Warshel, Y. (2007). As though there is peace: Opinions of Jewish-Israeli children about watching *Rechov Sumsum/Shara'a Simsim* amidst armed political conflict. In D. Lemish and M. Götz (eds), *Children and Media in Times of Conflict and War* (pp. 309–32). Cresskill, NJ: Hampton Press.

PART III

A Sustainable Future: Community and Partnerships

8

OPENING NEW DOORS

Community Engagement in India

Ameena Batada, Sashwati Banerjee, and Mathangi Subramanian

Something special's going on . . . So come along.
There's a whole new world inside . . . Let's take a ride.
We're heading for a place . . . You'll want to stay.
Ready or not climb aboard . . . We'll be singing all the way!
Galli Galli Sim Sim . . .

These opening lines of the theme song from India's adaptation of Sesame Street—Galli Galli Sim Sim—demonstrate the excitement about more than a children's television show. The lyrics are indicative of the positive momentum of early childhood development and education in India in the mid-2000s, when Galli Galli Sim Sim made its debut. Reaching millions of children annually with educational content, the Galli Galli Sim Sim television show has been, for close to a decade, very successful as one of India's only originally produced early childhood educational programs; additionally, it is Galli Galli Sim Sim's community-based interventions that meet a unique need and opportunity in the Indian context. Focusing on engagement with schools and community partnerships, this chapter describes how a local subsidiary of Sesame Workshop known as Sesame Workshop India (SWI) is inspiring early childhood education in the country through its multi-platform approach that combines education and entertainment.

Early Childhood and Education in India

In India, as in much of the world, child survival rates, prevalence of communicable diseases, opportunities for early childhood education and development, and other indicators of child wellbeing have improved over the past century; however, many Indian children continue to face daily challenges. Nationally, about 59 children of every 1,000 born will die before their fifth birthday as a result of infectious and other diseases, injuries, poisoning, and other causes (Ministry of Statistics and Programme Implementation, 2012). Malnutrition contributes to poor health and development. About 70% of children aged six months to five years suffer from anemia, which can cause impaired cognitive functioning, behavioral and motor development, language development, coordination, and academic performance.

In addition to physical health issues, there is a need to address social issues such as girl-child empowerment and child labor as well as socio-emotional topics such as self-esteem and coping with stress. Although educational approaches are limited in the face of structural challenges such as poor sanitation or lack of access to healthy foods, efforts to offer ways to practice healthy habits within existing systems and when possible, pairing education with interventions to improve access to physical environments and resources, can be effective. As early childhood experts Venita Kaul and Deepa Sankar state in the conclusion to their 2009 report on Early Childhood Care and Education in India, "Given the synergies among health, nutrition and education aspects of development, convergence of initiatives through different sectoral programs, particularly at the ground level, is an important way forward" (p. 42).

The Educational Context

About four in ten children between the ages of two and five years attend pre-primary school in India (UNESCO, 2006).[1] There are about 67,000 pre-primary schools in India, with nearly half of them government-run (*anganwadis*), a quarter run by local organizations, *balwadis*, and the rest private (both subsidized and not subsidized) (Ministry of Statistics and Programme Implementation, 2012). According to the Ministry of Women and Child Development (2013), in 2013 India had 1.4 million *anganwadis* run by the Integrated Child Development Services Scheme (ICDS), half of which provided preschool services to over 35 million children aged three to six years.

Non-formal preschool services at *anganwadis* follow a draft national curriculum that is developmentally appropriate, field-tested, and based on the input of national and international early childhood experts (Ministry of Women and Child Development, 2014). However, due to mismanagement of funds for staff and supplies, inadequate training, and a lack of supervisors with the capacity to monitor and improve pedagogical practices, few states actually administer a high-quality program within their ICDS centers (Sharma et al., 2008; Kaul and Sankar, 2009; Rao, 2010). Even within the states, services remain highly variable due to the fact that *anganwadis* are locally administered, and thus dependent upon the quality of area leaders. Private early childhood education settings, driven by parent demand, are often a downward extension of the primary curriculum. Children as young as two years are taught to count to 1,000 and to recite their varnmala (alphabet), long before these milestones are developmentally appropriate, which may actually be detrimental because the students learn to recite without understanding. Moreover, such instruction potentially takes them away from more productive age-appropriate learning. Indian researchers recognize the need for locally developed quality standards that are realistic but rigorous within the Indian context. Several early childhood education researchers also suggest ways to both evaluate and improve existing systems, both public and private (Sharma et al., 2008; Rao, 2010).

In the last decade, education advocates worked to pass Right to Education (RTE) legislation, which in 2010 mandated free and compulsory education for all children. However, the policy only applies to primary and secondary schools (which children don't typically enter until age six) and experts agree that a national policy on early childhood education is also of critical importance and need. While the Ministry of Women and Child Development, in collaboration with Indian researchers, the government, and multilateral NGOs, published a draft early childhood education policy in 2012, as of this writing the movement to extend RTE to children below the age of six continues.

With increasing value placed on appropriate, high-quality early childhood education in India and international attention to the United Nation's Millennium and Sustainable Development Goals, transnational-level commitments to improve education levels, improve health status, and reduce poverty, there is growing political will and public support for new learning approaches to educate young children (United Nations, 2014).

Opening New Doors: Sesame Workshop India

Sesame Workshop gained an initial presence in India with a new, indigenously created television co-production, Galli Galli Sim Sim (GGSS). Galli Galli Sim Sim began, like other international co-productions of Sesame Street, with a meeting to plan the project's education framework. According to Asha Singh, GGSS's first education content director, advisors from diverse disciplines came together,

> striving to make an idea and an ideal come to life . . . what emerged was a collective resolve to create socio-culturally rooted content appealing to children growing up in the contexts of Indian pluralism—multi-ethnic, multi-lingual, encountering multiple cuisines and cultural forms. The lived experience of plurality and multiplicity, we felt, would be the first steps for the youngest citizens to learn to build bridges playfully through the medium of television.
>
> A. Singh, personal email communication, October 1, 2012

This vision emerged from the potential to reach a large and diverse young Indian population combined with the critical need to re-shape early childhood education in the country, as identified by Indian child development experts. Over 160 million children aged zero to six years live in India (Ministry of Statistics and Programme Implementation, 2012). India also is a diverse country, with hundreds of languages and culturally distinct groups, a vast range of topographic and climactic regions, urban and rural communities, and many religious traditions.

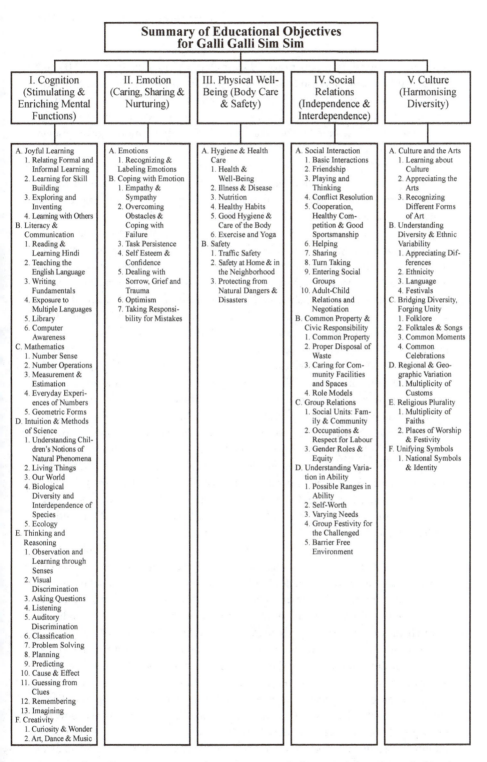

FIGURE 8.1 Galli Galli Sim Sim curriculum: summary of educational domains and objectives

In its early years, the project was managed similarly to that of other Sesame Street international co-productions. With development funding from USAID and ICICI bank, Sesame Workshop partnered with an Indian production company, Miditech, and worked collaboratively to produce the first episodes which were broadcast both by Turner Broadcasting (which provided significant funding for the production phase) and by Doordarshan (DTV), India's national, government-owned broadcaster.

The project's early success led to a desire to ensure its long-term sustainability. Accordingly, Sesame Workshop pursued a new model of on-the-ground management, resulting in the creation of the first-ever, independent Sesame Street entity, known as Sesame Workshop India (SWI). Based on the belief that an initiative in India could be most effective if managed locally, Sesame Workshop India applies a management strategy that leverages the opportunities the contemporary infrastructures in India afford. The set up contributes to more efficient operational structures, greater access to local funding streams, and is more contextually relevant.

As with all Sesame Workshop endeavors, education is at the heart of SWI's work. Its educational framework, which was originally conceived for the GGSS television series in 2005 by Miditech and an Indian educational advisory group, includes five key domains of learning: 1) cognition (stimulating and enriching mental functions; 2) emotion (caring, sharing, and nurturing); 3) physical well-being (body care and safety); 4) social relations (independence and interdependence); and 5) culture (harmonizing diversity). These domains—which support SWI's overall objectives of 1) providing accessible, high-quality educational content to prepare children for school and life, 2) promoting good health, safety, and nutrition habits for a positive impact on child survival, and 3) embracing diversity and inclusion to promote social equality, especially those of gender, caste, color, religion, and disability—are consistent with national and international development milestones, including India's National Early Childhood Education Curriculum Framework (Ministry of Women and Child Development, 2012) and the Millennium and Sustainable Development Goals.

Figure 8.1 provides more detail on how the curriculum was envisioned within each of these domains. As this framework serves as the foundation upon which all educational content developed for SWI is based, the document is a central aspect of SWI's educational achievement. The core strategies of SWI incorporate development of content for children from ages zero to eight years that is grounded in research, distribution through partnerships, and public education and advocacy.

Over the years, Sesame Workshop India has developed entertaining educational content for distribution through three broad approaches: popular media, schools, and community engagement (see Figure 8.2). Popular media include television and radio programs as well as a website and other web- and cell-phone based applications. School initiatives include educational kits for NGOs and government preschools and primary schools, and educator training and support. Community engagement includes mobile community viewing activities in urban areas and community radio and related programming in rural areas.

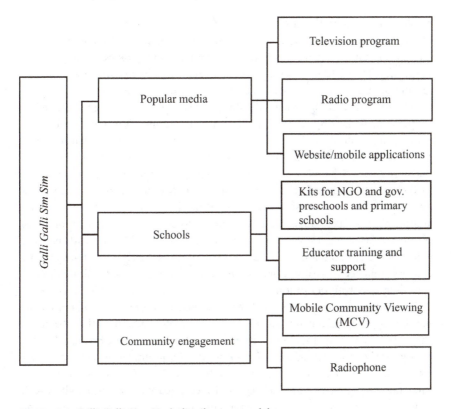

FIGURE 8.2 Galli Galli Sim Sim's distribution model

From Screen to Street: GGSS Community Engagement Takes off on Popular Media

The Galli Galli Sim Sim television program is one of the only contemporary originally produced children's educational shows in India. According to a review of Indian mass media, most of the children's television programs aired in India, including both Indian cartoons and imported programs, display aggression and violence (Wijesundara, 2011). Since few Indian educational television programs exist specifically for younger children, Galli Galli Sim Sim fills a niche among children's media in India.

As with all co-productions of Sesame Street, the setting and characters for Galli Galli Sim Sim were carefully planned to enhance children's overall educational experience. The program takes place on an Indian neighborhood street, or *galli*, so viewers from a variety of locations in India may relate to the characters and their stories. The *galli*, with its variety of homes, a park with a large tree, a basketball court, a garden, nurse's office, and a shop, provides writers a setting in which to set stories that engender naturalistic learning experiences within a range of curricular domains. Healthy lifestyles, such as promoting being physically active and healthy eating, are easily emphasized in stories that take place in the park, the court, the garden, and the nurse's office. Pro-social learning, such as community involvement, communication, social interaction, culture, and the arts flow from activities in the homes, at the park, and in the shop. Thus, just as the setting has been designed to be attractive and engaging, specific educational purposes are integrated into its architecture.

The *galli* has lots of human and Muppet characters who were developed to support curricular objectives. Chamki, the star Muppet, is a five-year-old girl dressed in a school uniform to promote education, particularly among girls. She enjoys karate, traditionally seen as a boy's activity, thus challenging gender stereotypes. Chamki's best friend Googly (named for a well-known move in the popular sport of cricket) is a furry blue Muppet who is enamored of outer space and has a sensitive side. Boombah, the seven-foot tall, lovable pink and purple lion-like Muppet, enjoys dancing to any type of music, promoting physical activity and a love of the arts. Aanchoo, a furry Muppet with hair the colors of the rainbow, is older than the others and has the ability to transport the cast and audience to various places around India, promoting multiculturalism and providing opportunities to learn key educational lessons in a variety of contexts.

The human cast represents the diversity and richness of India itself. For example, the shopkeeper Ahmed Chacha is Muslim and often educates other characters about the customs and foods in his household. There is also the Christian "Doctor Aunty," as she is known in the neighborhood, who promotes gender equity as a woman in a traditionally male profession. In addition, live-action segments feature children, not actors, from all over India, engaged in everyday activities such as visiting their parent at work or preparing and eating a meal, promoting the central focus of cultural diversity. The combination of the characters and segments provides viewers with a rich introduction to the range of personal experiences within India and brings children with different languages, families, and realities into each other's homes and closer together.

Annually, the original show was viewed by over 18 million children and the newer animated series is viewed by over 30 million. While sizable, this is still not the majority of young children in India. With between 47% and 60% of households with televisions in India (Ministry of Home Affairs, 2012; KPMG, 2014), there is potential to reach additional Indian children through other mass media channels. As such, the Sesame Workshop India team developed content for distribution through additional popular media, including radio, websites, and mobile applications. All of these media were originally produced in Hindi, one of the official languages of India.

Modeling the success of Sesame Workshop's Takalani Sesame radio program in South Africa, Sesame Workshop India again broke important ground by producing the first entertaining educational radio show for children in India to use missed call interactive voice response to reach children without access to television. The radio format also is unique—with Grover, a popular Sesame Street character who was adapted to the Indian context—hosting the program and providing humor that resonates with both children and adults. Each episode consists of multiple segments including stories, songs, parenting advice, and interactions. The interactions, which are presented in a call-and-response structure, are particularly popular with children, allowing them to follow along and participate by clapping, naming, stomping, and so forth. Further, the interactions are particularly well suited to the radio format which, unlike television with its visual components, depends solely on auditory novelty to maintain attention. The topics addressed in the radio program span a wide range, fitting under three curricular areas: physical health (e.g., nutrition, physical activity, hygiene, etc.), social health (e.g., sharing, conflict resolution, etc.), and emotional health (e.g., feelings, coping, etc.). As the project evolves, Galli Galli Sim Sim television and radio reach more and more children and families, with additional languages and expanded broadcasting planned.

School Programs

Sesame Workshop India's school programs include educational materials for non-government organization and government preschools and primary schools and educator training and support.

Teaching and Learning Materials

Sesame Workshop India is inspiring many changes in classrooms, communities, and policies through its preschool program. Galli Galli Sim Sim materials, teacher training, and multi-modal activities are transforming how children, parents, and experts think about and conduct early childhood education. What started with the provision of innovative materials to community-based preschools has developed into a set of multi-platform initiatives tailored and distributed to a range of educational and other settings. Though SWI now also franchises its own preschools, this section focuses on support to other providers.

In 2007, Sesame Workshop India began developing educational kits that could be distributed to non-governmental partners running preschools in New Delhi and Mumbai. SWI staff also trained the classroom educators on how to use the materials in the kits. Over the years, the program expanded to over ten cities and states. SWI has partnered with over 50 organizations around the country and with the ICDS in four states (Maharashtra, Rajasthan, Tamil Nadu, and Gujarat) and the Delhi National Capital region.

Each educational kit focuses on a thematic content area and builds developmentally appropriate skills across domains for a range of ages and abilities. In its first five years, Sesame Workshop India developed 14 kits, on topics from personal hygiene to financial literacy, including various learning materials from puzzles to books to sequencing cards. Each kit also includes basic written instructions for activities for use by educators, some who might have limited literacy themselves. The range and number of kits is unprecedented, particularly since the kits are translated into multiple languages (see Table 8.1 for a full list of kit topics).

TABLE 8.1 Preschool educational kits: title, domain(s), learning objectives, and components

Kit	Domain area(S)	Specific concepts/skills	Components
Aanchoo Teaches Letters	Literacy and language	• Vocabulary • Letter sounds • Letter recognition • Sighting words • Phonological awareness • Narrative skills • Constructing short sentences • Print motivation • Print awareness	• Alphabet posters • Alphabet book and guide • Letter and picture cards • Laminated board and double-sided tape
Scribbles to Stories	Cognitive, motor (fine motor)	• Prewriting skills • Expressing emotions • Fine motor skills • Hand–eye coordination • Creativity • Narrative skills	• Storybook 1 • Storybook 2 • Storybook 3 • Chalkboard
Story Pond	Socio-emotional, cognitive, language	• Vocabulary • Narrative skills • Opportunities for self-expression • Creative expression • Turn taking • Relational concepts • Self-confidence	• Floor mat • Caregiver guide

(Continued)

TABLE 8.1 Continued

Kit	Domain area(S)	Specific concepts/skills	Components
All My Friends kit	Socio-emotional, cognitive, language	• Modeling decisions and behaviors around friendship • Resolving conflicts that arise in friendships • Appropriate words to express themselves	• A set of puppet characters (12) • Situation cards (6) • Caregiver guide • Packaging box
Googly's World of Shapes	Cognition and language	• Mathematical skills • Creativity • Hand–eye coordination • Visual discrimination • Narrative skills	• Storybook 1 • Storybook 2 • Shape cut-outs
Numbers Are Everywhere	Mathematics cognition and language	• Number sense • Identifying written numbers • One-to-one correspondence • Number operations like addition and subtraction	• Floor mat • People cards • Instruction cards
Chamki's Wonderful World	Science and cognition	• Various life processes • Concept of metamorphosis • Observational and comparing skills • Properties of living and nonliving objects	• Flash cards • Storybook
Googly's Green Party	Science cognition	• Reasoning and memory skills • Visual discrimination • Skills in problem solving • Observational skills	• Story/activity book • Cut-outs of gardening materials
Animals kit	Science cognition and language	• Wild animals and their habitats • Distinguishing characteristics of wild animals • Logical reasoning	• Flashcards • Storybook • Animal puzzles

(Continued)

Kit	Domain area(S)	Specific concepts/skills	Components
Ready for School kit	Hygiene	• Elements of a healthy morning routine • Various good health practices	• Healthy habits flash cards • Storybook 1 • Storybook 2
Dhamyawad, Shukriya, Thank You	Hygiene	• Discovery of how to take care of their own health • Proper hand washing • Sequencing ability	• Sequencing cards • Poster on hand washing • Flash cards • Caregiver guide
Nutrition kit	Health	• Concept of a balanced meal • Value of regular meals • Three main food groups • Informing that food habits are linked to family, tradition, and culture	• Food flash cards • Nutrition wheel • Nutrition dice • Story accordions
Financial Literacy kit	Math cognition, social relations	• How money is earned, spent, and saved • Coins and notes worth different amounts • Pictorial representations for numbers • Spending decisions • Use of numbers, the context of spending • One-to-one correspondence • Encourage children to save money in safe places	• Storybook • Vendor stands and cards • Coin-counting cards • Savings poster
Human Body kit	Science cognition, health, literacy, and language	• Body part names and locations • Identifying matching shapes (visual discrimination) • Location, basic function, and sound of their heart • Print awareness • Print motivation • Vocabulary • Body movements	• Body reveal flipbook • Body poster • Heart booklets for caregiver and children • Movement floor mat

Galli Galli Sim Sim educational kits are more colorful and fun than the materials typically available in low-resource preschools. As such, they make learning and coming to preschool more fun, and may even increase enrollment and attendance. Furthermore, parents see high-quality materials as a strong incentive to register their children in these centers. Perhaps the most popular GGSS educational kit material is the *Story Pond* floor mat (see Plate 8.1). Made of vinyl and measuring five feet by five feet, this educational innovation is essentially a large mat with an image of a large pond filled with stones, each containing a picture of a person, food, or object. The *Story Pond* may be used for a range of skill-building activities, from basic vocabulary to sentence and eventually story construction. This simple material provides numerous fun activities with groups of children of varying sizes and is a big hit in classrooms. In addition, though the *Story Pond* is intended to increase literacy skills, there are no letters or words on the material, making it both inviting to children and easy to use by educators who themselves have lower written literacy skills. Ease of use and appeal have generated great interest in the *Story Pond* both across India and in other countries. Several other international co-production projects have adapted the concept by changing the icons to reflect culturally relevant images, making the *Story Pond* flexible and useful in different locations. There are now *Story Ponds* in Indonesia and China, a *Story Quilt* in Bangladesh, and a *Story Tree* in Nigeria.

Sesame Workshop India is continually exploring new ways to distribute GGSS content. In 2012, SWI distributed small portable projectors for use in preschool centers accompanied by GGSS print materials. Educators received the projectors pre-loaded with secure digital cards that contain themed audio-visual content from the television program, and which reinforce the contents of the kits that are simultaneously distributed to preschool centers. The projectors enable educators to screen the television program with its powerful and enjoyable messages. These projectors function even in centers where there is limited electricity available as they require a charge similar to mobile phones. With three to four hours of viewing capability from a one-and-a-half-to-two-hour charge, communities find solutions to keep them charged and to rotate them around to centers located close together.

Educator Training and Support

Educator training is an integral part of the educational kit, particularly since the prevailing pedagogy has been primarily didactic in most Indian preschools. Moreover, scholars throughout India recommend teacher training as one of the key ways to improve the pre-primary system (Sharma et al., 2008). Training modules emphasize the importance of child-centered learning and manipulation of materials. In many preschools, materials are so scarce that educators feel that the best way to preserve materials is to prohibit children from holding or playing with them; rather, they opt for showing the materials to the children. Consequently, we learned to include many copies of materials in the kits, and in the training sessions educators have the opportunity to role play and practice ways to engage children with the materials.

While Sesame Workshop India team members have provided training directly to educators, we now engage primarily in a "train-the-trainer" (TOT) model to build capacity with organizations to continue to provide and support this type of training for their educators. The TOT model involves training of supervisors, who oversee the educational activities at several *anganwadis*, so that each supervisor may train many educators (see Figure 8.3). As such, SWI trains supervisors on both how to promote learning with GGSS kit materials and how to conduct a GGSS training

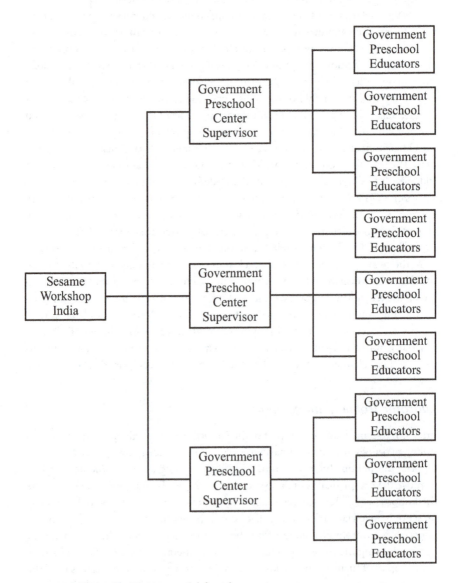

FIGURE 8.3 Train-the-Trainer model for educators

session for educators. Since GGSS educational materials focus on child-centered learning through discovery, the trainings are often fun-filled and different from what educators have experienced during other training programs.

Similar to the use of portable projectors, in 2011–12, Sesame Workshop India piloted an innovative model for educator training and support using cell phones in the large urban center of Mumbai. In conjunction with Awaaz De, an organization that develops and maintains interactive voice response systems, SWI delivered weekly voice messages to educators, describing how to conduct specific educational activities. In addition, we sent out reminder calls and provided an archive that educators could call to listen to previous activity descriptions. We surveyed educators using polls they could follow and complete using their touch-tone phones and we also encouraged participants to call in and leave messages about how the activities were received and pose questions they had related to the materials and/or activities. The GGSS field staff person then responded to questions and shared success stories in the weekly outgoing messages.

The telephone training enhances existing educator training by providing ongoing reminders and support after the initial training. Indeed, one of the challenges with the ICDS is the lack of supervision available to provide consistent monitoring and professional development support of non-formal preschool activities (Gragnolati et al., 2005). Cell phones help address this challenge. The approach also provides educators a network and way to connect with other educators, especially when they hear their colleagues' success stories broadcast each week. Without this approach, it would be very costly to provide ongoing support to large school districts with thousands of educators.

Community Engagement

In addition to the work in schools, Sesame Workshop India engages extensively with communities in non-educational settings. Sesame Workshop India's community-engagement activities include mobile community viewing (MCV) in urban areas and a radiophone program in rural areas.

Mobile Community Viewing Program

The MCV program brought Galli Galli Sim Sim to the *gallis* (streets) of India. Nearly a third of India's population lives in urban areas (Ministry of Home Affairs, 2012) and many of those areas are so densely populated that it is too difficult to drive a car down the narrow streets. The MCV was originally designed to promote the GGSS television show but, over time, Sesame Workshop expanded the objectives of this popular program to include preschool enrollment, good nutrition, and healthy hygiene practices.

The MCV intervention involves a partnership between SWI and Banglanatak, a community theater organization. Banglanatak trains and employs local performers to be part of its troop, which rolls vegetable carts fitted with televisions and

DVD players into urban neighborhoods. Once a crowd gathers, the troop screens a 20-minute thematic compilation of GGSS video segments and then leads playful activities that engage audience members and reinforce the messages in the episodes. The troop also distributes printed educational activity or recipe booklets or calendars related to the program's topic. Each troop with an outfitted vegetable cart can hold eight to 12 screenings in a day, sometimes just blocks from each other. MCV interventions included one or sometimes two screenings in one location, with weeks between the screenings and each focused on a different topic.

Though now only implemented occasionally, in its first five years, the MCV program was implemented in a total of eight cities around India and reached over a million children and their caregivers, based on SWI program records. The MCV program was extremely popular, with crowds of sometimes more than 100 children and adults gathering to watch together. The combination of the communal viewing, the interactive games, and the take-home materials provides participants with a multi-sensory and extended intervention that was cost-effective; according to SWI's estimates, the MCV costs about 11 cents per person per screening. And, whether it was to increase viewership of the television show, to demonstrate increased awareness of the importance of preschool, to recall ways to incorporate more iron- or calcium-rich foods into daily dishes, or to remember the steps of the proper hand-washing technique, the intervention had an impact on the short-term participant knowledge (BGM Policy Innovations, 2011a).

The GGSS MCV and preschool programs have grown quickly and in innovative directions in terms of content and distribution. The content, though primarily focused on improving cognitive skills, also focuses on the important dimensions of physical, social, and emotional health and wellbeing. The materials themselves are durable, withstanding exposure to monsoon rains, as well as fine dry dust, both common in preschool centers. The distribution of materials began in coordination with small NGOs and has expanded to government partnerships with thousands of centers. With increasing size has come new challenges to train educators, and SWI has met those challenges with telephone-based instruction and support. Through the outreach activities, both the program and the messages of Galli Galli Sim Sim have become better known in many communities and highlight the value that GGSS has to children and their caregivers.

Radiophone Program

In 2010, after producing 30 radio episodes focused on promoting healthy habits for life and airing episodes in 11 Hindi-speaking cities with over 22 million listeners, Sesame Workshop India began work on a new model of community radio. The radiophone program brings together mass media, which by nature is more general in its approach, and community radio, which is inherently localized by nature. The pilot project involved *Gurgaon ki Awaaz*, a community radio station in Gurgaon, just south of Delhi, and was supported by Qualcomm. The Gurgaon project has become a model for nine additional sites, where a similar approach is utilized in rural communities with a multi-platform, early childhood education experience using Galli Galli Sim Sim.

The full program includes the production and airing of radio content featuring Galli Galli Sim Sim episodes, as well as classroom-based materials and educator training, a digital application (described below) and community advocacy. The program is innovative in that it combines pre-produced radio content (the episodes) with live radio host commentary, as well as on-location activities that supported the content in the episodes. The radiophone program also utilizes the Gramin Radio Inter-Networking System, developed by an organization called Gramvaani, which allows the server to call back numbers with an interactive voice response system menu where children and parents can listen to the full episode, segment, songs, and even leave their suggestions and feedback. Thus far, the radiophone project has reached an estimated 1.4 million community members and has provided a community platform for the discussion of and advocacy around important and timely local issues. The radiophone program provides listeners with the opportunity to connect the messages of girls' and child rights, nutrition, hygiene, and education, among others, with resources offered in their own communities, and to advocate for additional resources with other community members and decision makers.

Digital Applications

Across popular media, schools, and community-engagement distribution platforms, GGSS continues to innovate in the areas of technology and preschool education. The rapidly growing digital presence in India provides an opportunity. Mobile and digital frontiers are expanding rapidly in India. About 59% of the population had cell phones in 2011 (Ministry of Home Affairs, 2012). Overall, mass media, cell phones, and other digital technogologies carry great promise as vehicles for social and educational messages, particularly for children, where there has been a limited amount of developmentally appropriate material. In addition, the radiophone project supported by Qualcomm, the Echnida Foundation and HSBC included a pilot that utilized video and radio segments and books in a mobile application. The MetLife Foundation supported content distribution through low-cost tablet platforms, and Qualcomm supported the development of ten literacy and numeracy games that are available on Google Apps and as HTML on the Galli Galli Sim Sim website. Sesame Workshop India's digital exploration is rapidly expanding with more and more ways to match technology with sound pedagogy.

Galli Galli Sim Sim's Impact

Commissioned research demonstrates multiple levels of impact of Galli Galli Sim Sim interventions, for children, caregivers, and communities. Researchers have documented the positive effects of the project in its many manifestations, including television, radio, school-based projects, and community-engagement initiatives.

Impact on Children

The research on Galli Galli Sim Sim's impact on children supports most strongly the intervention's impact on children's school readiness, literacy-related knowledge and skills, and health knowledge.

School Readiness and Literacy

School readiness is an important outcome of preschool and a predictor of success in primary school. In India, the World Bank developed and piloted a School Readiness Instrument (SRI), which includes a child assessment (World Bank, 2009). A 2010–11 intervention study in Mumbai assessed the level of children's readiness for school at age 4.5 years and using the SRI. Study findings suggest that the percentage of children who met the benchmark of 80% correct on the tool increased two-fold among children attending *balwadi* and *anganwadi* centers participating in the multi-pronged Galli Galli Sim Sim program versus children at centers who did not participate in the program (BGM Policy Innovations, 2011a).

Studies also indicate that GGSS has an impact on children's literacy levels. In a multi-year study of the impact of the GGSS television program, exposure to the program was associated with improved Hindi literacy skills, including recognizing and identifying letters and words and naming pictures, providing children with a head start in understanding and communicating within the world around them, among children living in non-Hindi-speaking households (GVT, 2009). In addition, the same study indicates that in small towns, three- and four-year-old GGSS viewers showed the greatest gains in literacy: four year olds with some exposure to the show experienced an increase in Hindi literacy knowledge twice that of children not exposed to the show. Watching GGSS also was correlated with improved visual discrimination among children living in low socio-economic classes (GVT, 2009). Another important aspect of literacy is narrative skill, which was assessed in a 2009 study of children in the *balwadi* program. In the study, one third of children in centers using the Story Pond were able to narrate at least one idea in a story about an event in their lives, compared to only one fifth of children in other centers (PrismWorld, 2009).

The 2011 primary school pilot project study also indicated that children who participated in the intervention were more likely to improve on key literacy skills, including print concepts, recognition of words in print, and emergent and early reading skills (Sambhu Singh Rathi, 2012). Research from the radiophone evaluation study also indicates that children exposed to the intervention demonstrated greater improvements in vocabulary and storytelling than those not exposed to the intervention (Ideosync, 2013).

Health Knowledge

Increasing nutrition and hygiene knowledge also are objectives of several GGSS interventions, with positive impact on children. For example, children in Mumbai where the mobile community viewing activities were conducted showed an increase in the average score on an assessment of good nutrition four times greater than among children living in the control area (BGM Policy Innovations, 2010). In the same study, the average number of correct responses on an assessment of children's knowledge of foods made from milk increased nearly twice as much among children in Mumbai slum areas, where MCV activities were conducted, compared to children living in the studies' control area (BGM Policy Innovations, 2010).

In addition, after a Healthy Habits for Life intervention in Jaipur, Rajasthan, children and parents in the treatment community showed greater improvements in their hand-washing knowledge and reported behaviors over the course of the intervention compared to those in the control community. Twice as many children in the treatment community were able to correctly sequence hand-washing steps and correctly identify soap as necessary for washing hands, catching up to children in the control slum, where the level of knowledge was higher at the beginning (BGM Policy Innovations, 2011b).

Results from the radiophone evaluation study also indicate that children exposed to the intervention were more likely to make gains in physical health (nutrition knowledge and hygiene habits), social health (sharing, gender equality, friendship, culture and diversity, and conflict resolution), and emotional health (task persistence and self-esteem), compared to children who were not exposed to the intervention (Ideosync, 2013). Figure 8.4 illustrates the health impact of the radiophone program, as well as the impact on other domains, for children exposed to the program (treatment) compared to children in communities who were not exposed to the program (control). These findings demonstrate the multi-layered influence of Galli Galli Sim Sim in the lives of children.

Impact on Caregivers

The impact of GGSS interventions on caregivers in the home is most evident in the areas of early childhood education advocacy and support. For example, in Delhi and Mumbai, where MCV messaging for caregivers focused on advocacy for early childhood care and education, caregivers exposed to the MCV showed significant gains in their attitudes towards progressive versus didactic pedagogy (GfK Mode, 2009). Similarly, in a study in Mumbai, parents whose children attended *anganwadis*, where GGSS materials were used, were more likely

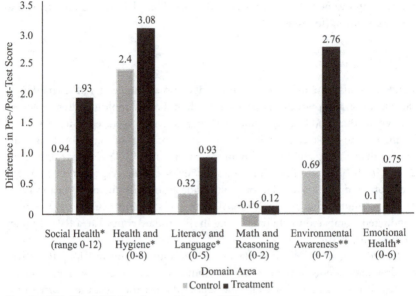

Note:*p<0.01, **p<0.001 Data Source: Ideosync, 2013

FIGURE 8.4 Radiophone project: average differences in pre-/post-test scores for treatment (n=59) and control (n=50) groups

to provide more educational and developmentally appropriate toys in the home than caregivers whose children attended *anganwadis* without GGSS materials. Additionally, parents who participated in the interventions showed greater gains in positive attitudes toward early childhood education (BGM Policy Innovations, 2011b). The many interventions involving educators also strive to promote more child-centered teaching techniques, and intervention research suggests that GGSS-trained educators do report more progressive attitudes and practices (BGM Policy Innovations, 2011a).

Impact on Communities and Systems

Although several GGSS interventions have likely influenced communities, the radiophone project has among its objectives to increase program-related community activities and outcomes and, consequently, research-evaluating program effects specifically examined this level of impact. In a 2012–13 evaluation study, researchers found that there were 60 community events held over the intervention period, on issues such as water conservation, girls' education, traffic rules, trash disposal, and many more, held across ten communities as part of the radiophone project. Findings from the qualitative portion of the study suggest changes in the communities as well, including stories of increased immunization, spending more time with children, appreciating the arts, developing better waste-management systems, using soap, saving money, and going to school. Even though Galli Galli Sim Sim is primarily intended to promote early childhood education, these secondary outcomes of the community radio programs help to improve social conditions and the contexts for educating young children. In one year, the program received over 70,000 calls about programming and community issues, and many of the calls came from women and children, suggesting a shift in the traditional roles related to community radio (Ideosync, 2013).

Sesame Workshop India mobile-based interventions have also strengthened ICDS, most notably through the implementation of an innovative program in the Surendranagar district in Gujarat. In this program, Sesame Workshop India provided training and materials to 150 *anganwadi* workers and an average of seven supervisors in Halvad and Dhangadhra blocks. During implementation, SWI monitored workers through weekly mobile phone calls, and created a helpline in which workers could phone in questions and receive timely responses designed to support improved pedagogy and practice. Qualitative evidence indicates that the use of mobile phones for monitoring improved quality of instruction helped workers feel empowered and motivated to improve their teaching, and provided a replicable and scalable model that would be useful in other ICDS areas throughout the country (Subramanian, 2014). This intervention is an example of how SWI's pioneering approaches led to an efficient and effective way to improve classroom practices in a rural area where prohibitive distances and a lack of staffing have made monitoring difficult in the past.

Data and findings on SWI's process, reach, and impact come from internal documentation, television and other media ratings, and external research. Specifically to measure impact, SWI commissions third-party research to understand the effect of programming on knowledge, attitudes, and skills of child participants, educators, and caregivers. Most studies assess the objective changes in populations exposed to a Galli Galli Sim Sim intervention (treatment group), against a similar but unexposed (control) group. However, some studies involve the collection of perceptions about the media and its effect. Working with external researchers has been a learning process in India. Most research firms focus either on marketing research or on social science research, and a limited number have experience conducting developmentally appropriate research with young children. SWI often educates research firms about our approach and appropriate measures and field techniques prior to conducting the research. In addition, the realities of intervention research in India pose challenges. Multiple factors, including inclement weather, changes in governmental structures and officials, outbreaks of communicable diseases, and extended closings of schools and other offices for holidays, are just some of the factors that contribute to unforeseen changes in interventions and challenges to research design and data collection. As a result, it can sometimes be difficult to understand fully the contribution of SWI interventions to learning and other outcomes among audiences.

Beyond individual-level change, an important goal and role of Sesame Workshop India has been to contribute to two paradigm shifts: first, the shift towards recognizing the period of early childhood as an essential developmental period during which children benefit greatly from receiving a developmentally appropriate education, and second, the shift from mostly didactic to child-centered joyful learning in early childhood. It is our belief that these paradigm shifts will take place through policy change as a result of advocacy and public awareness. To this end, Sesame Workshop India has been involved in major national and international discourse on early childhood, with organizations such as the World Conference on Early Childhood Care and Education and the India-based Center for Early Childhood, Education, and Development.

Sesame Workshop India team members also have published articles in national, regional, and international publications, such as *Navtika* (journal of early childhood in India), *ARNEC Connections* (of the Asia-Pacific Regional Network for Early Childhood), and *Young Child* (of the US-based National Association for the Education of Young Children) and presented at many national and international conferences, such as the International Communication Association meeting in Singapore and Boston, the ARNEC meeting in Dhaka, and the Designing for Children meeting in Mumbai. Sesame Workshop India increases the organization's reach to systems-level decision makers, who in turn hear about the on-the-ground success of a newer paradigm of early childhood education.

Through Sesame Workshop's network, SWI has also been able to extend its impact internationally. The Indian team is an invaluable resource for co-productions in other countries in the global south facing similar challenges, including populations of children and caregivers that were linguistically, religiously, and ethnically diverse. These audiences also often lack access to basic amenities such as power and television sets, both of which are necessary for televised distribution. Schools have huge class sizes but few facilities. Members of SWI travel to countries such as Nigeria, Saudi Arabia (to meet the Afghanistan team), and Bangladesh to help advise local teams. Outreach programs in Jordan, Indonesia, Spain, and other countries adapt Indian materials for use in their own programs as well.

Conclusion

Building on the success of the Galli Galli Sim Sim television program, SWI's school- and community-based activities leverage popular media, inspiring a wave of positive change in early childhood education in communities around the country. Recognizing the limitations of solely television's impact in diverse communities around India, community-engagement activities were part of SWI's plan from the beginning, and the Galli Galli Sim Sim school-based and mobile community viewing approaches have grown and been re-defined and re-imagined in exciting and innovative ways over the years. SWI is taking advantage of the digital revolution that is connecting people even in remote areas through the successful radiophone project and offering high-quality preschool education materials and training for large numbers of children and their caregivers through partnerships with the Indian government. SWI's approaches have inspired not only individual- and community-level changes but system changes as well, through its role as an advocate for a child-centered approach to early childhood education around the country. In a country with a rich and diverse set of cultures, languages, landscapes, and experiences, as well as a host of health, educational, and social challenges and opportunities, Galli Galli Sim Sim has become a household name, bringing laughter and learning into the lives of children and their families throughout India.

Notes

1. In India, preschools are usually referred to as pre-primary schools. They are called *bal-wadis* if they are run by non-governmental organizations (NGO) or *anganwadis* if they are run by the government's Ministry for Women and Children.
2. This figure is based on a combination of data and age projections from Television Audience Measurement (TAM), the 2011 census, and a multi-country study commissioned by Sesame Workshop.

References

BGM Policy Innovations (2010). *An evaluation of the educational impact of Galli Galli Sim Sim mobile community viewing in Mumbai.* Hyderabad: PI.

BGM Policy Innovations (2011a). *An evaluation of the educational impact of Galli Galli Sim Sim anganwadi intervention in Mumbai.* Hyderabad: PI.

BGM Policy Innovations (2011b). *An evaluation of the educational impact of Galli Galli Sim Sim mobile community viewing in Jaipur Rajasthan.* Hyderabad: PI.

GfK Mode (2009). *Evaluation of mobile community viewing reach: Final report.* New Delhi: GfK Mode.

Gragnolati, M., Shekar M., Das Gupta M., Bredenkamp C., and Yi-Kyoung L. (2005). *India's undernourished children: A call for reform and action.* New Delhi: World Bank.

GVT (2009). *The reach and impact of Galli Galli Sim Sim television show in India: Endline report of a naturalistic longitudinal study.* Hyderabad: Gyan Vriksh Technologies.

Ideosync (2013). *The impact of Galli Galli Sim Sim's radiophone project.* New Delhi: Ideosync.

Kaul, V. and Sankar, D. (2009). *Early childhood care and education in India: Education for all—mid decade assessment.* New Delhi: National University of Educational Planning and Administration, http://www.educationforallinindia.com/early-childhood-care-and-education-in-india-1.pdf.

KPMG (2014). *The stage is set: FICCI-KPMG Indian media and entertainment industry report 2014.* Mumbai: KPMG, https://www.kpmg.com/IN/en/Topics/FICCI-Frames/

Documents/FICCI-Frames-2014-The-stage-is-set-Report-2014.pdf, accessed January 29, 2015.

Ministry of Home Affairs (2012). *Houses, household amenities and assets: 2011*. Delhi: Government of India, http://www.censusindia.gov.in/2011census/hlo/Data_sheet/India/HLO_Indicators.pdf, accessed January 29, 2015.

Ministry of Statistics and Programme Implementation (2012). *Children in India 2012: A statistical appraisal*. Delhi: Government of India, http://mospi.nic.in/mospi_new/upload/Children_in_India_2012.pdf, accessed May 10, 2013.

Ministry of Women and Child Development (2012). *Early childhood education curriculum framework (draft)*. New Delhi: Government of India.

Ministry of Women and Child Development (2013). *Status report of the ICDS*. New Delhi: Government of India.

Ministry of Women and Child Development (2014). *Annual Report 2012–2013*. New Delhi: Government of India.

PrismWorld (2009). *Longitudinal education impact survey: Balwadi outreach*. Delhi: PrismWorld.

Rao, N. (2010). Preschool quality and the development of children from economically disadvantaged families in India. *Early Education and Development*, 21(2), 167–85.

Sambhu Singh Rathi (2012). *Galli Galli Sim Sim primary intervention study: Final report*. New Delhi: Sambhu Singh Rathi.

Sharma, A., Sen, R., and Gulati, R. (2008). Early childhood development policy and programming in India: Critical issues. *International Journal of Early Childhood*, 40(20), 65–83.

Subramanian, M. (2014). *Integrating multi-media to strengthen partnerships/system in ICDS Gujarat*. New Delhi: Sesame Workshop India, unpublished report.

UNESCO (2006). *Strong foundations: Early childhood care and education*. Paris: UNESCO, http://www.unesco.org/education/GMR/2007/Full_report.pdf, accessed May 17, 2013.

United Nations (2014). *We can end poverty: Millennium Development Goals and beyond 2015*, http://www.un.org/millenniumgoals/.

Wijesundara, T. (2011). Indian mass media: A sociological analysis. *International Journal of Communicology*, 1(1): 20–30.

World Bank (2009). *Early childhood education: Program evaluation package*. New Delhi: World Bank in India.

9

BUILDING RELEVANCE AND IMPACT

Lessons of Sustainability from Plaza Sésamo in Mexico and Beyond

Jorge Baxter

With over 43 years in Latin America, Plaza Sésamo, a Spanish-language version of Sesame Street, continues to delight, engage, and educate millions of children throughout the region.[1] Plaza Sésamo reaches approximately 15 million children a week through cable, private, and public television in countries such as Mexico, Colombia, Argentina, Chile, and many more (Radius Global, 2013). Plaza's vibrant and popular characters, fun approach to learning, educationally rich and culturally relevant content, ongoing research, and partnership model are all key ingredients in one of the longest and most successful experiments in children's television.

Plaza touchpoints include television, digital platforms, social media, community engagement, consumer products, and themed entertainment (amusement parks, live shows, and museums). Plaza program content is co-designed and distributed by a variety of public and private partners throughout the region including government ministries, local non-profit and foundation organizations, and through private-sector channels.

Today, the children's media space in Latin America is flooded with hundreds of programs, many produced outside of the region and with little or no educational value. Most of these are backed by large marketing campaigns that target young children and their families. They become popular fast and disappear just as fast. Very few transition from a media property into a recognizable brand. So how does one educational television program, backed by a non-profit organization, with no direct marketing to children, survive and remain relevant in an increasingly competitive commercial marketplace? Where, from whom, and how does it get the support it needs year after year to carry out its mission to use media to help children reach their highest potential?

Plaza Sésamo faces more challenges today than it ever has. Some of these challenges are internal and organizational, dealing with the need to balance Plaza's heritage and core values with the need to promote new ideas and innovation; others are external, dealing with the need to revitalize a 40-year-old brand in an increasingly crowded marketplace by connecting with new generations across diverse markets and educational contexts.

Despite these challenges, Plaza remains a strong and viable brand in the Sesame Workshop global portfolio. This chapter examines Plaza from a historical perspective identifying key milestones in the brand's development and exploring issues related to sustainability, including funding, impact, relevance, and brand management. The analysis incorporates views from stakeholder interviews conducted both within and outside of the organization as well as market and research studies conducted over the last decade. It offers a model of engagement that has valuable implications for building business strategies for lasting impact in other contexts.

Plaza Sésamo Milestones

Over the past 43 years Plaza Sésamo has undergone significant changes in content, format, and delivery. These changes are situated within broader societal and technological changes. The section below identifies key milestones. These are related to important shifts in Plaza's business model over the course of its history (see Figure 9.1). In its earliest phase, the model primarily focused on TV production

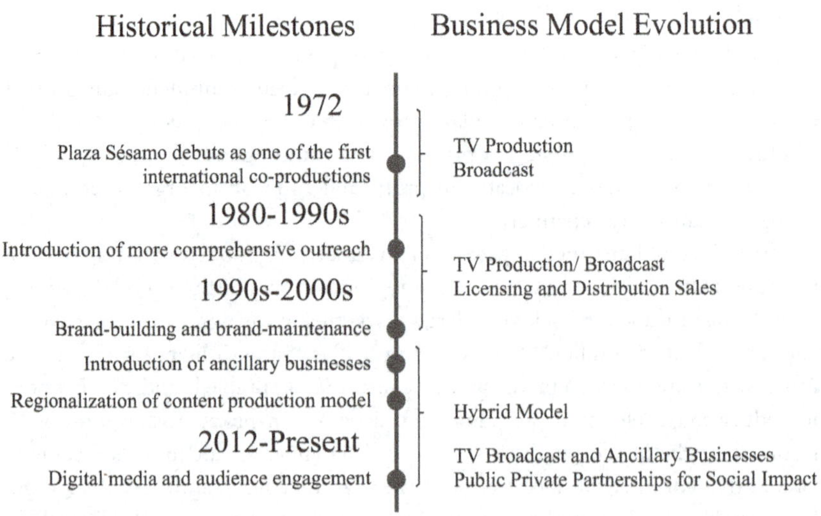

Historical Milestones   **Business Model Evolution**

1972

Plaza Sésamo debuts as one of the first international co-productions

TV Production
Broadcast

1980-1990s

Introduction of more comprehensive outreach

1990s-2000s

Brand-building and brand-maintenance

TV Production/ Broadcast
Licensing and Distribution Sales

Introduction of ancillary businesses

Regionalization of content production model

Hybrid Model

2012-Present

Digital media and audience engagement

TV Broadcast and Ancillary Businesses
Public Private Partnerships for Social Impact

FIGURE 9.1 Historical milestones and business model evolution

and broadcast. It evolved to include licensing and distribution sales, and emerged in its current form as a complex social impact and commercial enterprise.

Milestone 1: Plaza Sésamo Debuts

Plaza Sésamo first came to Mexico through a fortuitous combination of individual entrepreneurship and alignment of macro political and business conditions. In the early 1970s, the Workshop hired Norton Wright to manage the newly formed International Division. Wright and Edward Palmer, vice president of research at the time, traveled to various countries in Latin America (Brazil, Argentina, Colombia, Mexico, and Venezuela) to explore a possible co-production. The Workshop settled on Mexico given its production capacity, television landscape, proximity to New York, and local interest from Mexican producers (Mayo et al., 1984). On the Mexico side, well-established Mexican television producers named Manuel Barbachano Ponce and John Page approached the Workshop during this same time with the idea of bringing Sesame Street to the newly formed Televisa channel. Televisa, founded by the Azcarraga family, was formed in 1973 when Telesistema Mexicano merged with Televisión Independiente of Mexico (Barrera, n.d.). During this same time, the president of Mexico, Luis Echeverria, and other public officials were strongly criticizing private television's content and advertising. Producing Plaza Sésamo was a way for Televisa to respond to these critiques given its educational and cultural approach (P. Arriaga, personal communication, July 23, 2014) (Mayo et al., 1984).

Plaza was first introduced to Mexican and Latin American audiences in 1972. Televisa, Xerox, and Sesame Workshop (or Children's Television Workshop as it was called at the time) produced and funded the first two seasons (1972 and 1974). The show integrated familiar elements from Sesame Street including Muppets, an educational curriculum, a colorful set, animations, live-action films, and production process that included formative research. To kick off the production cycle Sesame Workshop and its partners organized the very first Plaza Sésamo content seminar in Caracas, Venezuela. The meeting included participation from creative producers, writers, media, and education experts from around the region and a select group of Sesame Street (New York-based) staff including producers and educators. They developed an educational plan or curriculum for the series that addressed the critical needs of all Latin American preschool-aged children. The first curriculum focused on early literacy and numeracy goals. Season 1 introduced local Muppets Abelardo (an ingenious, soft-spoken orange and yellow crocodile) and Paco (a grumpy bird), joined by a human cast.

The show's first two seasons were well received by the general public in Mexico with its premiere reportedly achieving the highest audience share of any television program broadcast in the country (Gettas, 1990, 58). Some intellectuals on the left critiqued the show as a form of cultural imperialism and as a "gringo import." This critique would come up again and again over the years in content seminars and elsewhere regardless of the fact that Plaza is designed and produced with local institutions and creative teams (Lesser, 1983). Despite the excellent ratings during the two first seasons, high production costs (1.6 million USD for two seasons) and lack of donor funding for Season 3 led to an almost ten-year period without new production (Gettas, 1994; M. Lambert, personal communication, June 5, 2014). Re-runs of the first two seasons continued throughout this ten-year period, helping to retain the show's reputation.

In 1983, Plaza Sésamo revamped the third season to create a show that appealed to markets across Latin America with a special emphasis on Argentina. Televisa, Coca Cola, and the Children's Television Workshop were some of the partners. They held a content seminar to kick off the season in Manzanillo, Mexico in May 1982. It included participants from ministries of education from Costa Rica, Venezuela, Colombia, Brazil, and Mexico. The educational curriculum maintained a strong focus on literacy and numeracy but expanded to include social, cultural, and emotional goals. They organized a second seminar in Argentina several months later to include Argentine educators who were not able to attend the first seminar because it coincided with the Falkland Islands War. The Argentine meeting included participation from the country's Ministry of Education, Ministry of Technology, and the Ministry of Foreign Affairs as well as many distinguished educators from around the country (Lesser, 1982b).

The third season introduced new Muppet characters including Serapio Montoya (a cousin of Big Bird with green and red feathers; later re-named Abelardo and replacing the previous crocodile version of Abelardo) and Bodoque (a cousin of Oscar the Grouch). Two child actors joined the cast as did guests from Argentina, Venezuela, Chile, and Mexico. Televisa produced 103 episodes that were broadcast throughout Latin America. The show included over 100 live-action films shot in different locations in Mexico, Peru, Colombia, Argentina, and Venezuela. The regional cast combined with live-action films from various countries in Latin America presented audiences with one of the first truly "pan-regional programs" (Lesser, 1982a).

When Plaza first premiered, there was nothing like it on television in Latin America. Its integration of both formative and impact research was one of its unique aspects. No other children's show at the time used research to measure its impact on engagement and learning (Lambert, personal correspondence, June 5, 2014). In Mexico, Diaz-Guerrero and Holtzman (1974) conducted an experimental study with a sample of 221 randomly assigned three-, four-, and five-year-olds in rural and urban environments. Children who regularly viewed the show performed better than non-viewing peers on a general test of knowledge of numbers, letters, and words. Another study by Diaz-Guerrero et al. (1974) did not show conclusive results, perhaps due to methodological issues that did not account for levels of exposure in control groups given the broad reach of Plaza Sésamo (Cole et al., 2001).

Over time, the show became an important reference point for educators and producers in the region known for its innovative model that combined entertainment, education, and research. By the early 1980s, Plaza had inspired several imitations throughout the region (M. Manrique, personal correspondence, May 23, 2014).

Milestone 2: Comprehensive Educational Outreach

Similar to Sesame Street, Plaza has always had a "whole-child" curriculum addressing the intellectual, social, physical, and emotional development and wellbeing of the child. As in the US, a local board of educational advisors from Mexico and later from all around Latin America developed a curriculum for the program that aligned with the needs and pedagogical practices in Latin America. The resulting educational framework differed from the US curriculum in important ways: it included, for example, greater emphasis on critical thinking; additionally, literacy was taught with a more contextual approach that stressed whole words, phrases, and sentences rather than individual letters. Like Sesame Street, each season focused on a new theme, backed by an updated curriculum that local educators, media experts, and producers developed. Each new season's theme, aimed at addressing the broader concerns of educators, parents, and society, helped Plaza tell a new story and remain relevant (see Table 9.1).

By Season 4, it became evident that to tackle these issues in a deeper way, Plaza would have to go beyond television and into communities through more comprehensive outreach. In the early 1990s, the Plaza team joined forces with UNICEF to evaluate the potential benefits of using Plaza Sésamo video content as a resource for early childhood classrooms. UNICEF provided a 1 million

TABLE 9.1 Plaza Sésamo Themes

Year	Season	Number of episodes	Theme
1972	1	130	Basic academic and social skills
1973	2	130	Basic academic and social skills
1983	3	130	Basic academic and social skills
1995	4	130	Health, hygiene, nutrition, and safety
1997	5	65	Ecology and the environment
1999	6	65	Literacy
2000	7	65	Human diversity
2001	8	65	Gender equity
2005	9	65	Basic academic and life skills
2006	10	65	Latin American diversity and health
2008	11	65	Latin American diversity
2009	12	52	Ecology and the environment
2010	13	52	Conflict resolution and social relations
2011	14	52	Latin American diversity (cultural, bio, etc.)

dollar grant for Plaza Sésamo research and outreach (M. Manrique, personal correspondence, August 9, 2014). Coca Cola rounded out the partnership. To support research for Season 4 and promote outreach throughout the region, UNICEF organized a series of sub-regional meetings in Santiago (Chile), Quito (Ecuador), and San Jose (Costa Rica) (M. Manrique, personal correspondence, October 7, 2014).

Researchers conducted a study on Plaza's educational impact in Mexico City and Oaxaca preschools with 960 four- and five-year-old boys and girls from middle-income homes. Pre- and post-tests measured the impact of viewing Plaza Sésamo on children's performance in areas such as symbolic representation and environmental conservation. Results showed significant gains in the experimental group on the recognition of letters, numbers, and geometric shapes as well as ecology, nutrition, and hygiene (UNICEF, 1996).

The Mexican Secretariat of Education conducted an additional study which showed that children performed better on some literacy and numeracy skills and comprehension on environmental knowledge increased significantly after viewing Plaza Sésamo (SEP, 1999).

Over time, outreach programs evolved to provide content packages for a variety of platforms including print, board games, posters, storybooks, and community events for different institutional settings including schools, community centers, and hospitals. These outreach programs included resources for children, families, caregivers, and educators. The Plaza Sésamo team made special efforts to reach marginalized communities and address linguistic diversity through alliances with EDUSAT (an educational television network implemented by the Mexican Ministry of Education) and CONAFE (National Council for Educational Development, the entity responsible for addressing the educational needs of rural and marginalized communities living below the poverty line in Mexico). Plaza partnered with Mexico's National Institute of Indigenous Languages to dub television content into Nahautl and translate outreach content into Mayan.[2] By the early to mid-2000s, Plaza Sésamo had launched several large-scale outreach programs in different countries throughout Latin America. These projects varied in theme, such as health in Colombia and Mexico; digital literacy in Colombia; road safety in Costa Rica and Mexico; and disaster preparedness in Chile, Mexico, and Colombia.

In 2007, Plaza outreach took a distinctive turn, developing deeper, more structured interventions in schools and communities. This new type of outreach, different from the earlier, less comprehensive campaigns, aimed to combine mass media and community-based approaches to generate behavioral change. This shift in emphasis from knowledge building towards behavioral change mirrored trends in international development focused on evidence-based approaches to policy and programs (UN/ECOSOC, 2014). To better capture this deeper work, stakeholders in Latin America recommended changing the word "outreach" to "community engagement," implying a more participatory grassroots approach.

The health promotion program in Colombian preschools called Colombia Si is an illustrative example of this shift. Plaza teamed up with Dr. Valentin Fuster at the Icahn School of Medicine at Mount Sinai Hospital and local public and private foundation partners including Fundacion Cardio Infantil, the Institute of Family Welfare, and other local health and educational institutions. The preschool program aimed at improving dietary behavior and physical activity and included a longitudinal cohort study. The researchers randomly assigned schools to intervention and control groups. Over 1,216 children, aged three to five, 928 parents, and 120 teachers participated in the study. Children in each classroom were provided with Plaza-branded healthy habit themed content in a variety of formats including videos, storybooks, a board game, and posters. Teachers in the preschool participated in three structured trainings totaling six hours and received a teacher's guide. Children used these materials at least one hour a day over a six-month period. In addition, workshops and complementary materials were designed to encourage participation of parents in a "Healthy Family Day" workshop. On a weekly basis parents received messaging that included practical tips on how to reinforce healthy eating and an active lifestyle in the home (Cespedes et al., 2013).

Researchers collected baseline data before the program began and took subsequent measurements at six months, 18 months, and 36 months. Results showed significant and long-lasting improvements in knowledge, attitudes, and behaviors related to healthy habits among children that received the intervention (Cespedes et al., 2013). This program demonstrated that major lifestyle changes could be generated through well-designed media education programs that start at an early age (Cespedes et al., 2013).

The program provided a new model of engagement for Plaza, one that included a deeper involvement in communities and global and local public–private partnerships. The Colombia Si program also contributed to revitalizing the brand, helping to differentiate Plaza from the competition and served as a platform to launch new public–private partnerships in Colombia and throughout the region (T. Carrigan, personal correspondence, October 23, 2014).

Milestone 3: Brand Building and Brand Maintenance

It took two decades and four seasons of Plaza Sésamo to go from a TV series to a full-fledged brand. A brand is a distinguishing name or symbol, logo trademark, with a package design intended to identify goods/services and differentiate it from competitors (Aacker, 1991). Building a brand is much more difficult today as the costs of advertising and distribution are higher and as certain segments of the market are saturated. An early entry into the market helped Plaza build brand equity and gave it a significant competitive advantage within the children's television space. Outreach also contributed to building the brand as an extension into the community to address locally relevant issues and provided Plaza with a key point of differentiation from other shows that emerged to compete with Plaza on television. This brand equity has both monetary value and social value as it can be leveraged for reach and impact, as shown in the section above.

To help create and refresh associations that lead to brand differentiation, Plaza Sésamo commissioned regular market research studies with children, parents, educators, and other stakeholders. These studies show trends in the health of the brand across different metrics such as awareness, recall, trust, top of mind, and engagement and help Plaza teams refine content, delivery, and promotional strategies.

Market studies conducted over the last decade provide important insights into Plaza's evolving brand equity. One of the most consistent findings across these studies is the high level of nostalgia associated with the brand from parents and educators. This multi-generational nostalgia, in particular among mothers, is an important driver of Plaza's brand equity. In a 2005 market study in Mexico, 96% of mothers interviewed were familiar with the program, 72% of these mothers watched the program as a child, 95% liked the show as a child, and 98% of these mothers wanted to share the program with their child (Gemark, 2005). The findings are consistent with research on other brands which has shown that early emotional engagement leads to brand longevity (Twyford, 2010). Another finding concerns the awareness and likeability of characters such as Abelardo, Elmo, and Lola who are key drivers of viewership and engagement. Finally, consistent associations with the brand include "trustworthy," "educational," "real," "traditional," "communicates important values," and "reflects native culture" (Gemark, 2005; Fluent Research, 2007, 2011; Radius Global, 2013).

These findings have been used to make changes or reinforce what is working in Plaza content, distribution, and promotion strategies. On the content side, market research pointed to the need to create more interactive elements that could appeal to children and promote increased engagement. In addition, market research has underscored certain themes such as diversity, learning to live together, and an emphasis on everyday moments in the child's life such as bedtime, hygiene routines, and play. In terms of promotional strategies, market research on character appeal led to the decision of including Elmo in the Plaza cast in the early 2000s.

By the early 1990s, leveraging Plaza's brand equity meant extending the brand outside of television into new areas such as outreach, product licensing, theme parks, and publishing. These ancillary businesses provided additional revenue that could be reinvested in brand building, content, and research. These brand extensions also provided new touchpoints for audiences to engage with the brand and contributed to lifting overall brand awareness.

Although a not-for-profit enterprise, to stay viable Plaza Sésamo exists within an arena of market forces. Its competition has grown over the past 15 years and studies with mothers and children demonstrate signs of Plaza brand erosion in certain areas. The most persistent finding across market studies is the perception that Plaza Sésamo is "outdated." This could be attributed to the brand's long history and relative lack of innovation in content and format. Recently, the Plaza team has addressed these issues by revamping the format and feel of the content, curriculum, and platform delivery process with the aim of reconnecting with new generations of children.

Milestone 4: Introduction of Ancillary Businesses

With the rise of cable television in the region, actors such as Discovery in the 1990s, and specific channels dedicated solely to children's content, the demand for children's content increased rapidly. In addition to cable TV, there was a proliferation of new television platforms both public and private throughout the region that were building children's programming blocks.

With the rapid growth of the Latino population in the United States in the 1990s, the demand for Spanish content grew rapidly and Plaza moved to sign distribution deals with UNIVISION, Public Broadcast System, and VME TV.[3] Sales of Plaza Sésamo and dubbed Sesame Street content to private and public broadcasters throughout the region became an important source of revenue. By 1996 regional deals with cable broadcasters such as Discovery Kids and TV sales to public and private broadcasters generated 42% of Plaza's revenue while licensing accounted for 31% (T. Carrigan, personal correspondence, October 23, 2014).

Plaza also built a publishing and home video business in the mid-1990s and added "themed entertainment" (live shows, museums, and a theme park) to its portfolio. On the licensing front Plaza teamed up with Tycoon enterprises to help manage the business. Tycoon was founded in 1990 to license products for the most famous personality in Mexico, Chesperito. As Tycoon grew its portfolio of brands, it moved to regionalize its operations in the early 2000s setting up offices in Colombia, Argentina, and Brazil. Sesame Workshop also signed a global deal with Mattel toys that included Latin American markets. These regional and global deals provided Plaza with growing revenues. Interestingly, toys and other products almost entirely leveraged the global Sesame Street brand and characters as opposed to local Plaza Sésamo characters and content. This fact generated a question around the degree to which the continued growth, relevance, and survival of Plaza could be attributed to other factors outside of Plaza such as the growth of the global Sesame Street brand and expansion of global product licensing (T. Carrigan, personal correspondence, October 23, 2006). By 2008 licensing represented 40% of Plaza's revenue and media distribution generated a combined 23% of total revenue. From 1996 to 2008 revenues for Plaza increased six-fold.

The growth in revenue from the early 1990s and the mid-2000s was fueled primarily by TV sales and the licensing business. Plaza's ability to develop multiple touchpoints (TV, licensing, theme parks, museums, outreach, etc.) also helped to generate new sources of income while contributing to brand equity. By the early 2000s, the children's television market became increasingly competitive and new pressures on traditional distribution channels and business models (TV sales and licensing) emerged. Plaza Sésamo, as well as many of its media partners, have adapted their business models to this new more competitive environment, proactively pursuing points of differentiation, new channels of distribution, and sources of revenue.

Milestone 5: Regionalization of Content Production

The emergence of regional cable broadcasters in the 1990s provided the impetus to develop a program model that could appeal to audiences throughout the region.[4] The shift from a Mexican to a regional Plaza Sésamo was incremental and began in Seasons 3 and 4 with changes in the set. The set included a "Mercado," or open-air market, familiar and ubiquitous throughout the region. It became more "urban" to respond to population growth in big cities like Mexico City, Bogota, Caracas, and Buenos Aires (M. Manrique, personal correspondence, September 13, 2014). The human cast included stars from other countries who began to make guest appearances. In Seasons 3 and 4 an Argentine family was featured in several of the street stories. More recently, new formats such as "Lola Aventuras" (introduced in 2005) gave the writers and producers a pretext to explore other cultures in the region.

Dubbed content from competitors in the US and Europe flooded the market in the late 1990s and early 2000s, increasing backlash in the cultural and educational sectors. Policies created quotas and fostered local content production. The costs of 100% locally produced content can be prohibitive for many producers/broadcasters in Latin America and so many of these policies have not been fully implemented. While some sectors and audiences demand local content production, new models to finance high-quality children's productions in the region are also needed.

One recent trend for content producers in the region, especially independent producers and public television networks, is to collectively pool resources through regional co-productions. These new models of production help distribute the costs of content production across partners who share similar content needs and sensibilities. A recent example of this regional co-production model is the puppet show loosely inspired by Plaza called "The World of Max Rodriguez." This program is a co-production of Tribu 70 (an independent Colombian production company, Señal Colombia, Paka-Paka (Argentina), TV Ecuador, and the Ministry of Culture of Colombia. The Plaza Sésamo production model is moving in this direction, leveraging its ability to bring both public–private partners to the table within countries and across countries to address specific issues common to all, including digital literacy, health, and school preparedness.

An internal review of business opportunities across Latin America shows promise for growth in reach, revenue, and impact in markets such as Mexico, Colombia, Ecuador, Argentina, Chile, and Peru. Public-sector demand is growing, in many countries a political mandate to produce quality educational television content that reflects local needs and cultural diversity. Responding to this demand implies creating content that better matches the preferences and needs of audiences and partners in each country. A more localized approach presents challenges from a cost/efficiency and production capacity perspective. However, a more localized approach has advantages from an educational and mission perspective (i.e., developing content that better reflects local realities and building capacity in partners). Today Plaza Sésamo faces the dual challenge of creating regional content that can compete in the commercial market while simultaneously delivering locally tailored content solutions to governments and foundations interested in social impact.

Milestone 6: Digital Media and Audience Engagement

Over the last decade, the emergence of new technology platforms combined with an explosion of new content in the market has produced important changes in content production and distribution models in Latin America. Today, just as in the United States, many of those once dominant channels are being challenged by emerging channels such as YouTube, Video on Demand, and Netflix. Latin America is now seeing spectacular growth in social media platforms such as YouTube, Facebook, and Twitter. According to a recent comScore report (2013), Latin America has the fastest-growing internet population in the world, with 12% growth between 2012–13 and one of the fastest-growing markets in social media users (Deans, 2013). By 2017 Latin America will outrank Western Europe in average time spent by users online (comScore 2013; Deans, 2013).

These new technology platforms are changing the rules of how content is produced, distributed, and consumed by young children and their families. In particular, the proliferation of content choices across platforms has meant that content producers interested in creating cultural impact and sustainable business models need to shift their thinking from "eyeballs" to creating "experiences" and "engagement" of core audiences with content and brand.

It is in this context that in October 2012 over 40 regional experts from the fields of child development, policy, media, and communications gathered to discuss the key educational needs of young children in the region and to provide recommendations on expanding reach, relevance, and revenue for Plaza Sésamo in the 21st century. Stemming from the stakeholder meeting, Plaza has focused on ways it can deepen engagement in the Plaza Sésamo ecosystem. Program content design and distribution strategies are now designed to create content and brand experiences across a 360-degree content ecosystem. A straightforward 360-degree approach implies creating multiple touchpoints where target audiences can have brand experiences (television, internet, apps, products, books, outreach, marketing, events, etc). A transmedia approach implies spreading story arcs and narratives across communication channels (TV, internet, digital and media print, etc.) with the aim of creating a more immersive content experience and increased engagement of audiences and partners (Jenkins, 2006). Recently Plaza has implemented this transmedia approach in a program developed in Colombia called *Plaza Sésamo: Monsters on the Web*. This program aims to promote digital literacy, understood as the beneficial and safe uses of new technologies such as the internet, mobile phones, and social media for young children and families. *Monsters on the Web* was produced in collaboration with the Ministry of Technology, Communication, and Information of Colombia and Canal Tr3ce of Colombia. The program started in its first phase with a special television series consisting of 26 12-minute episodes and 30-second public service announcements starring Plaza Sésamo Muppets and local celebrities. The program's second phase focuses on creating a digital experience that leverages video content produced for TV and deepens the experience through interactive video games, e-books, and resources for educators and parents. *Monsters on the Web* was nominated for an International Emmy in the category of best international children's program in 2014.

Business Model Evolution

As highlighted above, Plaza evolved in content, format, and distribution to adapt and respond to key changes in society and the market. Plaza had an advantage with its early entry into the market. Unfortunately, Plaza did not have a robust business model when it first launched and production of new content and activities were put on hold for almost a decade (between Seasons 2 and 3). In the 1980s, Plaza resurfaced, taking advantage of changes in the media and education landscapes to refashion itself as one of the first truly pan-regional television programs. With the rise of regional cable broadcasters, Plaza gained momentum in the 1990s and adapted and leveraged its brand equity to extend its reach and impact through outreach, products, and themed entertainment. This more diversified business model fueled Plaza growth in reach and content production for over a decade. By the turn of the century an increasing number of shows, brands, and programs competed for children's and families' attention. Plaza has had to innovate and evolve its business model in order to remain relevant. In particular, Plaza is looking at re-aligning with local needs and developing more endurable partnerships with like-minded public and private partners to produce innovations in Plaza content format and delivery and drive long-term educational and social impact. An important part of this new emerging business model involves redefining the relationship between Plaza content and audiences to produce deeper engagement in a 360-degree content ecosystem across platforms (TV, new technologies, print, social media, products, and live community events).

In the non-profit context, sustainability implies attaining the support needed (financial and other) to generate social impact in the mid and long term. In the for-profit context, sustainability relates to generating a financial return on investment in the mid and long term. In the case of Sesame Workshop, the sustainability model is rooted in producing long-term social impact where the key drivers of the business model have differed over the course of the history of the brand as the context, market conditions, and broader strategic considerations have changed.

Traditionally, Sesame Workshop looks at different markets as either "market-driven" or "mission-driven." This categorization is an internal short-hand to refer to the fact that different markets require different strategies. Market-driven countries such as Germany, Spain, Japan, and Australia demonstrate sufficient brand recognition matched by a base of consumers that are willing to pay for Sesame programs, experiences, and products. The business model tends to focus on mass media broadcast followed by licensing. In mission-driven countries such as Nigeria, Bangladesh, and Afghanistan there is a need (development, educational, social, etc.) that Sesame Workshop programs address and funding opportunities, usually from international donors, are needed to support the work. In some of these countries a long-term sustainable presence is unlikely given the lack of conditions to build a local institutional presence sustained by local sources of funding. A few markets, mostly emerging economies such as Brazil, Mexico, India, South Africa, and China, combine great educational need with market conditions that can drive local revenue-generating activities such as public–private partnerships and product licensing needed for sustainability, long-term growth, and impact. An example of a successful public–private partnership model is Sesame Workshop's South African co-production Takalani Sesame. Long-term support for Takalani Sesame has been provided by Sanlam (a South African financial services company), Mai Family Foundation, SABC, and the Department of Basic Education. Plaza Sésamo fits into this last category with its focus on partnering with local institutions that can design and deliver educational and social impact while providing consumers (children and parents) with appealing content and product experiences (D. Mintz, ongoing conversations, 2012–14; R. Knezevic, ongoing conversations, 2012–14).

Funding trends help illustrate how Plaza's business model has shifted over time. As noted above, the first three seasons of Plaza were funded by large corporate donors such as Xerox and Coca Cola, with contributions from Televisa, the main producer/broadcast partner. This corporate sponsor and broadcaster received high visibility for associating with an innovative and upcoming media children's program that already had begun to prove its popularity in the United States.[5] While initially successful, the business model failed to support the longer-term sustainability of Plaza and enabled the production and broadcast of only three seasons. In part, the breakdown of this model could be attributed to the lack of attention to cultivating local institutional capacity in partners who shared Sesame's longer-term social impact vision and who had the incentives as well as the political, financial, and technical resources to manage the brand's evolution. Mayo et al. (1984) attribute the initial lack of sustainability to Sesame Workshop's failure to focus on local institution building, to asymmetries in know-how between Sesame New York and local partners in producing children's television, and to a transactional approach that focused too much on a "product" as opposed to "process" orientation.

In the second phase, from the 1990s to the mid-2000s, the business model shifted from simply a television production/broadcast to a broadcast/licensing model. New seasons of Plaza Sésamo were produced and broadcast about every year and a half. Promotion around each season created the brand visibility required for growing and sustaining ancillary businesses. A regional co-production agreement with Discovery, a distribution deal for the Hispanic market with UNIVISION and VME, as well as the globalization of the Sesame Street toy product business with Mattel helped generate the additional revenues required for ongoing content production and brand management activities such as promotion and research. During the period from 1995 to 2008, revenues increased by five times and consisted roughly of a third licensing, a third TV sales, and a third TV co-production deals. This business model generated a healthy net margin that could be re-invested in content and brand maintenance. However, many of the brand's activities were still managed in New York. Production costs rose with the increased staff in New York required to manage the various aspects of the project and as the market shifted Plaza was slow to adjust locally to new emerging opportunities and challenges.

By the mid-2000s the media landscape changed as content and global children's brands from abroad flooded the Latin American market. Large commercial broadcasters were less incentivized to invest in producing their own children's content and the larger more commercial brands provided more attractive financial packages to ensure a more robust presence on air and off air. Despite the increased competition, Plaza's ratings remained consistently steady (within the top-ten programs in the preschool block), but it was only a matter of time before the brand showed signs of erosion on other fronts such as licensing.

The business model is shifting once again as Plaza looks to partner with local governments and foundations to create new sources of support. In addition, Plaza is focused more aggressively on developing content and distribution opportunities on the digital front on platforms such as mobile phones, YouTube, and Netflix, with the forward-looking projection that in three to five years these digital platforms will surpass TV as the principal content platforms for many Latin American children (Deans, 2013).

Over the last five to seven years revenues from public–private partners increased steadily and now represent at least a third of total revenues and contribute about 15–20% of total net margin.[6]

To better capitalize on these local opportunities, Sesame established a more permanent local project management presence in the region in 2014 with local staff in Colombia, Mexico, and Brazil. The goal is to create a self-sustaining entity in Latin America by the year 2017 supported by long-term public–private partners and to become the go-to source of sound, innovative, and fun educational solutions for the critical needs of Latin America's youngest generation.

The Way Forward

Plaza's history can be characterized by the tension between staying true to its heritage and core values while innovating and evolving at an increasingly more rapid pace. In today's media-saturated world, where children and adults have more choices, where attention spans are shorter, where message channels proliferate, where products and platforms are created and destroyed in shorter cycles, the challenge of staying relevant has become increasingly difficult, yet vital.

With Plaza Sésamo, early entry into the market and 40 years of brand building has generated a unique set of opportunities and challenges. Plaza Sésamo could have easily disappeared after Season 3 in the early 1980s. However, Plaza leaders and teams were able to take advantage of emerging business, technological, and social trends and built a more viable business model that included revenues from ancillary businesses, namely licensing and content distribution. More recently, with increased competition in these commercial channels Plaza has a renewed focus on local public–private partnerships, content innovation, and building new channels of revenue on emerging platforms.

Part of Plaza's enduring relevance and impact can be attributed to the growth of Sesame's overall global management of the brand's equity. Market research, sound financial analysis, and ongoing educational research have informed strategic decision making around the brand. One of the challenges in today's fast-paced world is for Plaza teams to integrate these various forms of information and analysis in a timely and effective manner.

Sustaining a brand goes beyond strategic marketing. Plaza has had to consistently produce on two fronts. On the first front, and perhaps the most important, Plaza has had to produce programs and products that children, educators, and parents find appealing and useful. On the other front Plaza has had to align increasingly with governments and foundations who understand the potential of media and well-crafted content to contribute to critical development issues. As a communication platform Plaza Sésamo has made important contributions to development efforts in the region for the past 40 years. Within the field of communication for development, Plaza stands out as a model that blends both mass media and grassroots approaches. Key components in Plaza's communication for development model include: leveraging the popularity and iconic nature of the brand and Muppets; insertion into popular culture; strategic partnerships with regional development agencies and governments; collaboration with young creative talent; and the use of various forms of research to ensure relevant and impactful messaging. With this unmatched blend, support has grown for Plaza over the past decade from development actors including governments, foundations, and international organizations. The healthy habit Colombia Si program that launched in 2007 is exemplary of Plaza's unique potential as a communication platform for development. It provides a new model of engagement rooted in a more comprehensive approach to addressing local needs and global and local public and private partnerships. The demonstrated educational and broader impacts of this program helped catalyze additional partnerships in Colombia and throughout the region, contributing to Plaza's renewed relevance and sustainability.

Today, Plaza is at another critical turning point, as some of these channels have become saturated and overall the market is increasingly competitive. Plaza will have to find a way to revitalize the brand by re-focusing on what it does best, do it better, while simultaneously innovating and creating new approaches.[7] A mature brand has certain advantages and disadvantages when it comes to relevance and sustainability. In the case of Plaza, a long-term consistent delivery of quality programs has generated trust among parents and educators. To cultivate and leverage this trust Plaza has had to think in the long term and consistently apply non-negotiables to maintain its educational integrity and quality. These non-negotiables have also helped create a consistent identity, differentiate the brand from others, and communicate a clear set of values to parents, educators, and partners. In addition, the presence of a clear repeatable model with concrete learning processes and practices has provided Plaza with a structured approach to experimentation, learning, and adaptation.

There are of course disadvantages to Plaza's maturity and increased organizational complexity. Rigidity in decades-old processes can shut down reflection and openness to new ideas and approaches. Unreflective adherence to blueprints and end products could undermine local capacity to resolve problems and build partnerships that will give Plaza long-term sustainability. The extent to which Plaza will remain relevant as a brand over the next few years is contingent on how fast it can adapt to changes in the marketplace and how successful it is in aligning its business model and organizational design (culture, policies, structures, etc.) to maximize performance. But beyond business models, sound management, and financials, the real test of Plaza's continued relevance will be its ability to continue to produce engaging, fun, and educationally sound content that resonates with future generations of Latin American children.

Notes

1. I would like to thank several individuals who made themselves available for interviews and who reviewed drafts of this chapter. Their contributions were vital. In particular, I would like to thank Manuel Manrique, Marcella Lambert, Patricia Arriaga, Taska Carrigan, Carolina Casas, David Albano, Daryl Mintz, Robert Knezevic, Lewis Bernstein, Lorenzo Dunoyer, and the editors Charlotte Cole and June Lee.
2. See the Nahautl version of Plaza Sésamo at https://www.youtube.com/watch?v=dPQvN30B3Ws.
3. VME TV is the first Spanish broadcast television network in association with public television stations created for the United States Hispanic market.
4. Discovery Communications launched its Latin American operations in 1994.

5. The ratings in Mexico from the first few seasons were higher than anything else on TV at the time (Gettas, 1994).
6. This coalition of public partners includes the Ministry of Technology and Communication in Colombia, the Secretariat of Health in Mexico, the Santo Domingo Foundation in Colombia, corporate sponsors such as Tetra Pak, regional organizations such as UNICEF, Inter-American Development Bank, and increased support from global corporate foundations such as Metlife Foundation and Pfizer.
7. Research on the revitalization of brands has shown that maintaining brand equity can be expensive. It is often hard to determine in the short term how an investment in one brand-maintenance activity may yield benefits over another. Increased marketing dollars in crowded channels does not necessarily translate into tangible results. One strategy that has worked for some enduring brands is a push towards a stronger presence in emerging channels (Aaker, 1991; Twyford, 2010).

References

Aacker, D. (1991). *Managing brand equity.* New York: Free Press.

Barrera, E. (n.d.). *Mexico.* Mexico, DF: Museum of Broadcast, http://www.museum.tv/eotv/mexico.htm, accessed September 11, 2014.

Cespedes, J., Briceño, G., Farkough, M.E., Vedanthan, R., Baxter, J., Leal, M., Boffetta, P., Hunn, M., Dennis, R., and Fuster, V. (2013). Promotion of cardiovascular health in preschool children 36-month cohort follow-up. *American Journal of Medicine,* 126(12), 1122–6.

Cole, C.F., Richman, B., McCann Brown, S. (2001). The world of Sesame Street research. In S. Fisch and R. Truglio (eds), "*G*" *is for growing: Thirty years of research on children and Sesame Street* (pp. 147–79). Mahway, NJ: Erlbaum.

comScore (2013). *Latin America digital focus in future,* http://www.comscore.com/Insights/Events_and_Webinars/Webinar/2013/2013_Latin_America_Digital_Future_in_Focus, accessed October 27, 2014.

Deans, D. (2013). *The internet is booming in Latin America, especially among younger users,* October 7, http://blogs.cisco.com/cle/the-internet-is-booming-in-latin-america-especially-among-younger-users/, accessed October 27, 2014.

Diaz-Guerrero, R. and Holtzman, W.H. (1974). Learning by televised "Plaza Sésamo" in Mexico. *Journal of Educational Psychology,* 66(5), 632–43.

Diaz-Guerrero, R., Reyes-Lagunes, I., Witzke, D.B., and Holtzman, W.H. (1976). Plaza Sésamo in Mexico: An evaluation. *Journal of Communication,* 26(2), 145–54.

Fluent Research (2007). Plaza Sésamo brand research: Topline report of qualitative findings (internal unpublished report). New York: Fluent Research.

Fluent Research (2011). Plaza Sésamo: A brand assessment (internal unpublished report). New York: Fluent Research.

Gemark (2005). Plaza Sésamo in Mexico: Findings from market research studies (internal unpublished report).

Gettas, G. (1994). The globalization of Sesame Street: A producer's perspective. *Educational Technology Research and Development,* 4(38), 55–63.

Jenkins, H. (2006). Convergence culture: Where old and new media collide. New York: New York University Press.

Lesser, G. (1982a). Trip report: Plaza Sésamo III Manzanillo, Mexico, May 13–15 (internal unpublished report), 17 May.

Lesser, G. (1982b). Trip report: Curriculum planning seminar for Plaza Sésamo in Buenos Aires, Argentina, November 24–6 (internal unpublished report), November 29.

Lesser, G. (1983). Trip report Plaza Sésamo III: Trip to Televisa, Mexico City, May 5–15 (internal unpublished report), May 16.

Mayo, J.K., Bautista Araujo e Oliveira, J., Rogers, E., and Dantus Pinto Guimaraes, S. (1984). The transfer of Sesame Street to Latin America. *Communication Research*, 11: 259–80.

Radius Global (2013). Multi-country reach study: Individual country report Latin America: Mexico, Colombia, Argentina, Chile (internal unpublished report).

SEP (1999). Proyecto Plaza Sésamo como Apoyo al Programa de Educación Inicial. Informe de Resultados. Mexico: Secretaria de Educación Pública de Mexico.

Twyford, C. (2010). Longevity: What makes big brands stay big? In *Nielson Featured Insights: Delivering Consumer Clarity*. March, www.nielsen.com.

UN/ECOSOC (2014). *Trends and progress in international development cooperation*. Draft report to the Secretary General, May 15, http://www.un.org/en/ecosoc/docs/adv2014/2014_dcf_sg_report_adv.pdf, accessed October 26, 2014.

UNICEF (1996). *Executive summary: Summary assessment of Plaza Sésamo IV: Mexico* (English translation of unpublished report). Mexico City: UNICEF.

INDEX

Page numbers in italic refer to figures, plates, and tables.
Page number followed by 'f' refer to figures. Thus, *14f1.2* refers to *figure 1.2* on page 14.
Plates are identifies by plate number only. Page numbers with "pl" or "pls" refer to plates appearing in the plate section located in the middle of the book. Thus, *pls 5.1–5.2* refers to *plates number 5.1 and 5.2* in the plate section.
Page numbers followed by 't' refer to tables. Thus, *18t1.1* refers to table 1.1 on page 18
Page numbers followed by 'n' refer to notes. Thus, 151n1 refers to note 1 on page 151, and *18t1.1n1* refers to note 1 on page 18 of table 1.1